THE GREAT DAYS OF THE CANALS

Anthony Burton

THE GREAT DAYS
OF THE
CANALS

DAVID & CHARLES
Newton Abbot London

ACKNOWLEDGEMENTS

(Page 1) *No amount of careful design can ever reproduce the accidental beauty that comes with age. The bollard is a purely practical device, but generations of users have shaped it into its sculptured form. It is such apparently insignificant details that add together to create the unique visual appeal of Britain's rivers and canals* (Anthony Burton)

(Page 3) *No matter what the future of canals may be it is unlikely that there will be a place for scenes such as this – a pair of narrow boats heading for home, their cargoes safely delivered* (Anthony Burton)

I should like to thank the following for permission to quote from published works:

M. & M. Baldwin for Emma Smith's *Maiden's Trip* and Susan Woolfitt's *Idle Women*
Eric de Maré for *The Canals of England*
Sonia Rolt for L. T. C. Rolt's *Landscape with Canals* and *Narrow Boat*

I should also like to thank Mikron Theatre Company for permission to quote from recorded interviews.

British Library Cataloguing in Publication Data

Burton, Anthony, 1934 –
  The great days of the canals.
  1. Great Britain. Canals to 1988
  I. Title
  386'.46'0941

ISBN 0-7153-9264-6

Book designed by Michael Head
and printed in Great Britain
by Butler & Tanner Limited, Frome and London
for David & Charles Publishers plc
Brunel House   Newton Abbot   Devon

CONTENTS

	INTRODUCTION	6
1	DAY TRIP	11
2	THE RIVER NAVIGATIONS	21
3	BUILDING THE CANALS	40
4	THE ENGINEERS	60
5	ARCHITECTURE AND ENGINEERING	79
6	THE CANALS AT WORK	99
7	THE CRAFT OF THE INLAND WATERWAYS	113
8	THE CARRIERS	126
9	LIFE ON THE BOATS	139
10	THE YEARS OF DECLINE	155
11	THE CANALS AT WAR	167
12	PASSENGERS AND TOURISTS	176
13	CANALS FOR PLEASURE	191
14	RESTORATION	203
15	CANALS IN THE FUTURE	212
	FURTHER READING	222
	INDEX	223

INTRODUCTION

What were the great days of canals – are they indeed over? For some, the best times came somewhere around the late fifties, when commercial traffic was still a reality but the holiday trade had not yet grown to any great proportions. This was the time that I began my own love affair with the canals – a time when taking a canal holiday made one feel like a pioneer. Others would look further back in time to the days when the canals were a vital part of the trading life of the nation, whilst others would go to the opposite extreme and praise a system which gives such pleasure to thousands of holidaymakers. Whichever slice of time one cuts, it is probable that most of us have come first to the canals as a form of leisure and relaxation. 'There is *nothing* – absolutely nothing – half so much worth doing as simply messing about in boats.' Those famous words are from Kenneth Grahame's *The Wind in the Willows*, and they are words which many of us are only too happy to echo. Certainly, over the years, I have enjoyed messing about in boats of every shape and size: I have canoed down rivers, and even an ignominious sinking when I ripped a hole in the hull going down rapids gave me a story to tell even if it seemed less than entertaining at the time. At the opposite end of the scale, I have crewed a Thames barge and spent many happy, if sweaty, hours shovelling coal into an old coastal steamer. They have all been tremendous fun and enormously rewarding, but if an edict was to come down saying that in future my messing about would be limited to just one type of boating, I should have no need to ask for time to consider – the answer would be immediate: I should opt for the canals. But why? Sailing in a stiff breeze can be one of the most exhilarating of pastimes, far more exciting, one would think, than a slow plod down a narrow waterway to the accompaniment of a noisy engine. Canoeing can also be thrilling, and has the added advantage of providing good, healthy exercise. And I have always been enthralled by steam engines, so that a day in the engine-room remains one of my favourite experiences. I should not wish to give any of them up – but I could if I had to, whereas with the canals I have to confess to an addiction.

The unique appeal of canals lies in the complexity of responses which they evoke. There are some things which pall after a time, but the more one knows about canals, the more one realises that one does not know. Canals take you to town and country, but then so do rivers. I enjoy river travel, but it is always with a happy sigh of anticipation that I turn off from, let us say, the broad waters of the Severn to the confines of the Worcester and Birmingham Canal – even though I know that lurking up ahead is the longest flight of locks in the country. The rivers remain essentially natural phenomena, even if man has tinkered with them and

changed them over the centuries. The canals are totally artificial creations, entirely the works of man. Phrases such as 'works of man', however, smack of anonymity. Here one is looking at works of the not-so-very-distant past, works whose characteristics began to develop when individual men – men we can usually name – took decisions on the line to be taken, the structures that would be needed. We do not have to travel long on the canals before we begin to recognise those differences. This makes them seem very human creations, and brings a sense of individual personality to a canal which we soon begin to associate with the particular engineer who built it. This is something which has gone from the world of transport today. We can sensibly say 'This is very much a Brindley canal', but whoever commented 'Ah, I see we've come on to a Smith motorway'?

There is another essential element to the canal scene. The canals we travel for pleasure were actually built for work and industry. If someone builds a boating lake, we might well enjoy it, but we seldom have any desire to know anything about its history. If we are told, however, that popular Hollingsworth lake in Lancashire is not really a pleasure-boat lake at all but a reservoir built to supply water for a canal that is not even anywhere in sight, our curiosity is aroused. Some will want to know a lot more and may go to see the distant Rochdale Canal. They might even take the trouble to find out why the engineer, William Jessop, decided to put a reservoir here and how it was built. But even those – and they are probably the majority – who are simply quite happy to be given the information and leave it at that, will have found something a little extra, perhaps a touch surprising, to add to the enjoyment of the place. All canal travel brings with it associations, sometimes powerful, sometimes faint, of the working life that thrived until very recent times. It has been my experience that the more I know about the canals, the more I enjoy travelling. I will not pretend that all day and every day when I stand at the tiller, I am peering about, looking for historical reminders, but the feeling of being part of an old working environment is never far away. It is the extra dimension that makes canal travel different and very special.

In this book I have tried to look at the canals in all their different aspects. Inevitably, the emphasis is more on the past than on the present, but I hope to show that giving at least a little thought to the past can make present-day enjoyment of the canals all the greater. It has certainly done so for me, and I have long since reached the happy conclusion that the subject is inexhaustible. I can travel a canal I thought I knew well and still find features I had missed, which bring out some new and sometimes unexpected aspect of the old life of the waterway. And the canals are not yet, thank heavens, museum pieces artificially stopped at one moment in their history. Change goes on all the time. There is the natural change – the change that gives a different look as the seasons alternate – and the change on a longer scale as the inevitable process of ageing continues. And there is change that reflects the different ways in which each age sees and uses the canals. How can one possibly tire of it or become bored?

this sort inevitably builds on the work of many other people des the author. It is probably tedious for readers to be presented with authors' 'thank yous', but I have a special reason for including just a few names in this list, for they show just what a mixture of strands are woven together to complete the canal picture. This is also, in its way, a personal history of my own growing involvement with, and understanding of, canals. I began, as we all begin, knowing nothing, and before I could start towards any sort of understanding my eyes had to be opened so that I could see that there was indeed something very special about this world of canals. For that I am indebted largely to Eric de Maré, whose photographs showed up the beauty to be found in the everyday, not just on the canals but in the industrial world that they served. Even more than *The Canals of England*, it was the book he produced with J. M. Richards, *The Functional Tradition*, which was to change the way in which I looked at the world. If de Maré taught me to see, others taught me to understand. L. T. C. Rolt was the first to people the canal for me, to bring the past to life, to give history a very human face. He wrote of the great engineers, not as models in some historic waxworks, but as people you might well find enjoying a pint in a canalside pub. It was Rolt as much as anyone who inspired me to begin writing, and who, with great kindness, encouraged me when I did begin. But when it came to delving into the past, I found myself – as I suspect everyone else who tries to write any sort of canal history – turning to the work of Charles Hadfield. Nowadays, when I want information there is a whole range of books and pamphlets written over the last two hundred years to which I can turn and all types of records that I can look up. I know what they are and I know where they are, because the pattern of historical research is there to follow. But it is only there because Charles Hadfield did the work on which all the rest of us have drawn. I cannot think of any research that I have undertaken on canals which did not involve taking a book of his from the shelf to look up a date or check a reference.

In working on this book I received help from a number of people. It is always a good idea to try to get fresh viewpoints on one's subject. Peter White, architect/planner for British Waterways Board, found his initial inspiration, as I did, in seeing the canals for himself and reading books, but he also has another way of looking at the canals now. He has to see them as a working architect with practical problems to solve. Travelling with and talking to Peter over the years has, I hope, taken me out of the academic study and put me in touch with the realities of preserving and maintaining – and even improving – a now decidedly aged transport system. Books are only one way of getting information, and only one way of presenting it. Mike and Sarah Lucas and Mikron Theatre Company have been travelling the canals telling the waterways story to an increasingly large and enthusiastic audience since 1972. They have also been talking to canal people about their working lives and have amassed literally hundreds of hours of taped interviews. Oral history is just as valuable as written history in bringing the past back to life, and they very kindly let me loose with their tape collection. Without it some sections of this book could hardly have been written, and would certainly be very much the poorer. Finally, the pictures: an old picture can be every bit as eloquent as the well-turned phrase of a writer describing a scene of many years ago. The picture research for this book was the work of my wife Pip, who has not only helped in this work but has been my companion in canal travels since my very first trip.

There are many people who have helped directly and indirectly, but to name them all would be to produce one of those never-ending credit lists that are tacked on to modern movies and which are still rolling long after the cinema has emptied. Instead, I shall end the introduction here and invite readers to join me for an exploration of the past and the present – and to take a quick glance towards the future – of Britain's canals.

The canals in their heyday: Limehouse dock busy with ships, lighters and narrow boats. The entrance to the Regent's Canal can be seen at the back of the basin (Bodleian Library/JJ Collection Canals)

1 DAY TRIP

It comes hard to an author to admit that anything could be better than reading his book, but it has to be confessed that travelling a canal will beat reading about it every time. What a book should be able to do is to help make the journey more interesting. The aim of this chapter is a simple one – to try to give some idea of the endless fascination of canal travel by concentrating on just one 10-mile (16km) section of canal – just the length for a very leisurely day's cruise or a slightly more energetic tow-path walk. The length I have chosen is on the Kennet and Avon between Bradford-on-Avon and Bath. There were several reasons for the choice. It is an outstandingly beautiful and interesting section, but, just as importantly, it is easy to arrange a day's outing. You can travel silently and smoothly on the water in an electrically powered boat, which can be hired from the Bath & Dundas Canal Company at Dundas aqueduct. Walkers and cyclists will find a tow-path in excellent condition and, having reached the far end, they are not faced with the prospect of turning round and coming back under their own power, as there is a railway station conveniently near to the canal at both Bradford and Bath.

This journey starts just below the lock at Bradford-on-Avon. Those arriving here on foot will have no difficulty spotting the start on the B3109, for a colourful sign showing a pair of boats announces the presence of the Canal Tavern. The pub was the centre of social life on the canals when the population was constantly on the move, and you can be sure that you will never have to travel very far before arriving at a spot to slake your thirst. The best of them, such as the Canal Tavern at Bradford, are history lessons in themselves, with canal memorabilia and old photographs covering the walls. Down by the canal is a small wharf below the locks, and a much larger one up above, but you might wonder what on earth Bradford had to offer that the canal could carry. Today, its main claim to fame is as a tourist spot, and that is certainly what you see from the vantage point of the canal set high up on the southern slope of the Avon valley. You look out across the river to a hillside, where ancient stone houses squash into terraces that rise one above the other so that it seems as if the foundations of one must rest on the roof of another below. Closer at hand is one of Bradford's most remarkable buildings, the massive medieval tithe barn approached by a track that runs across a delightful low stone bridge. It is just the sort of place that the cynical dismiss with the one damning word 'quaint'. The cynical should be made to look at the real Bradford, and anyone with time to explore will find a place that may well surprise them. But this is to be a canal trip, not a general history exercise, and in any case, we shall soon

The Kennet and Avon Canal between Bradford-on-Avon and Dundas is everybody's idea of what a rural canal should be, with shady trees leaning over the sun-sparkling water (Anthony Burton)

11

be seeing just what it was that made Bradford-on-Avon an important medieval town.

So it is time to start, and there is no better place to start than Bradford, for it was here in 1794 that the first sod was cut heralding that work was under way in building the Kennet and Avon Canal. That was a day of high optimism, although optimism was to fade somewhat over the years, for it was not completed until 1810. As soon as you start travelling you get a notion of the problems facing the canal builders. The Avon cuts a narrow way through the hills, so that the canal seems to cling precariously to the slope, occupying the narrow ledge that has been carved out for it. Down below, by the river, is the railway – and how the canal owners must have dreaded the appearance of this puffing, steaming rival. It began life as the Wilts, Somerset and Weymouth Railway in 1845, but independence was short lived and it was soon swallowed up by the mighty Great Western. It may all seem very far away down in the valley, but the railway world is closer than you might think. Dotted along the way are distance posts, recording the mileage from Reading. A few can still be read and show miles and fractions of miles such as the one at Avoncliff. They are just simple chunks of wood stuck on metal posts – but these are not just any metal posts, but lengths of rail. They are not all quite the same, but the majority are shaped like this in cross section ⊓ and these are very special indeed. They were the rails of Brunel's famous broad-gauge track, with its lines set 7ft (2m) apart. So, in fact, the railway has crept up to the canal after all, just as the Kennet and Avon Company feared it would, for, in the event, they found the competition too much to bear, and the GWR that had absorbed the Wilts, Somerset and Weymouth Railway down in the valley, gobbled up the canal as well in 1852. For almost a century, the Kennet and Avon had to relinquish its proud independence to become a minor part of a massive railway empire.

To describe a canal is only to describe it in one mood. I travelled on one of those days when winter is just beginning to slide away into the past, and new leaves are forming the palest of green hazes that blur the sharp, dark outlines of twigs and branches. The trees leaned over the canal from the high southern bank, but were scarcely reflected in the still, muddied water, opaque and khaki like an old army blanket. Little stirred except the birds; mallards in pairs, a solitary swan scavenging for titbits among the reeds and a head-bobbing, scuttling moorhen. The boating season had not yet begun, but the tow-path was far from empty as people strolled in a pallid sunlight that was more a promise of better things to come than a true mark of spring. It would be hard to imagine a quieter spot, and it is the easiest thing in the world to slide by boat or amble on foot through such scenery and think of the canal as a natural part of the countryside, or if its nature does make it appear a touch artificial, to conclude that it could only be put there for our pleasure and enjoyment.

If you are a boater, you go almost a mile (1.6km) before you meet the first obstruction, a swing-bridge. The very natural-seeming canal was once a major intrusion in the landscape, cutting off farmers from their land, dividing villages and hamlets. The canal company had to meet the needs of the community through which they passed – they had to accommodate them, hence accommodation bridges. Some bridges are the familiar hump-backed affairs of brick or stone, but where traffic was likely to be light, it was cheaper in the short term to make a simple, pivoting wooden platform such as this. One of the reasons the canal took so long to complete was shortage of funds, so any cost savings were welcome. In the long term, the swing-bridge would require regular and sometimes expensive maintenance, but for anxious penny-scraping canal builders, the first essential was to get the work completed.

All the time as one travels west, the valley seems to be closing in, and the River Avon comes to take an ever-more prominent part in the landscape. The peaceful, day-dreaming world of the canal quickens into life as a steady roar of water drifts up from the other waterway down below. Avoncliff looks from the map to be no more than a couple of buildings, a brief interlude to a tranquil journey. It turns out to be packed with interest. The first thing that I noticed was, in fact, across the river by Avoncliff station, which is really little more than a halt. There, rusted to a vivid orange, was the firebox and boiler of an old steam locomotive. The canal, it seems, does not have a monopoly of nostalgic glimpses of the past. Nearer at hand, the cause of the noise appears in a great stone weir spanning the whole river, with stone buildings set at either end. The one on the far side still has a waterwheel in place under a ramshackle covering of corrugated iron. The nearer of the two is altogether smarter, having been converted into a private house, but you can still see where sluices controlled the water flow, while a tall chimney bears eloquent witness to the fact that at some time water power had been replaced by steam. We have arrived at industry – textiles to be precise. For centuries, the waters of the River Avon turned the wheels of woollen mills – not the mills of the Industrial Revolution, which made yarn and cloth, but fulling mills where the cloth made in homes throughout the district was pounded under giant hammers to felt it, shrinking and compacting the material. Bradford-on-Avon was a wealthy textile town when Bradford in Yorkshire was an insignificant hamlet. These particular mills were somewhat lowly members of the textile fraternity – flock mills which broke up old material for reuse as stuffing for furniture. But it was all undeniably industry, a busy spot where raw materials, coal and finished goods had to be carried, and it was areas such as this which brought trade to the canal.

Seeing the mills and the wharf alongside helps one to understand why so much effort and money was expended on the canal in the first place. Little details tell other parts of the story. The canal bends at a right angle to head across the valley, and right on the bend is a stone pillar, scarred with grooves. It takes us back to the days when the horses did the work of hauling canal boats. The tow-rope was slipped around the post to make it easier for the boat to negotiate the bend. How many plodding horses came this way to dig those deep cuts in the hard stone? This was a busy little spot with its wharf, its cottages and its inevitable pub, but by far the grandest sight is the stone aqueduct that carries the canal across the river. Truth to tell, it looks at its best when seen from a distance, for it was another save-money-now-and-repent-later job. It

The Kennet and Avon at the Beginning of the Century

P. Bonthron, a member of the newly formed British Motor-Boat Club, travelled the canal in the years before World War I. His sensible suggestions were to become reality more than half a century later.

As far as I could judge, the opening for a motor boat service between Bristol and Bradford-on-Avon struck me at once as being excellent. With a good draught of water, generally speaking, lovely scenery, and without too many locks, there is ample scope for a canal cruise on these waters. Apart from the scarcity of general business on the canal, it seemed to us strange that there were so few pleasure craft about with such capital opportunities for good sailing and boating. Bristol is a large commercial city, but, as the tourist remarked about Glasgow with its beautiful Clyde attractions, 'It was a fine place to get away from,' and so in this case it was – under motor boat conditions . . . After a spell of fine water we approached Bath, a really fine town and health resort, as everybody knows. We saw rather an unusual craft just about this point. An enterprising barge-owner had fitted up a canal boat and furnished it throughout – with an awning on top – as a pleasure craft, the haulage being done by horse. The intention was to run trips from, say, Bath to Bradford-on-Avon and back, some 20 miles, without any lock obstacles. The idea is a good one, as the route is through fine country, and it reminded us of the old times one reads about when passenger traffic was conducted on the canals, coaching then being so costly.

(P. Bonthron, *My Holidays on Inland Waterways*, 1916)

13

looks fine at first sight, with its bold arches, striding across the valley, but close up you can see where the inferior stone has crumbled away and the spaces been filled in with brick. It is rather like a Savile Row suit inherited by a tramp – something of the original elegance still shows through the patches. A notice-board on the aquaduct gives details of its history, and includes the information that a tramway, or horse-drawn railway, once ran along beside the canal. Most of us, however, tend to forget, if only temporarily, about history when crossing an aquaduct. No matter how many times you do it, there is still something magical in the experience of floating in a boat high in the air; something distinclty odd about the whole notion of water passing over water. No wonder that when the idea of an aquaduct was first put forward at the beginning of the canal age it was greeted with a good deal of scepticism.

Avoncliff marks the start of 3 miles (4.8km) of some of the most beautiful canal scenery you can hope to find. Having crossed the river, the canal swings round again to continue the journey westward. On one side trees climb up the hill above the canal, while on the other, the land seems simply to fall away to give views down to the twisting river, each bend of which is echoed by the canal high above it. A pair of canalside houses seem perfectly at home here, and certainly earn the estate agent's cliché award as 'desirable residences'. Desirable they certainly are, and one at least has a built-in memento of the past: a GWR boundary post beside the drive. Everything seems idyllic, and so it is, but there are telltale signs that this was not always so – signs that what seems like paradise to the holiday boater was often more like hell for the engineers and the maintenance gangs. All along the way are grooves in the stone banking designed to take stop planks – baulks of timber that can be slotted in place to isolate a section of the canal. The other notable features are small rollers by the tow-path. Chains wound round them were fastened to a plug in the canal bed which could be pulled to empty the water out, much as you would empty a bath-tub. The water simply drained away through rock crevices, for the steep hillside which makes the canal so delightful to cruise was also responsible for a succession of land slips and cracks in the bed of the canal. The problem has been solved – or so it is hoped – by modern technology. The bed of the canal has been given a concrete and polythene lining. This could have been effective but drab, and the British Waterways Board who did the work recognised the problem. Above the water-line the bank has been given a facing of stone which has already weathered to blend with its surroundings, while mosses are creeping across the edge, softening the hard outline. It is an example of caring for small details repaying the effort many times over.

Even on this tranquil section there is ample evidence that this was once an important part of a busy, commercial waterway. Fractured cliffs poke through the tree cover, marking old stone quarries, and for every quarry there is a wharf area for boats. There is also a last glimpse of the textile industry, once again announced with a crashing, watery overture. Down in the valley is a lovely example of a textile mill, close by the road-bridge over the Avon, unmistakable with its water course and regular rows of arched windows. It also becomes clear why the canal's engineer, John Rennie, crossed to the other side of the valley, with all the expense of building an aqueduct. First, he was able to keep his canal on the same level, and second, if he had stayed on the west side he would have had to build an aqueduct anyway to cross the River Frome which joins the Avon at Freshford. Near Limpley Stoke the road builders also found problems with the awkward terrain and built a grand viaduct. We should be glad that Rennie took the decision that he did, for it resulted in the Kennet and Avon's grandest moments. As at Avoncliff, a worn post – iron this time not stone – stands like an exclamation mark by a sharp bend and around that bend is the Dundas aqueduct.

Dundas aqueduct seems to have been inspired by its nearness to elegant Bath. It is a reminder that the Georgian age, renowned for the refinement of its architecture, was also the age of canals. The style that seemed to flow so easily in the work of the best architects and builders did not leave the canal engineers untouched. The aqueduct is, in its own way, as graceful as a Bath crescent. It is seen at its best in bright sunlight when what can otherwise seem rather wan stone glows as if it had an inner light. But its form is stately at any time. A single, central arch spans the river, with smaller arches on the bank to either side. The applied decoration of Doric pilasters, deep cornice and balustrade combine with the lightness of the stone to give Dundas its appeal. Even structural necessities have their notes of grace, such as the buttresses built in long, sweeping curves.

On approaching Dundas you could be forgiven for thinking that the canal was about to do a complete U-turn, for you can see boats lined up across the valley. At the end of the aqueduct, you do find the Kennet and Avon bending again, but heading off towards Bath. The boats you saw were not on this canal at all but on another which is, as a notice at the entrance announces, 'The Somerset Coal Canal, opened 1801, closed 1904, restored 1985'. The notice brings you down to earth: after daydreaming and thinking poetic thoughts of sylvan glades, rural retreats and other suitably pastoral notions and then imagining Regency dandies and fashionable spas, here you are faced with a mundane coal canal. But this was the reality of the canal world: the surface dressing might, on occasions, be very beautiful, but in the end it all came down to shifting the heavy cargo of an increasingly industrialised world. To a canal subscriber, hoping for profits, the phrase 'Somerset coal-field' had a far richer ring to it than 'Beau Nash and the Pump Room'. This canal now has its own little tale that exemplifies a larger story. Built to carry coal, it fell into disuse. The old lock cottage at the canal entrance was bought by Tim Wheeldon, who set about clearing the lock chamber and digging out the canal – not for coal boats, but for pleasure boaters, the new cargo of the twentieth century. Private boats line the waterway and a hire fleet is moored under the shadow of the old wharf crane. The Somerset Coal Canal can also boast a new bridge, which is very much in keeping with the canal tradition – even if it did start life as a fire escape.

The canal continues its hill-hugging way beside the Avon, but opens out more than on the way to Dundas. There is much to see, much to admire: the river valley with its green meadows, a grand mansion on the hill and the odd curious feature to catch the eye. A typical stone hump-

The beauty of the canal near Claverton (Anthony Burton)

15

The interior of Claverton pumping station. The fly wheel and gears of the beam pump are in the foreground and the huge waterwheel can be seen through the arch. Working at its best, it could lift nearly 2½ million gallons of water a day from the river to the canal (Derek Pratt)

backed bridge carries an odd diamond-shaped sign, placed there by the GWR Paddington, which turns out to be cast iron. It informs drivers of 'heavy cars' that they must take due note of the Motor Car Acts of 1896 and 1903 and not drive over the bridge. Just beyond is another oddity: water gushing out of a culvert into the canal. When a canal such as the Kennet and Avon has such a long run without locks in such a rural setting, it is easy to forget that it is an artificial not a natural waterway. It contains water because the engineers have taken trouble to fill the canal and keep it topped up where necessary. It is not too difficult these days to pump up water from the nearby Avon, but what did the eighteenth-century engineer do? A sign-board points the way to Claverton pumping station.

There was a mill on this site when the canal builders arrived, and the weir across the river makes this a popular place for summer paddling. From the top of the weir a leat carries the water off to a plain stone building and here the water vanishes through a hole in the bottom of the wall. Plain it may be on the outside, but the inside is pure magic for all lovers of mechanical ingenuity. The engineer wanted to lift the river water up to the canal, and he had his power source right on hand – the river itself. Water falls on to a waterwheel over 17ft (5m) long and 24ft (7m) wide. When the sluices are open it turns with a steady throb as the water hits the paddles. Inside the building, cranks swing rhythmically, turning over to work a pair of beam pumps. It might sound a touch

16

Heath Robinsonish, but when the waterwheel turned at a steady 5 revolutions per minute, nearly 100,000gal (455,000 litres) of water were lifted 48ft (15m) up the hillside every hour and fuel costs were absolutely nil. Nowadays, the old machinery turns over only on demonstration days, but what a beautiful sight it is.

By a little canalside cottage are reminders of two aspects of canal life and it is difficult to decide which is the more attractive. One is a traditional canal narrow boat in all its glory, its working days over but finding a new role as an exhibition centre where the canal story is told. The other, peeping out from under a makeshift boat-house, is a most beautiful launch, the *Lady Lena*, built in the days when the name launch still conjured up an image of gleaming, varnished timber and even brighter brass. The mood of the canal, however, begins to change. The valley is opening and widening, and if Bath is not yet quite in sight, there is at least a feeling that it cannot be far away. The houses which appear in greater numbers now are built of the distinctive Bath stone, and the arrival of Bathampton marks the nearest thing to a built-up area since leaving Bradford. The place is an odd mixture of the old and the new, rural village and suburbia. The George Inn, below the canal bank, was clearly there long before the canal was built, but it is now viewed from across the water by a regular army of garden gnomes, and a feeder down to the canal has been turned into an ornamental screen through a rock garden.

Bathampton is the last stop before Bath, and there can be few better introductions to the city than the arrival by canal. The first glimpse, with rows of terraces, is reminiscent of Bradford, but as one continues, the whole of the city down by the river begins to appear as if a map has been unfurled. When walking through the streets one has a particular view of Bath, but from up on the heights it is remarkable how the city is still dominated by the great abbey church of St Peter and St Paul. Founded in 1499, the church was to be the last of its kind, for Henry VIII was soon to take the throne and the monastic world would be brought to an end. But there it stands, totally dominant, looking down over the terraces and crescents which have made the city famous as if they were so many newcomers.

A wharf and wharf cottage have a touch of the everyday, but the canal becomes involved with, almost absorbed into, that very special world of Bath where one still half expects to meet characters from Jane Austen out for a stroll or hear the clip-clop of hoof beats as a family drives by in a smart phaeton. A wide arched bridge suggests something a little grander than usual, but it is only when you are through and have a chance to look back that you see how grand the bridge really is. Officially, it does not qualify as a bridge at all but is listed as Sydney Gardens No 2 tunnel. It marks the entrance to the passage through the formal gardens with their classical pavilions, and the tunnel end, which is visible from the grounds, is highly decorated. Swags droop beneath the cornice, niches wait to be filled in the abutments. In the centre of the arch a fiercely bearded figure looks out from under the drapery, as though he was peeping round the stony curtain not quite sure whether he should be there or not. Once in the gardens, the canal is crossed by iron foot-bridges, very delicate and proudly announcing in suitably classical style that they were 'Erected Anno 1800'. The exit is through a second tunnel topped by a very grand house, once headquarters to the Kennet and Avon Canal Company but now home to the Department of the Environment. It is a splendid place with a front door which still has its glass lantern built into the fanlight. Beyond it, the tow-path changes sides on another reminder of horse days, for there is a long ramp doubling back on itself for the four-legged animal to get on to the bridge, and a flight of steps for the more manoeuvrable boatman.

A lock cottage is not quite so plain as the other canal houses, for Bath exerts its influence on everything, which here means pointed, Gothic windows. It marks the end of the lock-free canal and the start of the descent down through Bath. It all seems timeless, but as plaques along the way remind you, the Kennet and Avon has known hard times. It fell into a state of virtually complete dereliction, from which it was only rescued by the efforts of enthusiastic volunteers who refused to let it die. They did some work themselves but the main task of the Kennet and Avon Trust soon became to raise money and to persuade others to help. Bath did its share in the work. Once a canal becomes derelict, however, others feel it can be ignored. Why worry about how you build a road across the old locks if no one is going to use them? That was what happened here, with the result that one of the locks that helped to carry the canal down the hill to the level of the River Avon simply disappeared. What was to be done? The answer was to make the next surviving lock twice as deep. The result plunges boats down nearly 20ft (6m) in the awesome deep lock, a combination of locks eight and nine. It looks absolutely terrifying at first sight – and one is not encouraged by the message painted on the roof of the Ebenezer Baptist Chapel alongside 'Prepare to Meet Thy God'. In reality, it all works out all right, but it is a brave soul that does not feel a twinge of nervousness when faced with the Deep Lock.

In its passage through Sydney Gardens in Bath, the Kennet and Avon matches the formal beauty of its surroundings with delicate iron bridges (Anthony Burton)

Locks eight and nine of the Widcombe flight at Bath have been combined to make the awesome Deep Lock: a small cruiser is hurled about in the churning waters (Anthony Burton)

Was all the effort of rebuilding and refurbishing worthwhile? It clearly was, and not just for those who want to use the canal. The locals have a splendid waterway where once there was a muddy ditch littered with old supermarket trolleys. As at Claverton, new methods have taken over from the old. Water supply was once by steam engine. All that remains of the system at the top of the locks is the isolated chimney, but down at the bottom the engine-house has been very successfully converted into a wine bar. It is a mark of just how much renewal has improved the whole feel of this area that a grand new hotel has been built to look out over the engine-house and side pond. Before restoration, a hotelier would probably have preferred a site by the abattoir.

So, the last lock appears. Beyond it is the River Avon leading on to Bristol and the sea. This one short section of canal was not just a small portion of the whole Kennet and Avon, but the Kennet and Avon itself is only a small part of a complex waterways network. It linked together the old and the new of its time. It joined a river navigation at Bath which had itself been improved at the beginning of the eighteenth century and it provided a means of joining the two ancient ports of Bristol and London. Over the years, the canal has seen enormous changes. The days of the working boat have given way to the days of the pleasure boat, but the wonder of it is that so much of the past has survived, so much character has been retained. In 10 miles (16km) of travel, I filled pages of a notebook with my jottings. I would have written as much on any other section of the canal – or, indeed, on any other canal. And I know if I repeated the trip tomorrow, I would fill yet more pages with the sights I had missed. And that will ensure, if nothing else does, that the appetite for canal travel will never be satisfied.

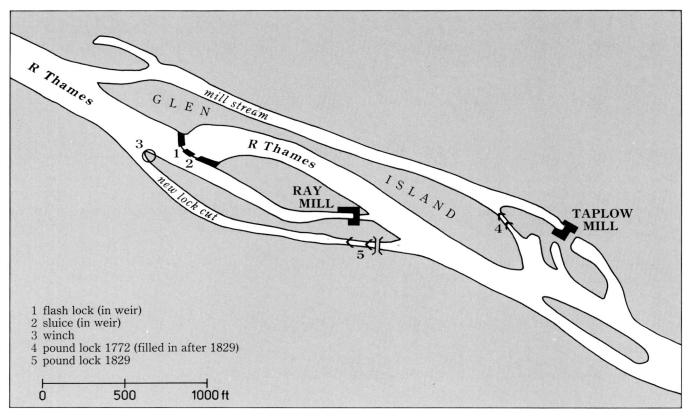

1 flash lock (in weir)
2 sluice (in weir)
3 winch
4 pound lock 1772 (filled in after 1829)
5 pound lock 1829

0   500   1000 ft

2 THE RIVER NAVIGATIONS

Boulter's, on a fine Sunday, is a sight to be remembered. The scene has been often painted and described, but it is impossible to convey to any who have not at some time formed part of the crowd, either on the water or as onlookers, an impression of its brightness and interest.

That brief description of Boulter's Lock at Maidenhead comes from a guidebook which was already past its prime when I took it on my first trip down the Thames in the 1950s. If anything, the scene today is even busier than it was then – as busy and varied as at any time in the river's history. Perhaps 'busy' is not quite the right word, for it suggests frenzied activity, and Boulter's on a sunny Sunday can more aptly be described as a scene of frenzied inactivity; the inactivity belonging to the boats forced to queue for their turn in the lock, and the frenzy belonging to their crews who often tend to bring the habits of a bustling working life with them to the river. There is activity on the fringes, however, as new boats arrive with the soft throb of a diesel engine and the deep, throaty gurgle of twin propellers or the insect-like whirr of a tiny outboard motor. Having arrived, there is the problem of finding space to wait among what can seem like the crowd at the start of the January sales. The one point of calm is the lock itself where the expert lock-keeper patiently directs each boat to its place and, as each fits into his pattern, the engines are stilled, and, like some giant composite raft, the boats rise or fall with the waters until the wonderful moment arrives when the gates swing apart and the boats are released to rush or dawdle to the next lock. And all this complex of manoeuvring or mooring and untying has to be carried out under the amused gaze of a crowd of spectators who, the boater feels, are only waiting for something really entertaining to happen, such as a collision or a capsize, to make their entertainment complete.

The people on the river are as varied as the boats that carry them: everything from suburban sea captains in regulation peaked caps 'Blighing' it over their fibreglass Bounties to the anarchic lads in Union Jack shorts. Yet they have one thing in common – they are on the river for pleasure. And if you turned back the clock a hundred years, you would find much the same to be true. Dress would be different, however, and most boats would be moved by oars or punt poles with only the occasional passing elegance of a sleek steam launch to break the pattern. This is the world we know from Jerome K. Jerome's classic *Three Men in a Boat*, which first appeared in 1889. It conjured up instant images of beefy young men in blazers made of material that could equally

The pattern of change at Boulter's lock (Gill Scott)

Boulter's Lock on the Thames in 1890, the age of Three Men in a Boat. *There is a typical mixture of punts, skiffs and steam launches – and the inevitable crowd of spectators* (Oxfordshire County Libraries)

Hambleden mill stands at the end of a long procession of weirs across the Thames. The medieval miller's weirs were a great hindrance to boatmen and a source of endless quarrels between these two important groups of river users (Anthony Burton)

well be used by a manufacturer of gaudy deckchairs, and somewhat droopy, muslined ladies sheltering beneath parasols. They were, in fact, a new phenomenon, and pleasure boating was just receiving attention from parliament who, as ever, wanted to regulate matters. They heard evidence from the old guard, who did not take kindly to the new generation of boaters, and among the complainers was the resoundingly titled Sir Gilbert Augustus Clayton East. In his evidence he spoke of the newcomers as savages, and wanted to know 'whether these people were naturally savages, or whether they become savages when they come on the river'. Pressed by the chairman to be more precise, he divided his savages between 'the London 'arry, recognised by the absence of the letter H', and 'a superior class'. The former dressed in shorts, and the others were even worse.

I should say that on a Sunday the majority are these objectionable people . . . one Sunday I was down at my Reach, and three lockfulls of boats came through one after another. A steam launch came through. I suppose they are not all as well behaved as they should be. There was a table fitted up in front, with two men and two women, and they went up sitting at this table with a bottle of Champagne; in another hour they came back. They had consumed two bottles of Champagne; and they were then followed through the lock by another launch which had a cabin to it. In this cabin was a middle aged man lying down fast asleep with an empty Champagne bottle by his side. I have not so much complaint to make of these steam-launches, because they do not offend very much; they pass by and are gone, but the rowing boats hang about. They come up from Marlow, and hang about all day.

THE RIVER NAVIGATIONS

One would dearly like to see Sir Gilbert Augustus Clayton East confronted by bikinis and Radio 1. The committee, showing remarkably good sense for a parliamentary body, seem to have found the apoplectic gentleman as absurd as we find him today.

Yet even then, when Maidenhead was at the height of its popularity, when the Guardsmen took their weekend train from London to visit their ladies' houses in the neat villas along the river bank, there was another aspect to river life of which you will find no mention in Jerome's book. But look up the waterways' Bradshaw of 1908, de Salis' *Handbook of Inland Navigation*, and you read of a busy trade of barges and narrow boats and of steam tugs that 'habitually tow barges to Reading, and at times to Oxford'. A century ago, the Thames was a working, as well as a pleasure, river. Yet if we could return, we should feel that Boulter's Lock was still the Boulter's Lock that we know today. The same would not be true were we to travel further back in time, to the end of the eighteenth century. It would not just be the river traffic that would have changed – there would be not a pleasure boat in sight – but Boulter's itself would have a totally different appearance. The lock is now on the west bank of the river, but then it was on the east. The familiar lock cut, so crowded with boats on our sunny Sunday afternoon, simply would not exist at all. To understand what had happened, we have to look further back to the 1770s.

In 1770 the Thames Navigation Commission, overwhelmed by complaints about the state of the river, put a plan to parliament for improving the navigation from Richmond to Abingdon. Permission was given for work to go ahead and Joseph Nickalls was appointed General Surveyor, or, as we should say, Chief Engineer. Eight new locks were planned, one of which was Boulter's. It was very different in appearance from the present-day lock. The lower part of the chamber was planked, but the upper part was a turfed slope, so that as the water rose it also spread out over the grass in an ever-widening pool. There was already an artificial cutting in existence which carried water to Taplow Mill, and the new lock was built in a short cutting from the end of the mill stream. It remained in use until, having fallen into a sorry state of disrepair, it was abandoned, filled in and replaced by a new lock in 1829. It is that lock in its new lock cutting which is, essentially, the one in use today.

The 'new' lock of 1829 was little different in essentials from that completed in 1772, apart, of course, from having hopped from one side of the river to the other. But if we continue our time travel back beyond that point, the scene changes dramatically. The familiar Thames lock with its massive gates has disappeared from view. Instead, all we should see would be the mill streams diverting water to mills on either bank, and to ensure that there was always a good head of water to keep the mill wheels turning, a massive weir stretched right across the river. The only obvious gap in the weir would have been the sluice which allowed the river water to pour in a torrent through its narrow gateway. If we could look over this scene of more than two centuries ago, we should also see a busy river traffic of barges, some driven along by square sails, others being hauled by gangs of men on the tow-path, for men rather than horses did the work on the Thames in those days. But we might also be faced with an interesting puzzle: how would the boats travel between the sections of river above and below the weir – there were no locks in sight, the mill streams were closed by the waterwheels and one could scarcely expect barges to shoot the rapids of the sluice like some slalom canoeists. The answer would be there, but not immediately obvious: the flash-lock.

Close to the sluice, a part of the weir was closed off by a complex system of removable paddles. The commonest system had a single gate, not unlike the familiar lock gate, except that the spaces in the sturdy frame, between the stout timbers – the rymers – were filled by the paddles. As these were removed, the water could run straight through the gate, which could then be swung open to create a miniature waterfall or 'flash' of water. Once the torrent had abated, barges could ride the flash downstream, but those travelling against the current had to be hauled up laboriously by means of a permanent winch on the bank. It was not, as the seventeenth-century Oxford historian Robert Plot noted, 'without imminent danger'. Indeed, in 1634 a passenger boat with about sixty people on board overturned in the flash at Goring: there were no survivors. It was, at best, an unsatisfactory system and, at worst, a dangerous one, and one that led to endless conflicts throughout the centuries it was in use until the new lock was built in 1772. The dangers now seem all too obvious. Who would willingly now take a heavy barge over a Thames weir, even if the waters were supposed to be under control? To understand the conflicts, you have to look at the scene in a little more detail.

Domesday Book lists more than five thousand mills in England, of which the great majority were water mills, and the River Thames had

The last remaining flash-lock in use on the Thames at Eynsham. To the left of the photograph, the tops of the movable paddles can be seen. The rest have been removed and the single gate swings open to allow the 'flash' of water to race down the river. Boats rode the flood of water downstream but had to be winched upstream against the current (Oxfordshire County Libraries)

its fair share. It was the millers who built the weirs to hold back the water, and only reluctantly allowed the boats to pass through. The miller's interest was in keeping his wheels turning, and when the flash-lock was in use, the water passed through there, leaving his mill streams useless and his waterwheel still. True, he could recoup some of the cost by charging for the use of the lock, but he regarded that as poor compensation for the loss of time. So the miller would wait until there was what he regarded as a decent number of craft queueing up before releasing the flash. This he felt was only fair and reasonable: the boatmen took a different view. John Taylor, the waterman poet, wrote a verse description of a journey from Oxford to London in 1632, with his objectives clearly set out:

> But I (from Oxford) down to Staines will slide,
> And tell the rivers wrongs which I espide.

Chief among those wrongs were the weirs set up by millers, which finally earned from the poet this exasperated condemnation:

> How can that man be counted a good liver,
> That for his private use will stop a river?

One can sympathise with both sides: mills remained still for hours on end while a procession of barges was slowly hauled up stream, and barge men might wait long hours or even days for the flash-lock to be opened. The new lock, the pound-lock – the familiar lock we all know today with its two sets of gates – was clearly a great advantage to all parties. The boatman could be on his way quickly and safely, and the miller could go on milling – although the latter having had several centuries of regarding boats as unpleasant nuisances, was not notably enthusiastic. This attitude earned the millers a reprimand from an anonymous commissioner of the Thames Navigation, who complained about high charges at the new locks or 'turnpike pounds'. In the old days, he wrote in 1772, the mill owner had

> to continue his Lock open for *three or four Hours or more*, during the tedious Passage of upward Barges through the Gull and Lock. Let him compare these incessant Damages with the immense Benefit, which he cannot fail to receive under the new Mode of Navigation; when, instead of the Wane of Water he usually sustained, the Loss to him will be no more than the contents of a Turnpike Pound; and, upon this comparative View, let the Miller himself be the Judge, who is injured, and who has most Reason to complain.

So, the scene at Boulter's changed over the centuries, just as the whole river scene changed with changing times. On some sections of the river change would seem almost infinitesimally slow. Flash-locks, which first appeared on the Thames somewhere around the end of the twelfth century, remained in use on the Upper Thames above Oxford for

This river scene at Abingdon on the Thames at the beginning of the nineteenth century is very different from that which one sees today. It is many years since any trading barges or lighters appeared this high up the river, and the many arched bridge has long since been demolished. St Helen's church spire, however, still dominates the scene and the old almshouses still stand beneath its shadow (Royal Commission on the Historical Monuments of England/Michael E. Ware Collection)

around seven hundred years, the last of them at Eynsham not being replaced until 1931. This loveliest part of the whole river can still seem to be meandering through a timeless landscape. The first pound-locks appeared between Oxford and Abingdon in the 1630s, so that progress here must have seemed almost indecently rapid by comparison. But the greatest change of all has been on the tidal Thames. As this has mainly been concerned with sea-going craft rather than inland waterways, it lies outside the scope of this work. The story of the rise and fall in the fortunes of London's river and docks needs a book to itself, but it is worth noting that there was a time when the river was not merely a route for cargo, but the principal thoroughfare of the capital. Londoners hailed a river boat as readily as they now hail a bus or taxi. There was, in Shakespeare's time, a brisk traffic between the Londoners who lived on the north bank and the theatres which were all built to the south, and the watermen were loud in complaint when the first theatres appeared in the north. They were eventually to get compensation of a sort, for Thomas Doggett, the manager of Drury Lane Theatre who died in 1721, provided in his will for a prize, Doggett's Coat and Badge, to be rowed for annually by young watermen. The race, between London Bridge and Chelsea, is the oldest rowing race in the country. The watermen were skilled and proud of their abilities and the Company of Watermen and Lightermen did their best to ensure that only the truly competent took charge of boats, by decreeing a minimum two years' apprenticeship. The company also had a complex set of rules, laying down just where and how boats could ply for hire, and setting out the conduct expected of a Thames waterman. The rules concerning language and sobriety do not, according to contemporary reports, appear to have been universally obeyed. A pamphleteer reported hearing men 'bellowing out their lewd and filthy jests, treating one another with all the approbious language their Wit can invent'. Perhaps so, but they provided Londoners with an efficient, pleasant and reasonably priced service, just as their descendants do today, for a trip by river boat remains the best way of seeing the capital. And the language of the modern waterman may not be opprobius but still shows inventive wit.

We have strayed some distance in both time and place from Boulter's Lock, but the excursion has at least shown that rivers have changed dramatically over the years, as man has changed and adapted them for his own purposes. Even the apparently simple matter of transport, which might at first seem to require no more than floating a boat out on to the water and cheerily setting off for one's destination, has been greatly affected by man's attempts to make journeys easier, safer and cheaper. So when did it all begin? When did man realise that these expanses of moving water might actually be useful and not merely a barrier to be overcome? There is no simple answer, because the use of rivers for transport takes us right back to the distant and only dimly understood years of prehistory.

Part of Britain's most famous ancient monument, Stonehenge, is constructed of blue-stones, weighing about 4 tons each from the Prescelly Mountains in Dyfed, Wales. They arrived in Wiltshire somewhere around 2,400BC. Now it is inconceivable that such massive stones could have been sent overland. On the other hand, the mountains are close to the sea and Stonehenge itself is close to Amesbury where the River Avon flows south to the sea in Christchurch Bay. Experiments have shown that it would have been possible to bring the stones by raft around the coast and then up the river. Possible confirmation for this theory is The Avenue,

Early in the twentieth century there was still an enticing mixture of trading vessels to be seen on Britain's rivers. Here steam tugs are towing spritsail barges on the Trent near Keadby with a lighter under tow behind them (Lincs Library Service)

A Proposal for Improving the River Thames

The city of Oxford, and the rest of your Majesties subjects and Barge-men are deprived of the benefit intended them by the said Navigation, and many times the Barges lye on ground three weeks or a Month together for want of water, which might be prevented by making three Holds of water in the River Sharwell near Oxford, to be let down as flushes in dry times, as also one Lock to be made at Swift Ditch, one pair of gates at Sutton, one Turn-pike a Mile below Sutton, with two flushes to be taken out of the River Kennet, with two near Chersey, all which being done, will so plentifully supply the River with water, that not only the Barges coming from Oxford and Abingdon, but many other places, will have the benefit thereof, and bring them clear to London without stay.

Andrew Yarranton, *England's Improvement by Sea and Land, 1677)*

One of the principal arguments in favour of the improvement of river navigations was the often atrocious state of the roads, as many travellers testified. Daniel Defoe, writing in the 1720s, described the road north from Dunstable:

You enter the deep clays, which are so surprisingly soft, that it is perfectly frightful to travellers, and it has been the wonder of foreigners, how, considering the great numbers of carriages which are continually passing with heavy loads, those ways have been made practicable; indeed the great number of horses every year kill'd by the excess of labour in those heavy ways, has been such a charge to the country, continued on page 29

which was laid out at the same time to link the main site to the river. It is pleasing to think of Britain's rivers as having been accepted as transport routes as far back as neolithic times, but the evidence is admittedly flimsy. But once we come up one rung of the prehistoric ladder, stepping off from the New Stone Age and into the Bronze Age, an altogether clearer picture emerges. We have the substantial remains of a boat – or rather three boats – built around 1500BC and first discovered in 1940 embedded in the Humber mud close to the new Humber bridge at North Ferriby. These were no mere rafts, but sophisticated wooden vessels – very definitely boat-shaped boats, over 40ft (12m) long with sides built up on a central plank, not unlike the keel of a modern craft. From here on the evidence multiplies of river use – peacefully for trade, less peacefully for invasion. Rivers came to be seen as crucial to the life of the country, and towns and cities grew and developed at the heads of navigations or at major crossing points.

At first, boats were restricted to the naturally navigable rivers and the improvements to river transport were mainly improvements to river craft rather than to the rivers themselves. As we have seen, it was the millers who constructed weirs to ensure a regular controlled water supply. The boating fraternity saw these as the creators of irritating delays, but they were, in fact, a considerable aid to navigation. A river left to its own devices seldom runs in a convenient, easy course. It collects gravel and soil from one spot and deposits it in another to create a shoal. It saunters along quietly and placidly for a while, then suddenly dives off steeply downhill, burbling and gurgling between rocks and splashing over ledges. It squeezes between the high cliffs of a gorge at one point and spreads out over a wide flood plain at another. All this may make the river picturesque, a delight to the artist or sightseer, but it is very little help to those who want move cargo on its waters. The river must inevitably flow downhill, but what the boatman wants is to see that descent kept under strict control. The weir and flash-lock provided an answer. The weir held back the water above it, cutting down the flow, allowing water to build up to cover the rocks and shallows. The river, instead of being an uneven slope, became a series of regular steps, the lock taking the boat from one level to the next. The fact that the weir benefited both boater and miller did not stop the endless arguments between the two, and there was a further irritant to the boater in the form of fishermen who built their own weirs of stakes and basketwork to trap their fish. The law tried to smooth the way between the factions, although if the amount of legislation is any guide, without any great success.

As far back as the reign of Edward the Confessor, a right of passage was established on those rivers which were considered always to have been navigable. Just as the citizens had the right to use the King's Highway on land, so too on the water, and contemporaries even spoke of the King's Highway of Severn or the King's Highway of Thames. That right was spelled out again in King John's Magna Carta. But stating that a right exists is not the same as ensuring that it is allowed in practice. It was not just the millers, fishermen and riparian landlords who wanted to use the rivers for their own purposes. Those who traded on the river

A busy river scene at Tewkesbury in 1804. A whole variety of craft can be seen, including a two-masted Severn trow of 99 tons. The scene also makes an important point about the early enthusiasm for river transport. In the background a heavily laden barge is being pulled by a single horse on the tow-path, while a team of three horses pulls a comparatively light cart away from the quay (Tewkesbury Town Council)

frequently demanded rights of passage for themselves, while attempting to deny the same rights to competitors. The different interests spread out along the River Severn almost gave the phrase 'cut-throat competition' a literal meaning.

In 1411, the burgesses of Bristol and Gloucester petitioned parliament over the town of Bewdley's attempts to monopolise trade by what can best be described as plain piracy. The Bewdley men had a fleet of vessels known as 'trows' (pronounced to rhyme with crows). What they were like is uncertain, but they were probably simple, square-rigged sailing barges not unlike those then in use on the Thames. In time, they developed into a very distinctive type of river craft (see Chapter 7). In 1411, however, they seem to have been new to the river and their owners were anxious to make as much profit as possible on their investment in the craft. Previously, much of the river traffic had been on large rafts or floats, but the trow owners decided, more than a little arbitrarily, that from now on all traffic past Bewdley would be on their vessels. The raft men, not surprisingly, ignored the demands, until the Bewdley men produced some persuasive arguments:

> On the eve of St Michael last past, lying in wait near Bewdley with great force and arms they had seized upon a great drag or float going to Gloucester, and made the masters of it cut in pieces the said float in the said river, or otherwise they would cut off their heads.

After Bewdley, it was Worcester's turn to try for an easy profit by charging tolls for boats going under their bridge. The excuse was the somewhat ambiguous definition of the charges known as pontage, usually taken as payment by those going over the bridge not under it. Parliament sorted that one out by firmly restating the rights of the king's liege people to carry merchandise freely on the river. The citizens were

continued from page 28
that new building of causeways, as the Romans did of old, seems to me to be a much easier expence.

Half a century later, the new roads seem no better than the old: In 1769, the agriculturalist Arthur Young wrote the following regarding the Wigan turnpike road:

> I know not, in the whole range of language, terms sufficiently expressive to describe this infernal road . . . let me most seriously caution all travellers, who may accidentally purpose to travel this terrible country, to avoid it as they would the devil; for a thousand to one but they break their necks or their limbs by overthrows or breaking downs. They will here meet with rutts which I actually measured four feet deep, and floating with mud only from a wet summer; what therefore must it be after a winter?

continued on page 30

continued from page 29
But nothing from these years can quite match this story, recounted by Mrs J. R. Green in her *Town Life in the Fifteenth Century*, of the perils of travel in medieval England:

In 1499 a glover from Leighton Buzzard travelled with his wares to Aylesbury for the market before Christmas Day. It happened that an Aylesbury miller, Richard Boose, finding that his mill needed repairs, sent a couple of servants to dig clay 'called Ramming clay' for him on the highway, and was in no way dismayed because the digging of this clay made a great pit in the middle of the road ten feet wide, eight feet broad, and eight feet deep, which was quickly filled with water by the winter rains. But the unhappy glover, making his way from the town in the dusk, with his horse laden with paniers full of gloves, straightway fell into the pit, and man and horse were drowned. The miller was charged with his death, but was acquitted by the court on the ground that he had had no malicious intent, and had only dug the pit to repair his mill, and because he really did not know of any other place to get the kind of clay he wanted save the high-road.

not going to give up that easily. They had been granted the right to charge for the use of the town wharf. Quite unreasonably, it seemed to them, some boat owners, not having any business in Worcester, simply sailed on by. The locals had the answer: they stoned the hapless boatmen from the town bridge and forced them ashore, where they demanded their tolls and even insisted that the cargo should be sold cheaply to pay the fees. Parliament had to intervene again to settle the dispute.

For many centuries river law was solely concerned with legislating for disputes, between miller and boatmen, boatmen and boatmen, toll payer and toll collector. In the sixteenth century, laws were not passed merely to prevent interference with the natural state of river navigations, but parliament began to concern itself with the notion of actual improvements. The most important of the general laws, the Statute of Sewers, 1532, sounds somewhat unpromising. This is because we think of sewers as underground pipes carrying a great amount of material that we would prefer not to see. In the sixteenth century, however, the name applied to any drainage channel, natural or artificial. The statute allowed for the appointment of six commissioners – 'substaunciall and indifferent personnes' – who had substantial funds of their own to reduce the temptations of bribery and who had no personal interest in the affairs they were soon to control. What made this statute different from others was that it specified that the commissioners were to concern themselves with navigation as well as land drainage. In practice, the commissioners concerned themselves solely with improving existing navigations rather than recommending new schemes. The sixteenth century did, however, see a number of purely local interests coming forward with proposals for new works.

The parliamentary acts from this period were particularly important. The first, in 1515, allowed the city of Canterbury to extend navigation on the Great Stour above Fordwich so that vessels could reach the city. This was the first time that an act had been approved for a river that had never previously been known to be navigable, and it gave wide powers to the improvers. They were given, in effect, rights of compulsory purchase, so that they could buy up mills or knock down bridges with independent assessors appointed to set the levels of compensation. This was a pattern that was to be followed in future river acts and in the canal acts of a later age. The second act of special interest was that for the River Exe of 1539. It is worth looking at this one in more detail.

In the twelfth century, the earls of Devon had cut off Exeter from the sea by building the Countess Wear right across the River Exe. This was a very serious matter for Exeter which was then a centre of the woollen cloth trade, but no amount of appealing and petitioning could have any effect when set against the might of the earls. Then, in 1539, Hugh Courtenay fell foul of Henry VIII and was executed for treason. Exeter promptly received the go-ahead to bring ships back to the city. Having waited some four centuries for this moment, the authorities did not exactly rush forward to start and little was achieved until 1546. It was not a propitious time. England had just finished a ruinously expensive war with France, which was paid for in part by debasing the coinage.

A trader's advert for the River Severn. The vessel is a trow, carrying a good deal of sail, with a basic square rig of mainsail and topsail and a small gaff-rigged sail on the mizzen. Such a vessel could, as the advert suggests, venture out into the Bristol Channel to cross over to South Wales (British Waterways Board)

The quay at the end of the Exeter Canal in the 1890s. The completion of the canal in 1566 and later improvements enabled large ships such as the brig Devonshire Lass seen in the picture to come right up to the city of Exeter (The ISCA Collection)

This led to rampant inflation and widespread rioting, ending in open revolt when rebel forces besieged Exeter. Eventually, in 1566, a new channel was completed, bypassing the Countess Wear and running up to the city quay. This was the Exeter Canal, paid for by local government funds and run by local government ever since. It earned a special place in the history books, for it was the first in Britain to be built with pound-locks closed by mitre gates, meeting at an angle, at the upstream end and single gates downstream. These were massive locks, 189ft (58m) long by 23ft (7m) wide, designed not only to allow for a change of levels, but to permit vessels to pass, for the canal itself was only 16ft (5m) wide. The new locks were not a local invention, for the modern lock began with the work of that greatest of all polymaths, Leonardo da Vinci, who was appointed ducal engineer for Milan in 1482. His sketch books show clear illustrations of pound-locks with masonry chambers closed off by mighty gates, containing small sluice doors for allowing water in and out. These were built on the Naviglio Interno and formed the pattern for all such navigations that followed on. On this occasion the British engineers were lagging more than a century behind their counterparts in Europe, so the claim to fame of John Trew, the Exeter engineer, is a purely local one.

The third important act legislated for a canal to run from the River Lea to the city of London. This was not an improvement of an existing river so much as an entirely independent canal. It could have marked the start of Britain's canal age two centuries before the Duke of Bridgewater but for the unfortunate fact that work was never begun. However, the River Lea itself can boast the distinction of having the first completely modern lock with two sets of mitred gates. This was considered sufficiently novel and impressive to merit a mention in a poem of 1577, 'Tale of the Two Swannes'. The poem makes up in accuracy what it lacks in literary value:

> . . . the locke
> Through which the boates of Ware doe passe with malt.
> This lock contains two double doores of wood,
> Within the same a cesterne all of Plancke,
> Which onely fils when boates come there to passe
> By opening of these mightie dores.

The work that was begun in the sixteenth century was continued with ever-increasing enthusiasm into the next and on into the eighteenth century and the start of the canal age. There were twelve river improvement acts in the decade beginning 1660, the most prolific period for legislation, out of a total of forty acts in the century from 1650 to 1750. There were also numerous books and pamphlets produced extolling the virtues of inland waterways. Some argued specific cases, such as Francis Mathew in his book *A Mediterranean Passage between Lynn and Yarmouth* (1656) in which the author proposes a new canal to join the Ouse and the Waveney. He also laments the state of the Fossdyke, the Roman drainage canal, which he claims was cut by order of Henry I. In fact, the medieval work was merely an improvement to

The idyllic rural canal: the Llangollen Canal near Llangollen (Anthony Burton)

make the dyke navigable by large vessels – not that the fact affects the nature of his passionate complaint:

> But what an unworthy neglect thereof hath been in these latter times I blush to write! To let it fall, to be of no use, and the Work (though yet extant) to lye empty, waste, and dry, far from the intention of the Royal giver! in so much as now Sheep and Cattel graze, where formerly Barks have sayled, and perhaps a King in them!

Mathew then proposed an even more ambitious scheme, another 'Mediterranean Passage', but this time from London to Bristol, anticipating the actual Kennet and Avon Canal scheme by well over a hundred years.

Another enthusiast, Andrew Yarranton, author of *England's Improvement by Sea and Land* (1677), had further ideas for profitable development. His schemes included damming the River Cherwell at Oxford so that it could act as a reservoir to supply the Thames in dry seasons; and improving the navigations of the Midlands with the aim of turning Stratford-upon-Avon into a major manufacturing centre, with two new towns – New Brunswick for malting and brewing and New Haarlem for linen. He also showed a perspicacity in foreseeing the end of Chester's role as a sea port:

> the Trade of Chester is much decayed, and gone to Liverpool; and that old great City in danger of being ruin'd, if the River Dee be not made navigable by Act of Parliament, and Ships brought to the City.

Yarranton was, however, more than just a pamphleteer; he was actively involved in new schemes. In 1662, work was authorised on the Worcestershire Stour, between Stourbridge and the Severn. There was no shortage of investors in the scheme, but sadly, very little overall control, and Yarranton stepped in with a thousand pounds, for which he received a one-third share in the enterprise. On completion, he had a successful business running coal boats, but the local population were less satisfied. Many bills had still not been paid and the agent for the navigation reported that people had stopped boats, 'some threatening to cut the lines, others to cut their legs; standing in their way with weapons, making them to forego their way'. The troubles passed and the navigations continued rather more peacefully until floods in the 1780s caused heavy damage. Trade passed to the new Staffs and Worcester and Stourbridge canals.

The early eighteenth century saw some major river schemes come to fruition, of which the most important was undoubtedly the Aire and Calder. The act to which it related was passed at the end of the seventeenth century and it received royal assent in May 1699. It opened up the Aire from the previous head of navigation at Weeland all the way to Leeds and made the Calder navigable to Wakefield, a total of 40 miles (64km) with fourteen locks. It was to become and remain one of the

The Thames at Abingdon: once this was a busy trading wharf (Anthony Burton)

The Advantages of Navigations

That the greatest advantages are derived by mankind from navigation, which establishes an intercourse, between all the different inhabitants of the earth, and enables them to supply their mutual wants, by exchanging their mutual productions, is a position which no one will dispute. To the improvements made in that most useful art are the commercial nations of Europe principally indebted for their superiority over the rest of the world in power and opulence, the consequence of their extensive trade, and the flourishing state of their manufactures.

But what the ocean is to the distant countries which it divides, navigable rivers and canals are to the different provinces and districts of the same country; and as navigation on the former effects an intercourse and mutual exchange of productions between different kingdoms, in like manner inland navigation facilitates a communication between, and consequently promotes trade and industry in the different parts of the same kingdom. It seems, indeed, totally unnecessary at present, to attempt to enumerate the great benefits that accrue to trade and commerce from inland navigation.

(John Phillips, *A General History of Inland Navigation*, 1805)

Opposite are the principal schemes for new and improved navigation schemes between 1600 and the building of the Bridgewater Canal in 1760:

most important navigations in the country. The engineer John Hadley proved to be efficient and prompt, completing all the work by 1703. Daniel Defoe, who visited the area a few years later on his *Tour Through the Whole Island of Great Britain*, wrote at length of the advantages to the Leeds merchants who could send out their cloth to Hull for shipping across the North Sea. Just as importantly, coal could be sent out to all the surrounding countryside without the tax that had to be paid on Newcastle coal, simply because the South Yorkshire coal did not go by sea. One reason for the speed and success of the Aire and Calder venture lay with its finance. It was paid for almost entirely by local merchants and manufacturers, who were more concerned with improving their main businesses than with any possible profits on the navigation shares. Other major schemes were less fortunate.

The scheme for the Kennet Navigation from Reading to Newbury was first brought to parliament in 1708, with the enthusiastic support of many important local towns, with one crucial exception – Reading. The River Thames was providing Reading with a steady and lucrative trade and the local inhabitants had no desire to see any goods bypassing them on a new waterway. Their opposition was fierce and so well co-ordinated that final approval and the transition of the bill into a fully authorised act had to wait until 1715. That, however, was not the end of the troubles. The work itself was particularly difficult. Where the change in level on the Aire in the 30 miles (48km) to Weeland was only 68ft (21m), that on the Kennet from Reading to Newbury was 138ft (42m) in 18½ miles (30km). Not surprisingly, the work needed on the Kennet was far greater than that on the Aire, and the engineer John Hore had to build twenty locks and dig over 11 miles (18km) of new cutting to bypass troublesome sections of the river. The work took nine years, but the delays were by no means all due to engineering difficulties. Again, there was a marked contrast with the Aire and Calder. Where support for the former had come from the local community, most of the Kennet finance drew on the funds of London speculators. The early eighteenth century was a great time for playing the market, when every speculation seemed destined to bring in instant returns. Then the bubble burst – in this case the famous South Sea Bubble, the company that was floated with government support to help bring down the national debt. When that collapsed, destroyed by a mixture of incompetence, corruption and greed, the consequences were catastrophic, as investors desperately tried to salvage funds from the wreckage. The many fraudulent schemes were the first to suffer, but such sensible plans as the Kennet Navigation suffered along with them.

The work was eventually completed, but the men of Reading were far from reconciled to the newcomer. When William Darvall of Maidenhead tried to take his barges past Reading and on to the Kennet, he received this blood-curdling threat:

Mr Darvall wee Bargemen of Redding thought to Aquaint you before 'tis too Late, Dam You, if y. work a bote any more at Newbery wee will Kill You if ever you come any more this way, wee was very near shooting you last time, we went with to pistolls and was not too Minnets too Late. The first time your Boat Lays at Redding Loaded, Dam You, wee will bore holes in her and sink her so Dont come to starve our fammeleys and our Masters . . . so take warning before 'tis too late for Dam you for ever if you come wee will doo it – from wee Bargemen.

It sometimes seems as if the canal age appeared by magic, growing from nothing but the inspired brains of the Duke of Bridgewater and James Brindley. It was, in fact, the next logical step for extending the benefits of inland navigation. Over the centuries, engineers, many anonymous and few now remembered, perfected many techniques that would be used on the canals. More importantly, perhaps, they demonstrated convincingly how valuable these watery highways were to the economic life of a country that was steadily moving towards industrialisation.

The factors that made water transport more efficient than land transport had been known for centuries. They were stated succinctly by the Speaker of the House of Commons in a speech of 1655:

It easeth the People of the great Charge of Land Carriage, preserves the Highways, which are daily worn out with Waggons carrying excessive Burdens; it breeds up a Nursery of Watermen which, upon Occasion will prove good Seamen; and with much Facility maintains Intercourse and Communion between Cities and Countries.

The roads obviously were used extensively. *The Carriers Cosmographie* of 1637 lists, for example, all the carriers' services for London, and very extensive they were, with different starting places for all the different routes. Goods for the Thames valley would be taken to The George in Bread Street; but if they were to be sent to Guildford, they would begin their journey from that still popular establishment, The George in Southwark. But river traffic was cheaper than road, simply because one horse could haul a boat carrying some sixty times the load of a cart on the rough, unmade roads of the time.

Looking around the river scene today, it might seem that river traffic could scarcely have been a threat to the roads since there are so many roads and so few navigable rivers. But two centuries ago there was far, far greater river traffic than would be possible today. In November 1987, Arthur Pagett took his pleasure cruiser up the Severn as far as Bridgnorth, the first time it seems that a vessel of such a size had travelled so high up the river this century. Yet in the eighteenth century, large cargo craft regularly traded beyond that to Ironbridge – indeed, one reason why Abraham Darby sited his famous ironworks there was to take advantage of the river traffic. And large vessels even went as high as Shrewsbury. Other rivers which are now scarcely used by boats of any description were once alive with trade. The 'picturesque Wye' for example, was once a thriving trading route, serving the tin-plate works of Redbrook, the paper-mills of Whitebrook and the iron and wire works of Tintern. Now the only reminders of those days are crumbling quays and the occasional pub name, such as The Sloop at Llandogo.

Date	River	Length (miles km)
1618–35	Great Ouse	24 (39)
1624–35	Thames	15 (24)
1636–39	Warwick Avon	32 (51)
1638–	Parret and Tone	12 (19)
1651–53	Wey	15 (24)
1662–	Wye	14 (22)
1662–65	Worcester Stour	12 (19)
1665–73	Welland	10 (16)
1672–74	Foss Dyke	11 (18)
1675–77	Warwick Avon	8 (13)
1675–80	Wiltshire Avon	30 (48)
1674–89	Great Ouse	15 (24)
1699–1703	Aire and Calder	42 (67)
1699–1710	Trent	23 (37)
1700–	Lark	14 (22)
1705–	Essex Stour	25 (40)
1718–23	Kennet	19 (30)
1720–22	Derby Derwent	10 (16)
1722–25	Mersey and Irwell	15 (24)
1725–27	Bristol Avon	16 (26)
1726–29	Don	23 (37)
1727–32	Yorkshire Ouse	35 (56)
1730–32	Weaver	20 (32)
1735–37	Dee	8 (13)
1738–42	Douglas	16 (26)
1740–	Medway	16 (26)
1755–57	Sankey Canal	10 (16)
1758–78	Weaver	20 (32)
1759–64	Calder	24 (39)

(Data taken from A.W. Skempton, *The Engineers of the English River Navigations, Transactions of the Newcomen Society Volume XXIX*)

THE RIVER NAVIGATIONS

The decline of river transport has taken something of the rich diversity out of river life. One has only to spend some time sitting by a river that is still in use to see how much the busy trade adds to the enjoyment of the scene. Recently, I spent an entertaining lunchtime in a wharfside pub in Ipswich, watching through the window as a coaster went through complex manoeuvres to turn round at Orwell Quay. For some, the saddest part of river history is the decline of the great river cities as ports. The official handbook for the Tyne for 1925 speaks with unconcealed pride of Newcastle's river:

To appreciate what the port of Tyne is, it is first necessary to realise what it was, for it is a distinction of this river that it is man-made. Literally, its tidal flow, no less than its busy banks, its capacious docks, its magnificent piers are the handiwork of a generation of Tynesiders who have snatched a port from the North Sea and converted what was little better than a ditch into a great river.

John Constable was not only a great artist but was also a knowledgeable and accurate portrayer of the river scene. This painting shows boatbuilding near Flatford Mill. The vessel is a Stour lighter, and the traditional crafts and tools of the boat builder are on display. The simple dry dock is closed off by gates, pitch is being boiled up at the bottom left of the picture, while to the right are two adzes for shaping wood and a caulking mallet (Victoria and Albert Museum)

After the purple prose, mundane facts and tables of statistics take over – but even these can make stirring reading. Among the twenty shipbuilding yards listed are such famous names as Swan Hunter and Armstrong. In 1924, over eleven thousand ships used the port, not counting small craft, tugs and fishing boats; and the most romantic list of all is the list of steamship services. In those days you could steam off anywhere from Aalborg to Valparaiso.

This was river traffic on the grand scale, only to be matched by the other great shipping rivers – Thames, Mersey, Humber and Clyde. But for many, the greatest charm lies with more modest waterways. Two river Stours have already been mentioned, but the most famous must be the Suffolk Stour, not because it was that important but because it was recorded by one of the country's greatest artists, John Constable. His paintings are primarily artistic masterpieces, but they are also a valuable and accurate record of the working life of the Stour in the eighteenth century. Constable himself wrote in a letter that 'I associate my "careless boyhood" to all that lies on the banks of the *Stour*. They made me a painter.' He showed Stour lighters being built and at work and, most interestingly, he showed the extraordinary versatility of the horses that pulled them. Life was not easy for these animals.

One famous painting, 'The Leaping Horse', shows what might seem an exercise in artistic licence – a barge horse performing like a Grand National runner. But the Stour tow-path was crossed by low fences that were designed to keep cattle within bounds, and the horses were specially trained to jump these obstacles. With the passing of the river trade such scenes also vanished and are retained now only as paint on canvas and sketches in a notebook.

Something at least of the variety of the river scene has survived, so a modern journey down, say, the delightful Nene with its imposing guillotine lock gates is very different from a trip down the tidal Trent with its massive conventional locks and still active traffic of small coasters and motorised barges. And, just occasionally, one can see one of the preserved trading craft – the wherry *Albion* out on the Bure or the Ant, the keel *Comrade* on its home waters of the Humber, or, most spectacularly of all, a whole fleet of spritsail barges competing in one of the annual barge matches on the Thames, the Medway or the Blackwater. Then one is being given a glimpse of what life was like when the rivers of Britain were the principal trading routes of the nation.

The guillotine locks on the River Nene can look alarmingly like instruments of execution. This example is at Cottistock Lock near Oundle (Susan Melhuish)

3 BUILDING THE CANALS

The Duke of Bridgewater and Barton aqueduct shown on a pub sign near the junction of the Trent and Mersey and Caldon Canals at Etruria (Anthony Burton)

It all began, so they say, with the Duke of Bridgewater's canal from his coal mines at Worsley into Manchester: yet travel the canal today and it is difficult to see what all the fuss was about. The actual beginning at the mines of Worsley Delph appears as a tomato soup-like waterway emerging from a nondescript hole in a rock face. Worsley Basin is undoubtedly more impressive, with its stepped wharf and attractive black-and-white timbered building, but after that there is a broad, almost dull, lock-free run into the city. The one really outstanding feature is the famous swing aqueduct at Barton, but that was no part of the duke's canal, for it was only built at the end of the nineteenth century to take the old canal across the new Manchester Ship Canal. So it is clear that one has to look back into history to discover why it was once the wonder of the age. Even then, the answer is by no means obvious. There was already an entirely artificial waterway at work in Britain, the Sankey Brook, and in France the spectacular Languedoc Canal, now known as the Canal du Midi, was already a century old. The latter was a truly major undertaking, 150 miles (241km) long with broad locks, including a staircase of eight interconnected locks, near Beziers at the Mediterranean end of France. It had splendid aqueducts, a tunnel, and a summit that was supplied by a feeder which was itself 27 miles (43km) long. The duke had nothing new to add to that and yet it is undeniably true that his canal was literally sensational, as important a stopping-off point on the gentlemen tourists' itinerary as the Derbyshire peaks or the stateliest of stately homes.

The answer to this paradox lies with the insularity of the English. There were fine canals in France, but the English had mostly not seen them, so for them the French waterways simply did not exist. The Sankey was a modern canal but it was described as a river navigation, so was thought of simply as a continuation of the general movement towards waterway improvement. The Bridgewater was seen from the first as a genuine canal, not another river navigation, since, as if to emphasise the point, it was actually planned to soar over one of those new navigations, the Mersey and Irwell, on an aqueduct. The English, paying no regard to the existence of such devices in France – not to mention the aqueducts built for water supply by the Romans – declared such a structure to be miraculous if not downright impossible. It was reported at the time that an engineer was taken to the site of the proposed aqueduct, where he drily commented that he had frequently heard of castles in the air but had never before seen where one was to be built. The scepticism with which the plans were received served only to make the triumph of the canal's completion all the greater. The aqueduct was built, boats did sail over boats and, most miraculously of all, the price of coal in Manchester was halved. In this lay the importance of the Bridgewater Canal. It solved no engineering problems that had not already been solved, but it caught the public imagination. One man had backed a scheme with his own cash against all the pessimistic forecasts of self-styled experts, and proved he was right. The scheme worked brilliantly well, both as an example of modern engineering and as a model of profitable entrepreneurship. The doors of the canal age had been thrown open.

The Bridgewater Canal has always been seen as having a very special place in British canal history and was held in far higher regard by contemporaries than it is today. The duke was spoken of as 'the great Duke' and 'the parent and father of all similar works in this kingdom'. Visitors practically swooned at the sight of Barton aqueduct, as one querulously anonymous tourist reported:

> While I was surveying it with a mixture of wonder and delight, four barges passed me in the space of about three minutes, two of them being chained together, and dragged by two horses, who went on the terras of the canal, whereon, I must own, I durst hardly venture to walk, as I almost trembled to behold the large River Irwell underneath me.

The reality of the canal and its building was a trifle more mundane than that somewhat overwrought writing might suggest, but its success was to have consequences which were to affect the whole development of canals in Britain.

The Duke of Bridgewater is an unlikely candidate for the role of canal builder. When the scheme began he was a young man in his early twenties, an age at which all that was expected of a nobleman was that he should be handsome, frivolous and a spendthrift. The duke at that time seemed to have met the first requirement, but failed absolutely with

The Navvy

In the making of canals, it is the general custom to employ gangs of hands who travel from one work to another and do nothing else.

These banditti, known in some parts of England by the names of 'Navies' or 'Navigators', and in others by that of 'Bankers', are generally the terror of the surrounding country; they are as completely a class by themselves as the Gipsies. Possessed of all the daring recklessness of the Smuggler, without any of his redeeming qualities, their ferocious behaviour can only be equalled by the brutality of their language. It may be truly said, their hand is against every man, and before they have been long located, every man's hand is against them; and woe befal any woman, with the slightest share of modesty, whose ears they can assail.

From being long known to each other, they in general act in concert, and put at defiance any local constabulary force; consequently crimes of the most atrocious character are common, and robbery, without an attempt at concealment, has been an everyday occurrence, wherever they have been congregated in large numbers . . . .

Peter Lecount, *The History of the Railways Connecting London and Birmingham*, 1839)

The famous Barton aqueduct that carried the Bridgewater Canal across the Irwell. It was demolished at the end of the last century to make way for the Manchester Ship Canal and replaced by the equally famous Swing aqueduct (Manchester Ship Canal Company)

The Opening Ceremony

This day the stupendous aqueduct of Pontcysyllte, upon the Ellesmere Canal, was opened with great solemnity . . . . The morning threatened to be unfavourable; but, before noon, the day cleared up, and the sun shone, adding, by its lustre, to the beautiful sight of various carriages, horsemen, and persons, descending by every road, path, and approach, leading towards that great work. Before 2 o'clock, the aqueduct having been filled, the procession began. The earl of Bridgewater's barge led the way, in which was his lordship and the countess; Sir Watkin Williams Wynne, bart. Sir Foster Cunliffe, bart. Col. Kynaston-Powell and lady, and several other ladies and gentlemen. In the prow of the barge, the sergeant-major of the Shropshire volunteers, in full uniform, carried a flag, on which was painted a representation of the aqueduct, the Dee, and the valley, and with the inscription:

'Here conquer'd Nature owns Britannia's sway, While Ocean's realms her matchless deeds display.'

Next followed other members of the committee, and Mr. Telford, the projector of the aqueduct and general agent to the company, in Col. Kynaston-Powell's barge, carrying two union jacks. In the third was the numerous band of the Shropshire volunteers, in full uniform, playing 'God Save the King', and other loyal airs. The fourth boat was filled with numerous ladies and gentlemen, the agents, clerks, and the heads of the departments employed in the execution of the work, and decorated with a handsome flag, on which was inscribed,

continued on page 43

the other two, and although it is said that he had fallen in love with the Duchess of Hamilton, it needed only a whiff of scandal to touch her family for the young man to turn his back on society and concern himself with the less emotional affairs of his coal mines. The 22-year-old duke found a willing assistant for his ambitious plans in his agent, John Gilbert. The only impediment to expansion lay in the exorbitant charges of the Mersey & Irwell Navigation Company, who also refused to allow the duke to build a short cutting from the mines to the river. They wished to maintain an absolute monopoly, but were to regret their decision. The duke and Gilbert, if they could not join the Irwell, took the momentous decision to leap across it, and the plans for the Bridgewater Canal were duly laid.

The Mersey & Irwell faction no doubt felt a little smug, faced by a 22-year-old nobleman, with no outside financial help and no engineering expertise, and the obstacles facing the would-be canal builder were indeed formidable. First, he had to obtain a private act of parliament to authorise construction, in the face of determined opposition by a wealthy and well-established navigation company. That obtained, he would then have to find the money from his own resources to pay for the enterprise and, even if the cash was raised, he still had to find someone to undertake the actual work. The journal of the House of Commons for 6 December 1758 duly noted that Mr John Gilbert had produced a plan for a new canal and in March 1759, after a period of fierce argument, the act was duly approved. The duke was wealthy, but still found it necessary to mortgage his estates to pay for the work – and the time had come to find an answer to the third part of the problem. An engineer had to be appointed. The man who filled that role was as unlikely a character as the duke – a semi-literate millwright from Derbyshire, James Brindley. He had made something of a reputation among the mining fraternity by the construction of an elaborate drainage system, involving the digging of underground channels, for the aptly named Wet Earth Colliery. Which of the three men should be given the credit for seeing the ambitious scheme through to completion is still a matter of debate. That the duke had the onerous responsibility of paying for a project which, like many of its successors, suffered from galloping price rises as work proceeded, was beyond argument. Having mortgaged his estate, borrowed from the bank and from his accommodating relatives, including a genuine canal enthusiast Lord Gower, he still frequently found himself all but bankrupt. Yet somehow the money was always found, or creditors successfully evaded, and the profits from the completed work more than justified the effort. As far as the actual construction is concerned, the work fell to Gilbert and Brindley. Contemporaries were all but unanimous in lauding the latter, and the duke's agent scarcely received a word of commendation. If one looks at the matter in terms of Brindley's later work, there is a boldness about the Bridgewater that was scarcely matched by him even in the grandest of his later schemes, which suggests that Gilbert's influence may well have been great. But when all was successfully completed, Gilbert remained with his employer and it was James Brindley who was free to take on new work. The success of the Bridgewater, the miracle of Barton aqueduct, were all the advertisements he needed, and his reputation was such that he was able to stamp his style and his authority on all the first generation of canals. The Bridgewater Canal made Brindley and James Brindley gave the canals of England the special character that they retain to this day.

There was no immediate rush to follow the Duke of Bridgewater's lead; in fact, in the five years following the completion of the canal in 1761, the only new project to be authorised by parliament was one for extending the duke's canal to the Mersey at Runcorn. But interest was stirring as the lessons, particularly the favourable financial lessons, of the pioneering work were learned. Soon, other major schemes were being put forward and a pattern of canal development was established that drew on the Bridgewater experience but altered it in a number of significant ways. The essential programme, however, remained unaltered: first formulate your plan and gather support; next obtain authorisation from parliament through an enabling act, then raise the money and then all you have to do is build the canal. As many a canal promoter was to find, the theory was simple but the practice far, far more troublesome. But let us start at the beginning with the planners and instigators. What kind of people were they and how did they set about their task?

In the first instance, they were men very like those who had promoted and paid for the river improvements – substantial businessmen, merchants, traders and manufacturers – men who were more concerned with the advantages that improved transport would convey to their various concerns rather than with any financial profits that might ensue – not that they were in any way reluctant to accept any profits if they should chance to come along. Of the different schemes that were begun in the 1760s, by far the most ambitious was that for a canal to unite the rivers Trent and Mersey, and that in turn was to be supplemented by other canals to form 'The Cross', linking this new waterway to the Thames and the Severn. By this means the Midlands, the developing industrial heartland of Britain, was to be linked by canal to the country's major navigable rivers and so to the sea. Such a scheme was first proposed by Lord Gower who employed Brindley to survey a possible line while he was working on the Bridgewater. That came to nothing, and the prime mover behind the revival of interest was a potter whose reputation was already spreading beyond the bounds of his native Staffordshire, Josiah Wedgwood.

Wedgwood's interest in the canal derived directly from his ambitious plans for his pottery. Staffordshire ware had previously been characterised as rather crude, although to modern eyes it has a splendidly robust simplicity. Wedgwood, however, wanted to make pottery for the aristocracy, confident that where they led, others of lesser rank but of greater numbers would follow. Aristocratic taste did not run to thick, heavily glazed earthenware, so he set about producing a lighter coloured body which could then be given a lighter glaze and be more delicately coloured. The result was his famous cream ware, but this could be produced only by using raw materials from outside the region: clays from the south-west of England and flints from East Anglia and the

continued from page 42

'Success to the iron trade of Great Britain, of which Pontcysyllte aqueduct is a specimen'

The fifth and sixth boats were filled with various persons, crowding, with anxiety, to have the satisfaction of thinking that they had been amongst the first to pass the aqueduct. As soon as the first barge entered the cast-iron water-way, which is 126 feet above the level of the river Dee, the artillery company of the Shropshire volunteers fired 16 rounds, from two brass field pieces . . . .

(*The Annual Register*, 1805)

Josiah Wedgwood tried to persuade Brindley to give the Trent and Mersey Canal a graceful curve as it passed his new house, Etruria Hall. As this old painting shows, Brindley was not to be persuaded to deviate from the straight and narrow (Josiah Wedgwood & Sons Ltd)

Canals and Landowners

The Shropshire Union Canal near Tyrley Locks passed through a private estate, and the owners were worried about the effects of the canal spoiling both the view and the shooting. There was also the worry among landowners of having uncouth characters moving across their land during the digging and afterwards when the canal was opened. Such worries were not, apparently, without foundation, as the owner at Tyrley complained to the company in 1844: 'The large gang of men repairing the locks has no provision whatever for purposes of nature. Consequently they are scattered all over the country looking for snug corners (like the Israelites searching for stubble instead of straw). This annoys my keeper, whose pheasants are nesting, and me too, for I am always putting my foot in it.'

south coast. Carrying costs for the overland journey from the nearest port were exorbitant, and that was only one part of the problem. Wedgwood planned to sell all over Britain, so he needed an efficient method of transporting his delicate ware from the potteries. Carts bumping over uneven roads offered a less than adequate answer. His enthusiasm for a canal is not difficult to understand and Wedgwood was a man who, once his enthusiasm was aroused, was quick to begin putting ideas to work.

In March 1765, Wedgwood had a meeting with Brindley and the two men found they had a great deal in common, for both had risen from comparatively poor beginnings and both were well on their way to fame and fortune. That talk was soon followed by a public meeting at which Wedgwood agreed 'to undertake a journey or two' to promote the idea of a canal. The modest statement disguises the truth which was that he had now become the chief promoter who was to find canal affairs almost dominating his life for the next year. There were friends to encourage and jolly along and enemies to discourage and argue down, and it is difficult to say which proved the more demanding task. The Liverpool interest argued with the Staffordshire interest and even Wedgwood's own personal friends and helpers were prone to jealous quarrelling. Wedgwood relied heavily on the solid good sense and taste of the Liverpool merchant Thomas Bentley, who was eventually to become his partner in the pottery. He also struck up a friendship with the mercurial and brilliant physician Dr Erasmus Darwin (the ties between the two were strengthened when Wedgwood's daughter married Darwin's son, the child of that marriage being the famous evolutionist Charles Darwin). Wedgwood was equally at home with either Darwin or Bentley, but his two friends did not always seem quite so happy with each other. They quarrelled over that most personal and aggravating of issues, literary style, for Bentley had been entrusted with the all-important task of writing a pamphlet to set out the case for the canal, while Darwin had appointed himself critic. Wedgwood had to step in to point out that what mattered was getting the words on paper and the paper in the hands of possible supporters, and not literary niceties. The pamphlet was, in fact, a very long and full exposition of the benefits not only of the particular canals but of canals in general. Its success eased the way for the many promoters who followed afterwards with their own schemes. The opposition consisted mainly of river navigation companies who saw the new canal as a potential competitor. They produced rival pamphlets, attempting to show simultaneously that the new canal was not needed, would never carry any trade nor make a profit but that, if allowed to open, this non-carrying, non-profitable waterway would totally ruin the river trade. Pamphleteers of the period were not noted for their sensitivity towards opponents. W. Hutton, writing of the rival promoters in Birmingham in 1801, summed up the situation perfectly: 'When two opponents have said all that is true, they generally say something more: rancour holds the place of argument.'

Wedgwood received his support and was appointed treasurer to the new company at, he wryly noted, 'a salary of £000 per ann. out of which he bear his own expenses'. He was also required to put up a security of £10,000, so that his personal contribution to the Trent and Mersey Canal was very considerable. His rewards, however, were also great. He built a new house, Etruria Hall, close to the canal (the property still overlooks the waterway) and his new pottery with its rows of workers' houses was next to the canal – a fact which greatly annoyed other local potters who had not shared Wedgwood's enthusiasm and vigour. The act was duly passed by parliament in 1766 and work began on construction. This pattern of argument and counter argument continued virtually throughout the canal-building period, for once the case for canals was well proven and the old navigation companies became less vociferous, planners then found themselves opposed by the proprietors of the older canals. Not every canal planner managed to clear this first hurdle, and their schemes fell usually from a failure to attract sufficient local support.

Signing petitions and making speeches were all essential parts of this early process, but the day came when cash had to be raised. The precedent set by the Duke of Bridgewater of personally financing construction was not followed. Instead, shares were issued, those for the early canals often being of quite large denominations – £200 each for example, in the case of the Trent and Mersey, which represented a whole year's fee for the organisation's chief engineer. Not surprisingly, a large number of shares went to the local landed interest, who invested an average of over £1,000 each. From the investors' point of view, investment in the early canals was sound. Some, notably the Birmingham Canal, regularly paid dividends of over 10 per cent, reaching 17½ per cent in the 1780s. It was returns such as these which drew the hordes of speculators eager to back each and every canal scheme, no matter how expensive or even preposterous it might be. This led to the years of the canal mania of the 1790s, with no fewer than nineteen new acts being passed by parliament in 1793 alone. But, as investors soon discovered, when they bought shares they were also taking on obligations. The original capital raised depended on the estimates of construction costs, and it seems to be an inescapable part of the human nature of the engineer, then as now, to be an unswerving optimist. A date for completion is confidently given, the costs of the work carefully set out

Contour cutting at its most elaborate: the extravagant twists and turns of the Oxford Canal near Wormleighton. The curious pattern in the fields in the foreground is the last remaining traces of a medieval village (Cambridge University Collection of Air Photographs)

and exactly itemised. Then, as years go by and inflation nibbles at the cost and unexpected delays and problems eat into the time, the money is spent and the estimated finishing date arrives with the canal only half dug. Then the company go back to the shareholders with an unpleasant piece of news: more money is needed and, when they purchased the shares, the investors undertook to supply that money when called for. But as the company found out, there was a distinct lack of enthusiasm on the part of investors who were asked time and time again to dip into their pockets.

There are few more striking examples of a stop-go, now-we-have-the-money-now-we-don't type of canal building than the Leeds and Liverpool Canal. It was the engineer John Longbotham who first suggested the trans-Pennine route in 1766, although the act to make it possible was not approved until 1770. Work started at a good pace under Longbotham's guidance, but soon began to falter. Longbotham resigned in 1775, and although he lived for a further twenty-six years, he did not survive to see the work he had started reach a conclusion. Engineers came and went. Money was spent and more money raised, and it was not until 1816, half a century after the first plans were laid, that the canal was at last officially opened.

One of the most thankless tasks in the canal world was that of the company secretary who was harassed by complainants demanding money – complainants who might include several hundred rough, tough, unfriendly navvies – and who was forced in his turn to collect the dues of recalcitrant investors. Of all those who celebrated a canal opening, few can have done so with such relish as the secretary who could feel that all he had to do now was to count the revenue – alas, not always as simple as it might have seemed.

At an early stage in this process of raising support and funds, an engineer was appointed to survey the line, decide where locks and bridges had to be built, cuttings and tunnels dug, embankments constructed, and then estimate the cost of the whole undertaking. In the years following the completion of the Bridgewater Canal there was, in the eyes of would-be canal promoters, only one man for the job, James Brindley. As there were no recognised qualifications, nor indeed any recognised training, for engineers, the only criterion a canal promoter could turn to was experience. Brindley had built a successful canal, therefore Brindley was the man for the job.

Popular versions of this period of canal construction, largely drawn from the somewhat romantic writings of Samuel Smiles, describe the bluff, down-to-earth, no-nonsense engineer shuffling across the face of Britain on an aged nag using techniques no more sophisticated than an eye for the land; relying, in short, on natural genius. That Brindley did spend a great deal of time travelling from canal scheme to canal scheme is undeniable, but he was not quite the solitary figure of legend. His accounts presented to the Chester Canal promoters for an early survey of the line in the winter of 1768–9 show that the work was principally divided between his surveyor, Varley, and an assistant surveyor, Allen, both of whom spent considerably more time on the project than Brindley himself. Others who worked with Brindley, notably Hugh Henshall, later became engineers in their own right. This was to become the accepted road forward for engineers: thus William Jessop, engineer of, among others, the Grand Junction Canal, began by working for John Smeaton, and Jessop in his turn took on an assistant, Thomas Telford, who later rose to success. But to return to the survey and the work of its chief engineer: this was the point at which the character of a canal was set.

An engineer faced with the problem of constructing a canal between two places is usually presented with a multitude of choices. If the land were conveniently flat, then all that would be necessary would be to take a ruler, draw a straight line and declare the job done. The landscape of Britain seldom co-operates quite so obligingly. One has only to look at the solutions favoured by different engineers for the waterways that link Yorkshire to Lancashire across the Pennines to see just how many variations are possible. The first to be started, the Leeds and Liverpool, avoids the worst of the hilly country by swinging in a great arc to the north, so that the distance covered by the waterway is approximately twice that needed by the proverbial crow. The Rochdale Canal from Sowerby Bridge to Manchester also swings north but takes a more adventurous route through the hills, involving many locks, but is only half as long again as the crow's route. The third canal, the Huddersfield Narrow from Ashton-under-Lyne scarcely deviates from a straight line, but does so only by charging straight at the hills, burrowing under the Pennines in Britain's longest canal tunnel, the 3-mile 135yd (5-km) long Standedge tunnel. Sometimes, choices were made easy. Thomas Telford had few decisions of this type to make when setting out the line of the Caledonian Canal from Fort William to Inverness, for there was a natural route up the glens that join together lochs Linnhe, Lochy, Oich and Ness. That, however, was very much the exception and choices had to be made – and they were choices which reflected the views of the individual engineers.

James Brindley was noted as a contour cutter. His ideal canal hugged the natural contours of the land as far as possible, so as to avoid what he regarded as excessive engineering work. This worked out well enough when he was following the line of a river valley, as in the section of the Oxford Canal that follows the Cherwell valley north from Oxford. Beyond that, however, and especially in the section above Fenny Compton, he was forced into a series of extraordinary convulsions, the canal twisting and turning as it wriggles around hillocks and dips, reaching its finest moment at Wormleighton where it almost encircles the hill. A similar wayward progress is made on the Staffs and Worcester between Wolverhampton and Kidderminster, where the natural River Stour can seem to be following a more logical course than the carefully designed canal.

The Brindley contour cutting method looks very like a lack of boldness in those early years of canal building, although all engineers found it a useful technique at times. When William Jessop laid out the Ellesmere Canal, now known as the Llangollen, in the 1790s, he included a short section of contour cutting near Ellesmere itself as extravagant as anything produced by Brindley on what, in every other

James Brindley's Workforce on the Bridgewater Canal

Brindley did not want for good men to carry out his plans. He found plenty of labourers in the neighbourhood accustomed to hard work, who speedily became expert excavators; and though there was at first a lack of skilled carpenters, blacksmiths and bricklayers, they soon became trained into such under the vigilant eye of so able a master as Brindley was. We find him, in his note-book, often referring to the men by their names, or rather bye names; for in Lancashire proper names seem to have been little used at that time. 'Black David', was one of the foremen most employed on difficult matters, and 'Bill o Toms' and 'Busick Jack' seem also to have been confidential workmen in their respective departments. We are informed by a gentleman of the neighbourhood that most of the labourers employed were of a superior class, and some of them were 'wise' or 'cunning men', blood-stoppers, herb-doctors, and planet-rulers, such as are still to be found in the neighbourhood of Manchester. Their very superstitions, says our informant, made them thinkers and calculators. The foreman bricklayer, for instance, as his son used afterwards to relate, always 'ruled the planets to find out the lucky days on which to commence any important work', and he added, 'none of our work ever gave way.' The skilled men had their trade secrets, in which the unskilled were duly initiated, – simple matters in themselves, but not without their uses.

(Samuel Smiles, *Lives of the Engineers*, 1874)

Speculators in Canal Shares

The canal speculator, who subscribes only to gain by selling his shares, I consider little better than a swindler; for all schemes in his estimation are extremely good, and he will ride from one county to another, to become a subscriber to the most ineligible plan, with no other view than that of selling his shares.

The public are little aware of the mischief which these men have done to the community; for subscribers to canals should be men of real property, who subscribe from no other motive but that of supporting the scheme.

(John Sutcliffe, *A Treatise on Canals and Reservoirs*, 1816)

way, epitomises the work of the second generation of canal builders. Brindley claimed advantages for his method in that the longer route enabled the canal to serve a greater number of communities – but this, to use a comparison with a later age, is to think of a canal in branch line rather than main-line terms. The canal users were mainly concerned in shifting heavy, bulky loads, especially coal, by as direct a route as possible. The early contour canals were to prove a liability, so that in time they were improved by straightening, as was done with the Birmingham Canal, while others were supplanted by new, improved waterways. But setting out the line was only a part of the job. Even the most assiduous contour cutter had to make some allowances for changes in level. Faced by a hill that cannot be bypassed, the engineer had three basic options: to build locks to go up one side and down the other, to burrow through the hill in a tunnel, or to slice into the top of it with a cutting and continue across the valley on an embankment.

Brindley used both locks and tunnels, but the way in which he used them was to have a profound and enduring effect on British canal development. When plans were drawn up for an extension of the Bridgewater Canal down to the Mersey at Runcorn, locks were needed to join canal and river. The size of these locks was mainly determined by the size of vessels that were to use them, the Mersey flats that were already in use in the region. So the locks were built 72ft (22m) long and 15ft (4.5m) wide to accommodate them. When it came to the new canals, the Staffs and Worcester, and the Trent and Mersey, there were no such restrictions, for no decision had yet been taken as to what craft would be used on these waterways. An obvious choice would have been to stay with the standard already set on the Bridgewater, since that canal was to be joined to the Trent and Mersey at Preston Brook. But Brindley did not take this option. Instead he designed locks to the same length but only half the width: why? The likeliest answer is to be found at Harecastle Hill, which had to be pierced by a tunnel. Brindley must have found the notion of building a tunnel nearly 2 miles (3.2km) long a daunting prospect when nothing similar had been attempted in Britain before, and a wide tunnel was far more daunting than a narrow one. But if he built a narrow tunnel it could only be used by narrow boats, and if the canal could only carry narrow boats it would only need narrow locks. Brindley took his decision: his locks from now on would be half as wide as those at Runcorn, and once the pattern was set for the crucial canals that crossed the Midlands of England, it was set for all the canals that were to join that part of the system. A special craft had to be built to fit the dimensions of the locks, the narrow boat, approximately 70ft (21.5m) long by 7ft (2m) beam with a maximum carrying load of 35 tons. This seemed more than ample in the days when the only competition was a horse pulling a cart with a load of, in the very best conditions, 2 tons: it was to look a good deal less satisfactory in the railway age that was to come.

No decision taken by any engineer had such a profound effect on British waterways history as did that of James Brindley in setting the size of the lock on the first generation of canals. But each engineering decision taken during the planning stage was important. When in the

J. C. Bourne's view of the barrow runs on Tring cutting during the building of the London and Birmingham Railway in the 1830s. It shows the horses at the top, pulling up the barrows through a pulley system. The men balance the barrows on the planks, while others dig and fill the barrows at the bottom. The scene on the nearby Grand Union cutting would have been very similar (Elton Collection: Ironbridge Gorge Museum Trust)

early 1790s John Rennie surveyed the line for the proposed Rochdale Canal, he suggested using the hill stream for water supply. This idea faced implacable opposition from the owners of the many water-powered cotton mills along the route who feared for their own water supplies. Two bills were brought before parliament and both were thrown out. Then William Jessop was called in and he proposed constructing new reservoirs high in the Pennines for water supply, and the opposition faded away. Many engineers developed their own styles, and travelling the canals today one can still recognise some of the more obvious

There was little change in building techniques over the years. When this bridge at Gayton was rebuilt in 1910, the wooden centring was first set up and the bricks were laid on top. Once the arch was formed the wooden framework could be removed (British Waterways Board)

characteristics. John Rennie may not have had much success with his Rochdale plans, but elsewhere he showed himself to be as much an artist as an engineer, designing some of the most elegant bridges and aqueducts to be seen in the country. Although Telford also prided himself on his architecture, he is now mostly thought of in terms of dramatic cuttings and embankments, such as those of the Shropshire Union main line, the original Birmingham and Liverpool Junction.

Sometimes, the chief engineer contributed little, if anything, to the work once the planning stage was complete. The demands on the best-known men were heavy, and they were forced to divide their time between many different projects. Companies often felt that they were not getting their money's worth. The Coventry Canal Company had a contract specifying that Brindley should spend at least two months in the year at the works, but getting him to meet his obligations was quite a different matter. They complained loud and long, but not quite to the effect which they intended: instead of reporting for duty, the great man resigned. The company hastily apologised and had to accept that a little Brindley was better than none at all. In these circumstances, the supervision of the actual work fell to the man one rung down the ladder, the resident engineer.

It must often have seemed to the resident engineer that the chief engineer received all the glory, not to mention the generous fees, while he himself did all the work. John Rennie, setting out his proposals for organising work on the Kennet and Avon, defined his own job as providing designs and specifications and inspecting the work once a quarter. The resident engineer's job was 'to superintend the work and to suggest improvements wherever possible' and to be 'responsible for purchasing timber, ironwork and so on'. That sounds reasonable enough, until one remembers that work was often spread out over many miles, involving hours of travel on horseback and, more importantly, supervision was not the simple matter the bald statement of duties might

Canal bridges needed to be tested, especially road bridges that might need to carry considerable traffic. The simplest way was to get as many heavy vehicles as possible on to the bridge. Here a Fowler traction engine pulling a loaded truck has been joined by an Aveling steam roller. The gentleman in the bathchair is presumably a spectator rather than part of the load (Michael E. Ware)

Thomas Telford, pictured with Pontcysyllte in the background (Institution of Civil Engineers)

*Caldwall Lock lies under the shelter
of sandstone cliffs on the Staffs and
Worcester Canal* (Derek Pratt)

suggest. Except in the earliest days, canal companies did not employ labour directly. Jobs such as bridge construction might go to local builders and tenders would be invited for other specialist jobs such as lock building. But the bulk of the work – the long, slow slog of digging out a canal – went to contractors who employed their own gangs of men. This was the cause of endless disputes. The contractors were paid by the distance dug and they in turn paid their men by the day – the fewer days taken per mile, the less that had to be paid in wages and the greater the profit. The resident engineer was there to ensure steady progress and sound workmanship: the contractors, in general, put speed first and quality some distance behind. The resident engineer, it seemed, was often in a state of open conflict with the contractors.

Archibald Miller, resident engineer on the Lancaster Canal, was taken to task for having had the temerity to give direct orders to the contractor's men. This was his curt reply:

> You complain our Agents gave directions to your Workmen instead of yourselves or your Agents. You well know your attentions have been very little employed in respect to the Masonry, and your only Agent if he knew anything about the business had little time to attend to it.

The list of complaints flowed on: contractors ignoring instructions, doing shoddy work and even advancing the canal forward before the company had completed negotiations for the land. Then there was the lack of consideration for the locals: gates were left open and roads and fences damaged. It is not surprising to find that the man who could unite the practical qualifications of a sound engineer with the tact of a diplomat in a hostile country was a rare creature, and there was scarcely a canal engineer in the whole of the canal age who did not complain at some time or other about the difficulty of finding and employing such a paragon.

In matters of patience, the resident engineer was only matched by the company secretary. As the chief administrator, his problems tended to be largely financial, running out of money being virtually endemic in canal building. His other principal occupation seems to have been conciliating the local population. Canal acts conveyed the then novel right of compulsory purchase along the line set out in the plans as approved by parliament. The local landowners, especially the aristocracy, found this to be a monstrous doctrine and could scarcely believe that the newcomers could take their land, whether they wished it or not, leaving nothing to argue about except the price to be paid in compensation. Powerful landowners could, however, force a diversion, and it was said that the extravagant loop around Wormleighton Hill on the Oxford Canal was to appease the local squire rather than to make for an easier line.

The post of company secretary was one that seemed designed to bring on ulcers or, as a colleague said of one long-suffering gentleman, 'the Dry Belly Ake'.

The engineers and administrators, however, formed only the apex of

Construction of the Manchester Ship Canal

Plant, &c., in use during the busiest period of construction.

Steam Excavators, &c	100
Including { 10 Floating Dredgers, 3 German Navvies, 2 French Navvies, 55 Ruston & Proctors	
Locomotives	173
Steam and other Cranes	194
Portable and other Steam Engines	182
Steam Pumps	209
Wagons	6300
Pile Engines	59
Length of Temporary Railways	223 miles
Number of Men and Boys	16,361
Number of Horses	196
Quantity of Coal used monthly	10,000 tons
Quantity of Cement	8,000 tons

The total amount of excavation is about 51,000,000 cubic yards (or 76 million tons,) about one-fifth being sandstone rock.

The total brickwork amounts to 175,000 cubic yards, or 70,000,000 bricks.

The masonry measures 220,000 cubic yards, and the concrete 1,250,000 cubic yards.

(*Manchester Ship Canal Handbook*, January 1894)

a broad pyramid. Beneath them were the contractors and, at the very bottom, supporting them all, the anonymous army of men, known at first from their work on the river navigations as navigators, a name later abbreviated to the more familiar 'navvy'. It was their muscle power that dug thousands of miles of canal with pickaxe, shovel and wheelbarrow. Mechanisation was virtually unknown at the start of the canal age, and even the simplest of tools could not be taken for granted. At the start of work on the Coventry Canal, a carpenter was sent to Staffordshire to copy the design for a barrow. At first workmen were recruited locally. The Duke of Bridgewater was able to call on miners from Worsley and estate workers who could simply go back to their own work when the canal was completed. But gradually, as canal work spread across the country, the diggers found that they had developed skills that were in demand and for which employers were ready to pay. It is extraordinarily difficult to estimate pay on the canals, and even more difficult to set it against pay elsewhere for similar jobs. The agricultural labourer was the closest in terms of work and skills to the navvy, and economic historians have been arguing over their rates of pay for years. There are added complications, such as ownership of small patches of land, tied cottages and the like, but if we look at the area of East Anglia we get a very close comparison. It was the practice there to employ large gangs of men, similar to the navvy gangs, and there were disturbances throughout the region in the 1810s related to demands for 2s (10p) a day. A little earlier, on the Lancaster Canal, there was a strike among one group of navvies because they were being paid less than another contractor's men. The demand here was 2s 6d (12½p) for a ten-hour day with overtime at 3d (1p) an hour. It makes sense to think that the navvy received high pay to balance the abandonment of a settled home life for one of constant wanderings from digging to digging, for that was what happened at some times, certainly by the 1780s, when a visitor to the workings on the Basingstoke Canal, the Rev S. Shaw, reported that although the contractors were keen to employ local people,

> such is the power of use over nature, that while these industrious poor are by all their efforts incapable of earning a sustenance, those who were brought from similar works cheerfully obtained a comfortable support.

The principal work of the canal navvy was digging a trench with sloping sides which, even on the most modest of early canals, was still a considerable affair. A typical Brindley canal would have a width of 16ft (5m) at the bottom with 5ft (1.5m) of water and 1ft (0.3m) clear above that to the top of the bank. It was estimated that the trained navvy could shift around 12 cu yd (9m³) of earth a day – a phenomenal amount as any gardener will know – but even such efforts would mean that one man could move the canal forward even in the easiest ground by less than a yard (0.9m) a day. Or, to put it another way, it would take a gang of a hundred men three weeks to dig a mile (1.6km) of canal, hence the need for a large workforce. And digging was not the navvy's only duty. When a section of canal was dug, it still needed to be made watertight

This illustration by Pugin appears to be the only one showing canal navvies at work. They are working on Islington tunnel on the Regent's Canal. Spoil is being wheeled along a simple plateway to be hauled away up the shaft. In the background is the timber frame supporting the arch and a gang of men working with pickaxes (Museum of London)

and that meant 'puddling' – working up a sloppy mixture of water and clay which was then trodden into the ground, layer upon layer, until it formed an impenetrable barrier. And, of course, not all canal cutting was simple and straightforward. At times rock might be met with, and the only means of shifting solid rock was to bore holes with hand drills and blow it apart with black powder, a slow, tedious and sometimes dangerous procedure. When Brindley met rock on the Staffs and Worcester, just north of Autherley Junction, he reduced the channel to a single boat's width, and so it remains today. On later canals, such as the Shropshire Union, where engineering work was on an altogether grander scale, you can still see the marks left by drills on the side of rocky cuttings.

As canal engineering developed, so the demands on the workforce increased, although there was no notable increase in sophistication in the tools available for the job. Later engineers, such as Rennie, Jessop and

The repair gang in Blisworth tunnel in May 1910. The simple tools are exactly the same as those shown in use a century earlier on the Regent's Canal (British Waterways Board)

The shafts sunk during construction were kept on as air vents, but during repair work they were used to move materials between the workings and the surface (British Waterways Board)

The Resident Engineer and the Canal Committee

To fit a man fully for this employment, requires so great a number of qualifications, that I look upon it as impracticable to find them united in one person. I therefore take it for granted, that he will, of course, be materially deficient in something; and as such, there is the greatest difficulty in the world to preserve good understanding between the resident Engineer and the Committee who directs him. His post is the post of envy. Not only all of the inferior departments are ambitious to be practical engineers, but even members of the committee have a propensity that way too; by which means all becoming masters, and he who ought to be so, being deprived of authority, it is easy to figure the confusion that may follow.

(John Smeaton, quoted in William Chapman's *Address to the Subscribers of the Canal from Carlisle to Fisher's Cross*, 1823)

Telford, turned away from contour cutting in favour of 'cut and fill' in which a deep cutting was driven through the hill and the spoil then taken away to build up an embankment across the next valley. Where it was possible for the navvies simply to wheel the excavated earth out of the comparatively shallow trench of a contour canal, the deep cutting presented a totally different problem. Boaters chugging peacefully through cuttings such as Tring on the Grand Union or Woodseaves on the Shropshire Union might care to try to think how they would get barrow-loads of muck up those steep slopes. The canal engineer's answer was the barrow run. Planks were laid up the cutting side and ropes led over pulleys to the workings down below. The rope was attached to the barrow which could then be pulled up by a horse at the top of the slope. A man guided the barrow up and down the greasy, slippery plank. There are accounts of those barrow runs but, it seems, no contemporary illustrations of them in canal workings. The Tring canal cutting, however, was paralleled in the 1830s by another cutting to carry the new London and Birmingham Railway and the artist J. C. Bourne was on hand to sketch the scene. The technique was precisely the same, and it is more than likely that most of the men shown labouring in the railway cutting had started their working lives digging the canals. The soil and rock was then carted away to the workers building up embankments.

The barrow runs of the cutting represented hard toil for the men, but by far the most difficult work was tunnelling. The first major canal tunnel was designed to take the Trent and Mersey Canal through Harecastle Hill to the north of Stoke-on-Trent. Brindley had assured the company that he would have the whole work completed within five years, and even wagered £200 of his own money to back the assertion. He lost the bet, for it took eleven years to complete and Brindley himself was dead before it was finished. The techniques used were comparatively primitive, mostly borrowed from mining. Water was at first removed using wind- and water-powered pumps, but these had later to be supplemented by a crude steam engine, for James Watt's improved, efficient engine still lay in the future. Foul air and gases were removed from the workings by an alarming system whereby a fire was lit at the bottom of one shaft which carried the foul air up with the smoke whilst sucking fresh air to replace it down a second shaft. Progress was by black powder blasting and the inevitable hard labour of the men. Even after those eleven years of hard labour, the tunnel soon proved inadequate and in 1824 Telford built a second tunnel alongside the first, this time equipped with a tow-path. Where the original took eleven years to complete, the new, enlarged neighbour required only three.

By the 1790s, tunnelling techniques had advanced somewhat and the technology of steam pumps had improved immensely, but even so it was at best a somewhat hit-and-miss affair. If one looks at the history of Standedge tunnel on the Huddersfield Narrow Canal, one finds a fairly detailed description of how work progressed, and just how haphazard the surveying techniques were. Setting out the line of the canal was not like setting out a modern road, and usually depended on nothing more complex than using a magnetic compass and having teams of men line up a set of long poles. Although that was satisfactory for canal digging in general, tunnelling added a new dimension-depth beneath the surface. Bench marks had to be established and hill height calculated. When that was done, shafts could be sunk down from the laid-out surface line to a pre-calculated depth. The workers could then tunnel out from the bottom of the shaft on agreed headings, meeting, in theory at least, the tunnellers working towards them from the next shaft. In practice, some workings were out by over 20ft (6m) from the true line. Spoil dumped from the tunnels was sent up the shaft by an ingenious water-balance technique. A horizontal tunnel, or adit, joined the shaft near the surface and a second short shaft was sunk down to the adit. A large bucket full of water with a valve in the bottom was dropped down the short shaft, which hauled a smaller bucket of spoil up the main shaft through suitable gearing. When the water bucket hit the bottom of the shaft a valve was opened and the water poured away down the adit. The spoil bucket was now the heavier so it went back down to the workings. As well as these simple machines, four steam engines were installed to pump water from the workings. This was all very well organised, but it did not prevent accidents, as the local paper reported in 1803:

> George Sharp, a canal contractor and three other men, employed in the tunnel of the Huddersfield Canal, near Marsden, having set what is technically called a blast, to blow up the fragments of rock, retired to witness the explosion. An unusual time having elapsed . . . they supposed it was extinguished and approached nearer, when the powder unhappily exploded and killed George Sharp on the spot; two of his fellow workmen were dreadfully bruised, and remained blind for some time, and the others received several wounds from the splinters of rock.

The reports of accidents in canal tunnelling at least do not suggest the wholesale slaughter of workers that was the darkest stain on the story of railway construction. There is no canal equivalent to the navvies' memorial that stands in the graveyard at Otley to commemorate the men who died in building the Bramhope tunnel on the Leeds and Thirsk Railway.

Canal building involved a whole range of activities besides the obvious one of digging a very long trench in the ground. The entire structure had to be filled with water, which in many cases involved the construction of extensive reservoirs – yet more spade work. In the 127 miles (204km) of the Leeds and Liverpool Canal there are, including the twin lock at the Liverpool end, 93 locks and well over 200 bridges. Not only did all have to be built, but the material for building had to be acquired. Quarries were opened up to supply stone and masons were employed to shape it for lock chambers and bridges. Carpenters, often working on site, were employed to build lock gates. At the famous staircase of locks at Bingley, the five rise, there was a saw-pit where the big timbers were cut. This was a particularly unpleasant job for one half of the team: the timber was set over the pit and one man stood above holding one end of the saw while his mate stood down below at the bottom of the pit in a constant shower of sawdust. On some canals,

Canal Con Men

The following item was probably intended as a satire on the canal mania of the period, – but such was the mindless enthusiasm for shares in each and every canal company, that it might just about have been feasible. The 'Grand Mere Canal' does, however, sound suspiciously like the Ellesmere launched at that time.

A few well-dressed *Sharps*, observing the *Navigation Mania* so prevalent among all classes of men, determined to make JOHN BULL pay for the frenzy of the moment. They in consequence took a room, and laying a map of *Botany Bay* (as the proposed line) upon the table, stiled themselves *Proprietors* in the intended *Grand Mere Canal*, and resolved that no person should subscribe for more than ten shares, nor less than one, and that an immediate deposit of one-half per cent should entitle the subscriber to be a proprietor. It was no sooner whispered abroad, than the FLATS flocked to the standard, and the SHARPS moved off with about 1500£.

(*Leicester Journal*, 14 September 1792)

BUILDING THE CANALS

Navvies of the nineteenth century. These men are working the Manchester Ship Canal (Manchester Ship Canal Company)

Mechanisation on the grand scale finally arrived with the construction of the Manchester Ship Canal. The steam excavator is dumping spoil into trucks being pulled by one of the 173 locomotives used in the works (Manchester Ship Canal Company)

extensive brickworks were established purely to serve the canal's needs. The works at Devizes beside the mighty Caen Hill flight of locks on the Kennet and Avon was a notably impressive example, for the brickworks remained in use after the canal was completed. Miles of fencing had to be erected and hedges planted. New buildings, ranging from huge warehouses to humble lock cottages, were constructed. Canal building was a mighty enterprise using vast resources, and the canal builders transformed the transport system of Britain in little over half a century, producing the most dramatic changes to be seen since the last Roman built the last road.

Towards the end of the period, technology began to show real advances as steam power found more and more application throughout the industrial world. When Telford set to work organising construction on the Caledonian Canal he ordered three new steam engines from Boulton and Watt. Steam dredgers were set to work and instead of a procession of horses and carts, trains of spoil were hauled by horses along specially laid railway tracks. The poet Robert Southey, who visited the diggings with Telford, marvelled at a new steam dredger that could shift 800 tons of spoil a day. But for all the mechanical marvels, the bulk of the work still fell to the navvies, almost a thousand of them at the busiest time. It was not until the end of the nineteenth century, when the canal age had its last late flowering with the construction of the Manchester Ship Canal, that mechanisation came to dominate canal building. But those of us who travel the canals today for pleasure should give our thanks to men not machines – thanks to the brain power of some notable engineers and to the muscle power of tens of thousands of anonymous navvies.

Navvy Riots

By the end of the eighteenth century, canal navvies formed a shifting army, moving about the country from one set of diggings to another. They were not easy to control. The records seem to be liberally spattered with references to strikes or the equally troublesome habit of workers suddenly vanishing off into the surrounding countryside at harvest time when local farmers were paying top wages. The navvies also gained a reputation for riotous behaviour – indeed, the easiest way of hunting out references to canal navvies in contemporary records is to look up 'riots' in the index. There is no shortage of entries. Two drunken navvies from the Leicester and Northampton Union Canal, for example, were arrested in 1795 and sent off for trial with an escort of sixty soldiers. The British army, however, proved no match for the navvy army which attacked them, defeated them and carried the two drunks back to their camp in triumph. Other riots were far more serious. This account comes from the *Morning Chronicle* and describes events in Nottingham in 1793.

A scandalous riot took place in this town on Wednesday evening and continued till midnight. A number of navigators, disorderly boys and others, were drawn together by the music of some recruiting parties, who were parading, as usual, in the evening. After various proceedings, which manifested a mischievous disposition, they attacked the Plough Ale-house, the Sun, the houses of Mr. Haywood, a plumber and glazier, of Mr. Keyworth, a respectable malster, in the Long row and of Mr. Homer, ironmonger . . . at length these daring miscreants proceeded to the house of Mr. Oldknow, our much respected Mayor, and the attack becoming very violent, his family were under the unpleasant necessity of defending the house with firearms. They fired upon the rioters and several were dangerously wounded, one or two of whom, we hear, is since dead. The mob, upon this spirited proceeding, dispersed.

A peaceful scene at Sampford Peverell on the Grand Western Canal. It was less peaceful in 1811 when some 300 canal navvies rioted for more than twenty-four hours and at least two of them died in the fighting (Anthony Burton)

Such accounts suggest that the local populace went in fear of their lives from the lawless navvies. Even canal companies were nervous of the men and the Oxford Canal Committee approved an order for a brace of pistols to be bought for the agent's use on pay day. But it is as well to remember that records show only one side of the picture. Newspapers will, of course, give full accounts of serious riots: they do not run headlines saying 'Men Work Peacefully All Day'. But newspapers were then – as they are now – prone to taking political stances which coloured the way they reported the news. It was often convenient to blame trouble on the outsiders, the strangers, rather than admit that a riot might have been started by local people as a protest against local conditions. Sometimes there was an even more direct political link. In 1796, the Lancaster Canal committee were told that a party of navvies had been hired by an election candidate 'for no other purpose but to riot and do mischief' – an early rent-a-mob. Company records, however, were just as limited as newspaper reports: they only mentioned the navvies when something out of the ordinary occurred – a serious accident or a strike. One would not expect an army of tough, itinerant workers far from home to spend their spare time in prayer meetings and sewing circles and what is so surprising is not that there is a record of troubles and disorders, but that the record is so scant. If the canal navvy deserves his reputation as an exceptionally hard man it is because of the work he performed and not because of the trouble he caused.

4 THE ENGINEERS

It was Samuel Smiles who first elevated engineers to the roles of heroes of the industrial age, with his highly coloured accounts of their lives. He was particularly attracted to those men who had come from humble backgrounds and then worked their way to the top – implying that if they could do it, so could anyone else. He failed to notice the many hundreds, possibly thousands, who, throughout the eighteenth century, toiled on the lower slopes of the engineering pinnacle without ever glimpsing the summit. Those few whose names are still remembered came from diverse backgrounds, mainly because there was no recognised formal training for engineers. Natural intelligence and practical skills, which were as likely to appear in a millwright such as Brindley as in an instrument maker such as Smeaton, were the main features that led to success. The lack of training often meant, however, that each engineer in the early days tended to view every problem as though it had never been tackled, let alone solved, before. This could be both time-wasting and costly. The French were well ahead of the English in this respect and, at the time of the Revolution in 1789, the School of Bridges and Roadways became part of a general school of public works, which in time developed into a polytechnic. British engineers such as Rennie and Telford learned French specifically to keep up with their publications. Despite their lack of formal training, British engineers do stand out, not just for their practical abilities but for the brilliance of their imagination. The short sketches that follow are intended to show how diverse a group they were, and also to dispel some of the mythology that has surrounded them in the past. They have no need of myths, for their enduring works are more eloquent than any apocryphal stories could be.

John Smeaton (1724–92)

Smeaton has been described as the first great British civil engineer, and it would be hard to quarrel with this description. His background was an unlikely one, for he was born to a wealthy family who intended that he would follow a career in the law. But the young man's interests and abilities clearly lay elsewhere, in practical mechanics and mathematics. He started work as an instrument maker and, by the age of twenty-six, he had his own business. His skills and innovations led to his appointment as a Fellow of the Royal Society before he reached his thirtieth birthday, in itself a remarkable achievement. The most important instrument he invented at this period was a dilatometer, a device for measuring the expansion of metal. But his interests were widespread and he soon showed a much greater enthusiasm for practical work for industry than for theoretical science.

The old lengthman's cottage on the partially restored Cromford Canal. It typifies the use of local materials and local style of building (Anthony Burton)

The barrel vaulted cottages of the Stratford Canal are among its most distinctive features (Derek Pratt)

60

Differing styles of aqueducts. Brynich aqueduct (left) *on the Brecon and Abergavenny Canal is a solid masonry structure, built in a style drawn from contemporary road bridges. John Rennie's aqueducts are altogether more handsome. His Lune aqueduct* (below left) *that carries the Lancaster Canal across the river at Lancaster is somewhat severely formal compared with the graciousness of the Dundas aqueduct* (right). *The arrival of cast iron gave the engineers an opportunity to indulge in fantasy. The Engine Arm aqueduct* (below right) *on the BCN is embellished with Gothic arches* (Anthony Burton)

The use of cast iron for bridges brought the advantage of ease of construction with standard castings. In the Horseley Iron Works bridges of the Oxford Canal it also brought elegance (Anthony Burton)

Power was a prime concern for eighteenth-century industrialists, and the major power sources – the waterwheel and, to a lesser extent, the windmill – had not changed for hundreds of years. Millwrights worked by rule of thumb and, on the basis of a long tradition, Smeaton set out to test efficiency by building models. He was able to demonstrate, quite conclusively, that the overshot wheel where water falls on to the top of the wheel is far more efficient than the undershot where water flows against the paddle at the lower part of the wheel. Similarly, he tried different types of windmill sails to establish the best design. But his interests did not end with the older form of power, and he was soon to turn his attention to the great wonder of the age, the steam engine. These early engines were huge, ponderous beasts, limited to pumping water and very inefficient. Once again, Smeaton went to work in a systematic manner isolating the problems and then attempting to solve them. One of these problems was inaccuracy in boring cylinders, so that pistons slopped about while steam hissed out all around them. Smeaton designed a mill that could bore to a reasonably high degree of accuracy for the Carron Ironworks in Scotland and he also invented a new blowing engine to improve the blast of air to the furnaces. With his various improvements he built what was in its day the most powerful steam engine in the country at Chacewater Mine in Cornwall. Its cylinder was a massive 6ft (2m) in diameter, and it was about twice as efficient as its competitors. This is not, in fact, saying a great deal since, if you think of thermal efficiency as the amount of work actually done for the available energy produced by burning coal, it comes out at a derisory 1 per cent.

A portrait of John Smeaton by Romney, showing the Eddystone lighthouse in the background (National Portrait Gallery, London)

Smeaton, then, was a man of wide interests, but the crucial event in his life came in 1754 when he visited the Low Countries and saw their impressive works of land reclamation, canal construction and harbour building. He came home, closed down his instrument business and embarked on a new career as a civil engineer, although that name was not then in use. The term 'civil engineer' only appeared when a group of men engaged in similar work founded a Society of Engineers, declared that engineering was a profession and acknowledged John Smeaton as its leading exponent. There was to be no branch of the profession at which he was not to prove a master, and his works can still be seen in all their rich variety: an elegant and handsome bridge across the Tay at Perth, the delightful Charlestown harbour in Cornwall, still in use today, and, most famous of all, the Eddystone lighthouse. There had been two timber lighthouses on the rocks off Plymouth, but the first was destroyed by a gale and the second by fire. Smeaton designed a stone lighthouse where each stone was dovetailed with its neighbour to form a solid bond. The great tower was only replaced in 1882 and the top section was reassembled on Plymouth Hoe as a monument to Smeaton's genius.

It was when work had just started on the lighthouse that Smeaton received his first commission for a river navigation, when he was invited to return to his native Yorkshire to devise a scheme for improving the navigation of the Calder between Wakefield and Halifax. In 1757 he drew up his plans, work started in 1759 and by 1764 the navigation was open to trade, but not, alas, for long. In 1768 a devastating flood swept over the banks and damaged the locks, so that much had to be done all over again. The navigation remains in use now in extended form as the Calder and Hebble, and a very impressive waterway it is, too. Perhaps the most important waterway that Smeaton worked on, however, was the Forth and Clyde Canal. The idea of joining Scotland's two great rivers, the Forth and the Clyde, to provide large vessels with a route from coast to coast that avoided the long, hazardous coastal route, was put forward as early as the seventeenth century. At that time it seemed too ambitious, but the resounding success of the Bridgewater Canal brought many dusty old plans down from attic shelves. The scheme was revived and Smeaton was invited to devise a plan for a ship canal, and his plans were duly accepted by parliament. Then, as so often happened, work was begun but then came to a halt for want of funds. Nevertheless, the canal that was built was substantially Smeaton's – even if with locks of only 68ft 6in (21m) length and under 20ft (6m) width, it scarcely qualified as a ship canal in the modern sense.

Smeaton worked on other canal and navigation schemes, but these never formed more than a part of his busy engineering career. He left, however, much fine work behind, and he also left a legacy of knowledge which was enthusiastically absorbed and put to use by his most able pupil, William Jessop.

James Brindley (1716–72)

The stories surrounding James Brindley are legion, and together they build up a portrait of an extraordinary person. His appearance was said to have remained that of the plain country man throughout his career – 'as plain a looking man as one of the boors of the Peak'. Together with a plain country appearance went a plain country speech and almost a total lack of education. Although Brindley was only semi-literate, it was said that he had remarkable powers of thought. As a young man he was reported to have completed a round trip of 100 miles (161km) on foot, during which he visited a mill, memorised all the details of the workings and was able to tell his employer at the end exactly what was wrong and how to put it right. It was said that he would solve practical problems by retiring to a darkened room where he would lie down, sometimes

The Forth and Clyde Canal was built to a scale very different from that of English canals of the same period. Here the Clyde puffer Anzac *is taking on cargo at Port Dundas (British Waterways Board)*

for days on end; to emerge with the solution complete in every detail, but all fixed in his brain, not set down on paper. An unsophisticated man, a visit to the theatre to see the famous actor David Garrick as Richard III so disturbed his peace of mind that he vowed never to go to such a place again. He emerges from such stories as something of a buffoon, a shambling figure in old clothes, redeemed only by a practical genius for things mechanical. Yet Josiah Wedgwood, a man who counted some of the leading artists and scientists of the day among his friends, declared that he received as much pleasure and instruction from talking to his good friend Brindley as he did from any, and he visited his friend daily throughout his last illness. Sadly, the side of Brindley's character that was so admired by men such as Wedgwood, remains unknown to us today. What we do have is an outline of his life and his works.

Brindley was born in 1716 in the Derbyshire Peak District. The young boy received little in the way of schooling, beyond what his mother taught him. He has often been described as illiterate, but this is not strictly true. He could both read and write, but his spelling was phonetic rather than accurate, and his notebooks would have delighted Shaw's Professor Higgins, for in them one can find his own dialect preserved: 'Engon at Woork' and 'Bad Louk'. In 1733 he was apprenticed to a millwright near Macclesfield and he proved himself a more than able workman – considerably better, it is said, than his master, who preferred the beer house to the mill.

James Brindley painted by Francis Parsons. The popular notion that he did everthing 'by eye' is belied by the theodolite. Barton aqueduct can be seen in the background (City Museums, Stoke-on-Trent)

In 1742 Brindley set up his own business, and soon established a sound reputation for good workmanship and a well-above-average share of mechanical ingenuity. He worked on conventional grinding mills for both grain and flints, the latter for the local pottery industry. He was also asked to undertake a major job for a waterwheel to power a silk mill. At this time, engineering was still an unformed profession and the millwrights with their dual skills in both mechanical devices and controlling water sources were as likely to succeed in the new field as were more scientifically inclined gentlemen such as Smeaton. And, like Smeaton, Brindley was interested in the new technology. He even tried his hand at steam-engine construction, but not, it has to be said, with any great success.

The turning point in his career – the moment that set him aside from the many other millwrights of the age – came when he was asked to help with drainage at the Wet Earth Colliery at Clifton in Lancashire. This is not as odd as it might seem today, for mine drainage still depended largely on pumps driven by waterwheels, so the millwright was a familiar figure on the colliery scene. Wet Earth, however, proved unusually difficult. To bring the water to his wheel, Brindley built a weir on the River Irwell and led the water away through a tunnel cut out of the rock for nearly ½ mile (0.8km). He then dug a pit down beside the river and took his water supply under the Irwell by a siphon. After that, all that was needed was a simple half-mile long channel to complete the watercourse. The work was completed in 1756. It was an elaborate system and a successful one and the mine owners were delighted with the results, so it was only natural that when the Duke of Bridgewater began to think of a canal that would link in directly with the

The Work of an Engineer

This letter was written by William Jessop to the proprietors of the Selby Canal in 1774:

I understand it to be my Duty as an Engineer to make Designs for the Locks Bridges Tunnels and all other erections necessary for compleating the Navigation, and after making the necessary contracts with Masons Carpenters Smith &c for their Execution I think myself bound to give due Attendance to see that the several Works are executed according to the Contracts.

I shall also think it my Duty to Mark out the Lines for the several Cuts, Banks and Back Drains and from Time to Time as I may be authorized by the Committee to make the necessary Contracts for those Works – and I do propose from Time to Time to give an Account to the Committee of the State that the Works may be in at those Times; and how the different Sets of Workmen are severally employed with such other Circumstance as may be necessary to come under their Consideration.

Without being more particular (as there may be many things necessary for me to attend to which I cannot at present Call to mind) I mean to make this Business the principal object of my attention and to give it every Degree of attendance that may be necessary to compleat it in the best manner I am able for the Advantage of the Proprietors and to my own Credit.

(Quoted by Charles Hadfield and A. W. Skempton in *William Jessop, Engineer*, 1979)

underground workings at Worsley, the name of Brindley soon came to his ears.

The Bridgewater Canal ensured Brindley's fame and fortune, although the question of how much credit for the actual design belongs with him and how much with the duke's agent John Gilbert may never be resolved. Contemporaries, however, were in no doubt: Brindley was the man of the moment. During the decade that followed the completion of the original Bridgewater Canal, there was a brief pause while the significance of its success was assimilated, then the deluge came – offers from all over the country from communities which, quite suddenly it seems, had discovered that they were in desperate need of a canal. All the canals on which he actually worked as chief engineer, following the Bridgewater, were narrow canals, with the exception of the Droitwich. This vital decision to opt for narrow locks (see Chapter 3) was to impose a pattern that still dominates the heartland of the British canal system. Five canals, the Trent and Mersey, and the Staffs and Worcester (begun in 1766), the Coventry and the Birmingham (1768) and the Oxford (1769) formed a cross linking together the Trent, the Mersey, the Severn and the Thames. Around this framework there was to be built an increasingly complex system of canals, short and long, on all of which, thanks to Brindley's decision, cargo would be carried in narrow boats. It was as decisive as, in a later age, George Stephenson's decision to set the rails on his Stockton and Darlington Railway 4ft 8½in apart.

Although Brindley was chief engineer for all these schemes, he was notoriously absent from many of them during construction: how could it have been otherwise? The Trent and Mersey, the Grand Trunk, received more of his attention than the rest whose proprietors might have complained but seldom received much satisfaction. And it was not just the canals with which his name is still associated which received his attention. As one of the few acknowledged experts in the land, he was called upon to advise on numerous projects. Inevitably, his surveys were occasionally somewhat perfunctory, and his views on the proposed Forth and Clyde Canal were treated with great sarcasm by John Smeaton. Brindley had claimed bad weather as an excuse, but Smeaton would have none of that:

but pray, Mr Brindley, if you were in a hurry, and the weather happened to be bad, so that you could not satisfy yourself concerning them, are the works to be immediately stopped when you blow the whistle, till you come again, and make a more mature examination?

It was a criticism that was no doubt well deserved and could be voiced because Smeaton was rightly confident of his own standing as an engineer. The gentlemen who made up the canal committees may have had expertise in their own fields but seldom knew anything of canal construction: for them the words of James Brindley were sacrosanct.

Brindley may have attempted too much, but what he achieved was remarkable. His Birmingham Canal was to prove the axis along which a whole new thriving industrial city was to develop. Leading industrial innovators of the day built new factories alongside Brindley waterways – Wedgwood at Etruria, Boulton and Watt in Soho, Birmingham. His canals even gave birth to whole new towns such as Shardlow, the transshipment point between the narrow boats of the Trent and Mersey and the barges of the Trent, and, most famously, Stourport at the junction of the Staffs and Worcester and the Severn. There is a story repeated by many authors, including, it must be confessed, by the present author, that Brindley originally intended to take his canal to Bewdley but that the citizens of that successful river port told him to take his 'stinking ditch' elsewhere, and lived to regret the decision. More recent work has shown that far from opposing the canal, the citizens of Bewdley petitioned to have it go there. In fact, it would be entirely typical of Brindley's methods that, having followed the line of the Stour from Stourton to Kidderminster, he should keep his canal in the same valley all the way to the Severn rather than take the shortest route to the river.

Brindley did find time in his busy life to notice that one of his surveyors, John Henshall, had a young and attractive daughter. They were married and James and Anne Brindley set up house in Staffordshire, close to the engineer's most time-consuming project, the Harecastle tunnel. They had two children, but the marriage was to be a short one. Brindley's friends warned him that he was overworking, but he paid no attention. What they and he did not know was that he was suffering from diabetes. He died in September 1772. Samuel Smiles, ever the author to provide a grand finale, tells his readers that at the very end a group came to him from the diggings desperate because the canal would not hold water. 'Puddle it,' said Brindley. They declared they had done so. 'Then puddle it again,' said the great engineer, and died. Wedgwood, who was with him to the end, wrote that he woke in the early hours of the morning, asked for a drink then simply said: ''Tis enough – I shall need no more,' and closed his eyes for the last time.

William Jessop sketched by George Dance in 1796, when he was most heavily involved in canal construction (National Portrait Gallery, London)

William Jessop (1745–1814)

The years immediately following Brindley's death were momentous in terms of world history, with revolution in France and the War of Independence in America. Events were somewhat less dramatic in the smaller world of British canals, with no more than a dozen acts being passed between 1772 and the end of the 1780s. Then, quite suddenly, the rate of progress quickened: one act in 1790, six in 1791, six in 1792 and nineteen in 1793 when the new wave of canal building reached its peak. The man who dominated this second phase of the canal story was William Jessop.

Jessop's father was a shipwright at Devonport who worked for John Smeaton on the Eddystone lighthouse, and when William finished his schooling he became Smeaton's apprentice. He worked his way up steadily from apprentice to assistant, learning his craft from the acknowledged master of the age: he could scarcely have found a better training. As an assistant he worked with Smeaton on a number of river navigations, but was soon being entrusted to do work on his own. In 1773, he went to Ireland for the first time to survey the works on the Grand Canal that was planned to link Dublin to Shannon. It is a fact

The Ideal Education for the Engineer

My father wisely determined that I should go through all the gradations, both practical and theoretical, which could not be done if I went to the University, as the practical parts, which he considered most important, must be abandoned; for he said, after a young man has been three or four years at the University of Oxford or Cambridge, he cannot, without much difficulty, turn himself to the practical part of civil engineering.

(Sir John Rennie, *Autobiography*, 1875)

that can be easily overlooked in a history of British canals that in Ireland major projects such as this were begun as early as 1756, although it was still very far from complete when Jessop went to inspect it on Smeaton's behalf. It was to prove a valuable experience and he was to return to Ireland as a mature engineer and supervise major works, including the construction of extensive docks in Dublin. In 1777 he was married.

Over the years Jessop became more firmly established as an engineer in his own right and worked on a number of canal and river projects. He was fortunate that when the canal mania hit Britain at the end of the 1780s, he had reached the stage in his career when he was old enough to have gained useful experience and a solid reputation, but was still young enough to have the energy and enthusiasm to throw himself into major undertakings. His first canal of this time was certainly one that offered more than its share of challenges. It was to be built to link Richard Arkwright's pioneering cotton town of Cromford in Derbyshire to the Erewash Canal at Langley Mill. It looks, and indeed is, daunting country for any canal builder, being dominated by the steep hills that rise up all around the narrow Derwent valley. It included three short tunnels and one major work, the 3,063yd (2,800m) long Butterley tunnel, and there were to be two big aqueducts. The tunnel was a great success, the aqueducts rather less so. Jessop was often troubled by failures in his aqueducts, but was at least always more than willing to accept the blame and even made good defects from his own funds. Yet in spite of the aqueduct problems, the canal as a whole was a success and it brought him into contact with another young man, Benjamin Outram, who was to make an engineering reputation in a slightly different field. Together, they established an ironworks on the canal at Butterley, which Outram supervised and which was to gain a fine reputation over the years.

Jessop now found himself with an immense work-load which included the Derby Canal, where Jessop and Outram's expertise coalesced, for it was built in conjunction with a horse-drawn railway or tramway. The canal was ideal for the flatter country, but on the hills the railway was more effective. An early form of containerisation was used, for coal was carried in wooden boxes which could be lifted off their wheels and dropped snugly into place in the boat. As well as this and other canal schemes, together with his work in Ireland, he also found time to work on drainage systems for the fens and marshes of East Anglia. But among this multitude of schemes, three stand out as those on which his reputation as one of the great canal engineers ultimately rests: the Rochdale, the Grand Junction (the main line of the Grand Union), and the Ellesmere, now known as the Llangollen. It says something for Jessop's somewhat self-effacing, self-deprecating character that for many years history gave the major credit for two of these projects to other men. The Rochdale was referred to as Rennie's, and the Ellesmere came to be associated with the name of Thomas Telford. Certainly, Rennie was the first engineer to survey a line for the Rochdale, but it was Jessop who was to lay down the line that was actually built. Its most remarkable feature is, paradoxically, that it has no remarkable features – no great tunnels, nor even very extravagant aqueducts on a canal that crosses the

Pennines at their wildest. And those who boat the sections that are now in water or walk the tow-path simply do not see the biggest works of all, the great reservoirs in the hills which are an essential feature of a canal with ninety-two locks in 33 miles (53km). No one, however, needs to be told which is the most spectacular feature on the Ellesmere Canal – the mighty Pontcysyllte aqueduct over the Dee near Llangollen – but simply because the aqueduct is so famous it is easy to overlook the quality of the rest of the canal. Here Jessop displayed the full range of the canal-builder's art: contour cutting around hills near Ellesmere and contour cutting again to follow the line of the hillside to Llangollen, cut and fill near Chirk, where the River Ceiriog is approached on a high bank, crossed on a stone aqueduct, after which the canal dives underground through a tunnel to emerge into a deep cutting. But Pontcysyllte is what everybody remembers, and who should have the credit – Jessop or Telford? Jessop was undeniably chief engineer and the final decision lay with him, while ironwork was no stranger to the Butterley partner; but it seems that the credit for first suggesting the iron trough should be given to the younger man. The story of how it came about is told in more detail in the notes on Telford. The Grand Junction, however, is indisputably Jessop's and it was clear from the first that it was to be one of the main arteries of the whole canal system, linking the industrial Midlands by a direct line through to London. It is still a majestic waterway, with its handsome, wide locks, even if, yet again, Jessop was plagued by aqueduct problems and had further difficulties with Blisworth tunnel. As on the Ellesmere, Jessop displayed the full range of engineering devices available to him, and at the end he had a canal which immediately proved its worth by becoming a busy and prosperous trading route.

Jessop continued to work on canals into the nineteenth century, notably as a consulting engineer on the Caledonian Canal, but his later years were more notable for other schemes, of which his harbour work

The Rochdale Canal in its Pennine setting near Todmorden is now almost dwarfed by the viaduct carrying the Lancashire and Yorkshire Railway (Anthony Burton)

The approach to Pontcysyllte. The illustration shows how the canal is banked up on the hillside, before turning sharply for the crossing of the Dee valley (Clwyd Record Office)

was by far the most important, and included the floating harbour at Bristol and London's West India Dock. He was involved, too, in the beginning of the movement that was, in time, to threaten his canals – the railways. In 1801, he proposed a line from the Thames at Wandsworth to Croydon, which was approved by parliament, making it the first public goods line in the world. It was built on the tramway principle with rails held on square stone blocks, to leave a space down the middle of the tracks for the horses that were to pull the trucks. The Duke of Bridgewater would have taken a dim view of a canal engineer involving himself in such a system, for he remarked with prophetic accuracy that canals would prosper 'if we can keep clear of those damned tramroads'. Jessop's Surrey Iron Railway was among the forerunners of the railways that followed in the age of steam locomotives.

William Jessop was never a flamboyant character, but a rather reserved man, happy in a settled family life with his wife and children. His name scarcely features in the lists of the great engineers, yet the scope of his work was vast and he, more than anyone else, took British canals from the rather tentative beginnings under Brindley into a new age of technological daring.

Thomas Telford (1757–1834)

Telford's fame rests only in part in his canal work, but that work seems always to be on such a grand scale that no list of the great canal engineers could omit his name. If Jessop bore the brunt of canal building in the mania years, then it was Telford who continued it into the nineteenth century, until canal building virtually stopped with the birth of the railway age. Telford, who worked as an assistant to Jessop, was to survive to advise on work by George Stephenson and to suffer the indignity of having one of his grand designs rejected in favour of that of an unknown engineer still in his twenties, Isambard Kingdom Brunel.

Telford was born in Eskdale in Scotland. His father died when he was a baby, but he was fortunate enough to have an uncle who ensured that he received a good, basic education and then set him on his way as an apprentice stone-mason. In 1782 Telford took himself and his ambition to London, where he worked on building Somerset House. His dream, however, was for a career in architecture and he was lucky enough to find a patron who was prepared to help him on his way. He worked for a time on harbour schemes in Portsmouth and then his career jumped forward in 1786 when he was appointed surveyor for the county of Shropshire. Road construction and bridge building all came under his control, and there were even opportunities to try his hand at his first love – architecture. He designed a gaol and even a church for Madeley, the latter a somewhat uninspired building. It was soon apparent, however, that the indifferent architect was a fine and innovative engineer. He was particularly fortunate in his position, for Shropshire was home to the great iron masters of the Severn valley, and the famous iron bridge stood as a monument to their pioneering attitudes. Telford soon showed that he appreciated the value of this new technology, and when he designed his own iron bridge across the Severn at Buildwas, it proved to be a great improvement over its more famous neighbour. But by this time he had

A canal-tramway interchange at Llanfoist on the Brecon and Abergavenny Canal. Trucks unloaded straight into the warehouse and boats floated in underneath (Anthony Burton)

Old woollen mills line the Leeds and Liverpool Canal at Skipton, whilst the Pennine hills rise up beyond the terraced houses (Anthony Burton)

already taken on a second job as assistant to Jessop on the Ellesmere Canal.

At this stage in his career, Telford seemed to be especially favoured by fortune, for he seemed always to be in the right place at the right time. He had only just grasped the fundamentals of his new profession as canal engineer when work stopped on the nearby Shrewsbury Canal with the death of its engineer, Josiah Clowes. Telford was given the job of finishing this modest waterway, which was to include an equally modest aqueduct across the River Tern. A conventional stone or brick aqueduct would have been quite satisfactory, but this was the heart of the iron-making country. An iron-trough aqueduct was proposed and the idea was eagerly taken up by Telford, who set to work with the iron master William Reynolds. The aqueduct was a success, largely because the light iron trough needed so much less support than a weighty masonry trough with its heavy lining of puddled clay. The advantages of iron were obvious, but especially for very long aqueducts, and it looked as if a very long aqueduct was what was needed on the Ellesmere Canal. Telford returned to Jessop full of enthusiasm for iron, and Jessop, with his own connections in the iron trade, was equally keen. The plans for Pontcysyllte were drawn up and the work authorised. Whoever deserves the credit for this work, it is undeniable that Telford's association with the great aqueduct assured his professional future.

Telford now returned to the native Scotland that he had left as a poor shepherd's son to undertake a major programme of road, canal and harbour building. This series of public works was designed to relieve the appalling condition the country still found itself in following the disasters of the 1745 uprising. Here some of his first memorable bridges

A pair of working narrow boats with traditional decoration at Hawkesbury Junction (Derek Pratt)

The impressive scale of the Caledonian Canal and the majesty of its setting can be seen in this photograph of Laggan bridge. To the right are the natural waters of Loch Oich, to the left, the deep tree-lined Laggan cutting (Derek Pratt)

were erected, including the first iron bridge in Scotland across the Tay at Aberlour. Its Scottish baronial stone towers still bear a plaque proclaiming that the castings came from Plas Kynaston in Wales – the foundry that had produced the iron-work for Pontcysyllte. The journey of these iron castings is not recorded, but it is tempting to think that the iron for Scotland started on its way by boat across the famous aqueduct. Telford developed his own techniques for road construction, which ensured a sound surface, and his harbour works were spread from Portree in Skye to Peterhead on the east coast. But the most ambitious plan was for a ship canal that would slice across the centre of Scotland from Fort William to Inverness – the Caledonian. On this project, Telford was reunited with his old master Jessop, but no longer as engineer and assistant but on an equal footing. The Caledonian was unique in the canal age for the resources used in its construction. It remains a wonderfully impressive waterway, but it was never a great commercial success.

When he returned to England other canal work came Telford's way, notably the Birmingham and Liverpool Junction, a canal which, with its high banks and deep cuttings, epitomised the final stage of canal development. Telford was also called in to improve Brindley's original Birmingham Canal. He carved a new straight route through the wriggles and curves of the old line, and over the deepest of the cuttings he threw one of his most elegant iron bridges, which was named after one of the Birmingham committee men – Galton Bridge. He also set about improving another Brindley work by constructing a new, improved

Telford's immense range of warehouses stand beside the entrance lock to the Ellesmere Canal at Ellesmere Port. The town grew up around this trans-shipment port between sea-going vessels such as that waiting at the quay and the narrow boats on the canal (National Railway Museum, York/Michael E. Ware Collection)

Harecastle tunnel on the Trent and Mersey. His fame even spread across the seas and he was invited to report and help on the proposed Gotha Ship Canal in Sweden. In spite of the importance of these late canals, they were overshadowed by his work on roads and harbours. On the important coach road to Holyhead he engineered a magnificent route that ended in triumph with his two finest bridges, the suspension bridges at Conwy and across the Menai Strait. At St Katherine's Docks in London he established a whole new pattern of building based on an enclosed dock, which was to remain influential for decades to come.

Telford ended his days full of honours, as founder-president of the Institution of Civil Engineers. But he was no longer in tune with the changing times. The railways came too late for him to make any real contribution, and what might have been his last great triumph became instead a fiasco. When a design was required for a bridge across the Avon Gorge at Clifton, the man who had produced the elegant simplicity of the Menai Bridge now brought forward a grotesque design based on useless Gothic towers. The work went instead to Brunel, who showed that he had learned the lesson that the old master had, it seemed, forgotten. But these last sad incidents in a somewhat cantankerous old age cannot diminish Telford's very real achievements. He never lost his love of architecture, but it is his engineering work that we now see as possessing the greater beauty and which still has as great a power to astonish by its daring and ingenuity as it did when it was new two centuries ago.

John Rennie, pictured in 1803 by George Dance (National Portrait Gallery, London)

Other Engineers

The four engineers whose lives have been briefly sketched were chosen because each seemed to epitomise one phase of the canal-building story. They were not, however, by any means the only engineers of note who worked on canals at this time, some of whom achieved considerable fame. John Rennie, for example, had a career which in its rich variety could match that of Telford and Jessop. His canals are notable for the beauty of their structures: no one could match Rennie when it came to sheer elegance in a stone aqueduct. Dundas on the Kennet and Avon with its sweet, classical simplicity is matched by the more austere beauty of perhaps the greatest of them all, the aqueduct across the Lune at Lancaster. Jessop's partner in the Butterley Ironworks, Benjamin Outram, was responsible for such fine works as the Peak Forest Canal with its superb flight of locks leading down from Marple to the aqueduct across the Goyt. His principal claim to fame must, however, be his plateways and tramways, the early railways that effectively extended the canal system into otherwise inaccessible places. There is an interesting connection here between the two fine engineers, for Jessop's Cromford Canal was eventually joined to Outram's Peak Forest by a tramway, the Cromford and High Peak Railway, for which the engineer was the young Josias Jessop.

Some engineers are scarcely remembered today, even when their works survive – Samuel Simcock who was mainly responsible for work on the Oxford, for example, or John Longbotham who saw the Leeds and Liverpool off on its long haul towards completion. Little is known of many of these names beyond what we can see of the quality of their work and the soundness of their ideas. But the canal-building age did not end when the first steam locomotive puffed along an old tramway. One other person at least deserves a special mention: Edward Leader Williams, whose father was engineer on the Severn Commission. The son produced what are perhaps the most remarkable structures on the whole waterway system. The old Barton aqueduct was in the way of the new Manchester Ship Canal which was about to swallow up the River Irwell. Williams designed a new aqueduct, but one which would pivot on a central support, swinging clear of the ship canal to allow big vessels through on their way to and from Manchester. Equally exciting is the boat lift he designed to take vessels between the River Weaver and the Trent and Mersey Canal at Anderton. Edward Leader Williams proved that the nineteenth-century canal engineer could show just as much ingenuity as his pioneering forerunners of the eighteenth century.

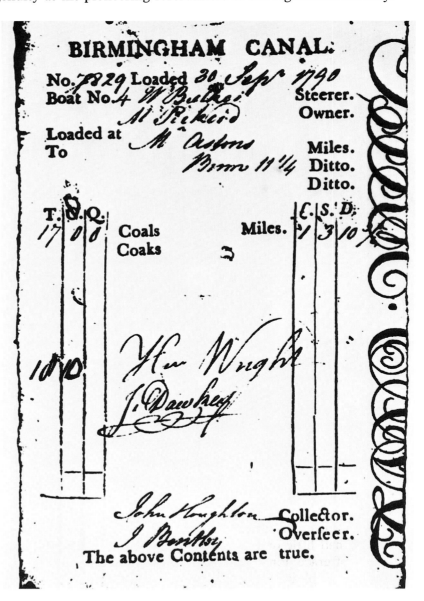

Toll receipt for the Birmingham Canal, 1790 (British Waterways Board)

5 ARCHITECTURE AND ENGINEERING

One of the great appeals of canal travel lies with the fact that each waterway has its own distinctive characteristics. You need no guidebook to tell you that you are on the Llangollen Canal when one of those typical lift-bridges comes into view around the corner, just as the sight of a barrel-vaulted lock cottage is a sure sign that you are travelling the Stratford. But this sense of identity goes even deeper. Travel a modern motorway and you often have no idea where in the country you are, but the canals send out clear messages: they belong to their own special place. To see why this is so and to understand what it is that is uniquely appealing about canal travel, one has yet again to step back in time and see them in the context of their own age.

The canal age came into being largely because of the difficulties and expense of moving heavy goods by land. This was a problem that not only affected the canal's potential customers but also confronted the canal builders themselves: until they actually had the canal completed they were faced by the same costs and difficulties as everyone else. And they turned to the same solution as the rest of their contemporaries: if it is very costly to bring in materials from far away, use what you can find close at hand. Where a canal passed through areas with good stone, that stone was quarried for building; where stone was scarce but good clay plentiful, then the clay was dug up and burned in temporary brickworks. The result is canal structures that belong, that fit into the countryside because they derive directly from that same countryside. And you can actually tell when you pass from one geological area to another as the canal-building materials change, and it is not just a case of brick giving way to stone, but of an infinity of subtle variations. In our age, the use of purely local materials has become a sign of luxury, for it is far cheaper and easier to opt for mass-produced materials and synthetics.

The eighteenth-century builder would no doubt have welcomed the modern materials, but they were not available. His misfortune is our good luck. Bricks fired in local kilns in a somewhat haphazard fashion emerge in a rich mixture of shades, so that even the most ordinary of canal bridges may have variations in colour from a yellowy-orange to the deepest of reds. Local stone weathers with age, it wears with use, so that a flight of steps at a lock once built of squared-off blocks becomes shaped into sinuous, gentle curves. Modern concrete merely stains with age and crumbles and breaks with time. The engineers and builders of the canal system usually had little or no interest in aesthetics: Josiah Wedgwood wanted 'a line of grace' for the Trent and Mersey Canal where it passed by his property, a pleasant curve to delight the eye. Sadly, he had to report that Brindley, the 'inflexible vandal', would have none of that: the best engineering line was dead straight, so dead straight it would be. And Wedgwood was actually paying for this stretch of canal himself! Later engineers might seek to impress and beautify, but not those of the first generation. Today, we speak quite naturally about the beauty of the canal, so if it is not due to deliberate acts by the builders, where does that beauty come from?

The basic character of any canal derives from the engineering decisions taken in the planning stage. Then, the line is fixed, positions for locks settled and the need for major engineering works, such as aqueducts and tunnels, decided. Even on the early canals there were marked differences in attitude between different engineers. Where Brindley was drawing his elaborate curves over the landscape to keep engineering works down to a minimum, in Yorkshire John Longbotham was taking a very different line. His Leeds and Liverpool Canal went charging up the Aire valley from Shipley on the outskirts of Bradford in a series of increasingly huge steps. At Dowley two locks are arranged as a double riser – that is, joined together so that the top lock gates of the first lock are also the bottom gates of the one above. That is the first step. This is followed by a short staircase of three interconnected locks and the whole process culminates in the Bingley Five, where the five interconnected locks lift the canal 60ft (18m) up the hillside to send the boats off for a 17-mile (27-km) long, lock-free ride all the way to Skipton. Bingley remains as impressive a piece of waterway engineering as it was when it was built, and if you want to see a complete contrast in attitude, then you need only compare it with Brindley's solution to the same problem of getting a canal up a steepening valley.

The Bratch lies just south of Wolverhampton on the Staffs and Worcester canal. At first sight it looks as if Brindley has opted for the same solution as Longbotham – three locks joined together to form a staircase. But a closer look shows that each lock is separated from the next by a short stretch of water or pound – considerably shorter, in fact, than a working boat's length. Now locks use a large amount of water, and in a conventional system, the boat coming downhill pushes a lockful of water into the next pound, which in turn will feed the next lock and so on until the lockful of water eventually gets lost into a river. If all were as it seems at the Bratch, then the pounds would be too small to take the rush of water, which would have to bypass the next lock on an overspill weir and run to waste. Then there would not be enough water to fill lock number two. But all is not as it seems: tucked away in the undergrowth are side ponds which act as reservoirs for the short pound. Why Brindley did not make the Bratch into a staircase proper will probably never be known, but he did produce one of the loveliest spots on the canal. The one advantage of the slow progress through the locks was that it afforded ample time for the boatmen to pay their dues at the handsome octagonal toll house at the top of the flight. Again, the curious shape derives not from any sense of whimsy but from the practical necessity for the toll-keeper to keep a look-out in different directions. It is all very fine, but what a contrast with Bingley where the five wide locks march boldly up the hillside to a four-square lock cottage of

Brindley's 'near staircase' at the Bratch. Side ponds are hidden away behind the hedge to the left of the picture. At the top of the flight is the octagonal toll house with the lock cottage beyond (Derek Pratt)

massive stone blocks. The latter is, in fact, something of a newcomer, for it was built from the remains of a demolished warehouse at Liverpool, and faded letters can still be seen on some stones, as though the whole structure was made up of oversize alphabet blocks from a baby's playpen.

Bratch and Bingley represent extremes, for most canals move upwards at a rather more leisurely pace, lock by lock, strung out at regular intervals over the length of the canal. It is worthwhile pausing – just as we all have to pause when out boating on the canal – to think about a typical lock scene. What is it that makes locks so appealing to so many people? The answer provides clues to the appeal of canal works in general. The details may vary from place to place, but the fundamentals remain the same.

First, there is the lock chamber itself, closed off by stout, heavy wooden gates. In order to move such massive chunks of timber you need to apply leverage, hence the balance beams. Now opening these gates still requires a certain amount of effort, and by far the easiest way to do so is to use one's strongest muscles, the legs. Lean your back on the balance beam, push with your feet and the job is done – although it helps to have something to push off against. So the builders provided quadrants on the ground, a little series of raised bricks or stones following the natural arc of the circle that the balance beam will follow as it moves. The contrast between the straight beam, blackened with preservative and painted white at the ends for visibility, and the curve picked out in natural stone or brick is very satisfying to the eye. But it

81

Principal Engineering Features on British Canals

The following list is intended to be representative rather than comprehensive: the order is alphabetical, rather than by any scale of importance, with the exception of tunnels, listed by length.

Aqueducts
Bridgewater
Barton swing aqueduct at Barton-upon-Irwell, Eccles. It crosses the Manchester Ship Canal and replaces the Brindley aqueduct, the abutments of which can be seen.
Caldon
Hazelhurst aqueduct is a canal flyover, carrying the Leek branch over the main line.
Edinburgh and Glasgow Union
This boasts three major aqueducts, of which the finest is the Almond near Broxburn.
Kennet and Avon
The Dundas aqueduct crosses the Avon, 1 mile (1.6km) north of Limpley Stoke.
Lancaster
The aqueduct at Lancaster across the Lune.
Llangollen
Chirk aqueduct beside the A5 and Pontcysyllte, Britain's longest aqueduct, 1,007ft (307km) long and 120ft (193km) high.
Peak Forest
Marple, at the foot of Marple locks, 90ft (27m) high.
Shrewsbury
Longdon-upon-Tern, the first iron-trough aqueduct, now isolated in a field (map reference SJ 618156).
Stratford-upon-Avon
Edstone iron-trough aqueduct, near Bearley.
Trent and Mersey
Dove aqueduct, near Burton-on-Trent, with twenty-three arches, it is the longest surviving example of Brindley's work.

continued on page 83

was built that way because the appropriate materials were at hand and they were then treated in the simplest possible manner. This same message of fitness for purpose is the key to so much that we admire on the canals today.

A lock is little use unless it can be filled and emptied to allow the boats to go up and down. The commonest solution is to have openings in the gates and in the lock walls, the latter being connected by a culvert to the canal above the lock for filling, while those at the lower end discharge through culverts to the canal below the bottom gates. These openings are then covered by movable paddles which can be raised and lowered by a simple ratchet turned by a windlass. The spiky metal outline of the paddle gear is as much a part of the traditional lock scene as gates and balance beams, although there are endless small variations. Well maintained, it is very easy to use and winding the gear produces a most satisfactory metallic rattle. It is not the only method for moving the paddles at a lock: on the Leeds and Liverpool Canal, for example, some locks are fitted with 'Jack Cloughs' where the paddles are attached to long levers which work directly to swing them across the face of the openings. Such devices are, admittedly, archaic, designed for a world where power mostly meant strong muscles. No modern engineer designing a lock for a transport route would dream of using such devices, but most of our canals are not transport routes in the sense of carrying cargo. They carry pleasure boaters who are looking for enjoyment, and that includes visual enjoyment. John Smeaton once said of James Brindley that 'every man, how great soever his genius, has a certain hobby-horse that he likes to ride; a large aqueduct bridge over a large river does not happen to be mine'. I had better confess at once that modern hydraulic gearing is a hobby-horse of mine – the bulbous excrescences that have sprouted like black, malign fungi at lock sides throughout the land. The excuse is that they are 'more efficient', but I do not want an efficient canal. If I was in a tearing hurry I should be out on the road. And they are not, in my view, very efficient anyway. Every regular canal user must have experienced the frustration of endlessly winding up one of these monsters, then going across to the next only to look back to see the first malevolently unwinding itself again, for there is no braking mechanism. A curse on them, say I, and with that I shall park my hobby-horse and return to the simple lock.

Lock users must be able to get from one side of the lock to the other, and the ready-made bridge is always available in the shape of the lock gates themselves, which need only the addition of a simple hand-rail. But bridges are an essential element on all canals. When the waterway was built, it would have run straight through old lanes and roads, and divided off one part of a farmer's land from another. Some form of bridge would then be needed to reunite the two parts of the country lane or to provide a route for the farmer's cows to amble from the fields to the milking shed. Engineers were usually cost conscious, and the tail of a lock with its built-up sides was the ideal place for a bridge which would need the minimum of building materials. Locks need to be well maintained, and when they were grouped together in a flight there was usually a lock cottage for the company's man. In the early days, no one would have contemplated anything as sophisticated as calling on an architect. The job would simply go to a local builder, who would be given rough specifications and then left to do the work. The result was a building using local materials and the local vernacular style, nothing fancy, simply another version of the country cottage that adds so much to the appeal of the landscape. These are the elements that establish the broad pattern of the lock scene, yet there are other details to look for which can prove just as pleasing. There is generally a need to supply some means for excess water to flow around the lock, an overspill weir. This may be no more than a subterranean culvert, but on some canals it can be a pleasure itself. Locks on the Huddersfield Narrow, for example, have stony staircases that create miniature cascades at the lock; while on the Staffs and Worcester there are curious circular weirs down which the water gurgles as if draining down some giant plug-hole. Even the simplest of devices, such as bollards, can show a rich variety: wood becomes worn and weathered and cast iron is sculpted by the wear of thousands of mooring lines. The list can, it seems, be almost infinitely extended. Each lock on a canal provides the boater with a new experience, not just in itself but because it acts like a shutter which, when released, displays a new scene, the next stage on the journey.

Simplicity was the rule with almost everything that touched the earliest canals. Bridges were built as simple arches constructed over wooden formers, with the resulting curves adding a graceful note to what might have been dull rectilinear slabs. In fact, the familiar hump-backed bridge is no more than the cheapest solution to the problem of providing the minimum of space for a boat to pass underneath while using the least possible material to enable the bridge to be used by pedestrians. The numerous bridges were expensive items in the budget, and a cheaper alternative for the farmer's cattle crossing was the movable bridge. On the Llangollen Canal, a simple wooden platform crosses the canal, above which is a more complex superstructure with a long balance beam. By pulling on a chain dangling from the end of the beam, the platform can be raised. These were easy and cheap to build, but not always so simple to maintain. Other engineers preferred swing-bridges, which pivot and swing in a horizontal plane, but could be rather more substantial as they do not have to be pulled up into the air. Again, maintenance can be a problem, for once the ends droop with age, the bridges can stick solidly – as the author well remembers, having spent a desperately tiring afternoon on the Peak Forest Canal between Marple and Whaley Bridge attempting to move the unmovable.

Over the years there were more subtle changes in bridge design, as engineers began to take a more direct interest in all aspects of their work. Where the early bridges were simply given out as jobs to contractors with a price attached, in later years complete plans and elevations with detailed specifications were supplied. It is with these that one looks for, and very often finds, workmanship and artistry of a very high order. John Rennie was noted for his design work, as one might expect from a man who was to give London some of its finest bridges. His Lancaster Canal work is particularly fine, but even that cannot match the work on the Macclesfield Canal, begun at the end of the canal period in 1825. It

continued from page 82

Earthworks

Birmingham
  Smethwick cutting on Telford's new canal.

Bridgewater
  Stretford bank, near Eccles, the first substantial canal bank.

Caledonian
  Laggan cut between Loch Lochy and Loch Oich, biggest cutting made in the pre-railway age.

Grand Union
  Tring cutting: compare with parallel railway cutting.

Leeds and Liverpool
  Burnley bank.

Shropshire Union
  The canal is noted for deep cuttings and high banks – for example, Woodseaves cutting near Market Drayton and Shelmore Bank, between Shebdon and Knighton.

Lifts and Planes

Grand Union
  Foxton incline on the Leicester section, undergoing restoration.

Shropshire Tub Boat
  Hay incline, near Coalport. The top of the incline lies in Ironbridge Gorge Museum.

Tavistock
  Runs down to the Tamar at Morwellham.

Trent and Mersey
  Anderton lift: Britain's last surviving working lift.

Locks

Caledonian
  A flight of ship locks known as Neptune's Staircase at Banavie and a five-lock staircase at Fort Augustus.

Grand Union
  Flight of 21 broad locks at Hatton and on the Leicester section, a 4-lock staircase at Watford and 2 staircases of 5 locks each at Foxton.

continued on page 84

ARCHITECTURE AND ENGINEERING

continued from page 83

Kennet and Avon
Caen Hill, Devizes, twenty-nine broad locks with side ponds.

Leeds and Liverpool
Bingley Five Rise: broad-lock staircase.

Staffs and Worcester
Near-staircase at Bratch, close to Wolverhampton.

Worcester and Birmingham
Tardebigge thirty-lock flight, longest in Britain.

Pumps

Kennet and Avon
Two working steam pumps at Crofton and working water-powered pump at Claverton.

Cromford
Lea Wood working steam engine.

Tramways

Brecon and Abergavenny
Numerous tramways, best example starts at the wharf, Llanfoist.

Caldon
A complex of tramways join the canal at Froghall Basin.

Cromford
Cromford Wharf has engine shed for Cromford and High Peak Railway.

Glamorgan
The Penydarren tramway ran from the canal wharf at Abercynon; the site is now occupied by the fire station. It was here the first steam locomotive ran on rails.

continued on page 85

was first surveyed by Telford but the actual work was directed by a little-known engineer, William Crosley, and to him must go the credit. The most famous works are the 'snake' bridges. A common problem in canal building was that of carrying the tow-path from one side of the canal to the other. It might not seem a problem to someone just strolling across a bridge, but for the person with a horse, a tow-rope and a boat at the end of it, the situation was quite difficult. No one wanted the bother of unfastening and refastening the tow-rope, so ways had to be found of devising a special turn-over bridge. The simplest solution was to provide a gentle approach ramp for the horse, a flat-topped bridge and a second long ramp which temporarily took the horse back the way it had come. Then the animal could turn again at the foot of the ramp to follow the tow-path back under the arch. In plan, such a bridge is shaped like a letter U with the two verticals as the ramps. These bridges required a great deal of land and a lot of material. On the Macclesfield Canal, the ramp curves up but then coils round to go back under the arch in a delightful sinuous curve. But as in so many cases, the beauty is incidental, the result of an elegant engineering solution to a practical problem. Just occasionally, however, a bridge is given special ornamentation, usually because the canal is passing through, or close to, the estate of some local big-wig. Avenue Bridge, just south of Brewood on the Shropshire Union, carries the driveway to Chillington Hall, a few miles away to the west.

The biggest change in bridge construction began some years after the canal age started. Abraham Darby's famous iron bridge across the River Severn was completed in 1779, and canal engineers came to appreciate that iron could be a useful material for their work. The most famous bridges are associated with an engineering company that set up in the

The sinuous curves of the turnover bridge at Marple on the Macclesfield Canal. By doubling back under the bridge, a horse can cross the canal without needing to have the tow-rope disconnected (Derek Pratt)

ARCHITECTURE AND ENGINEERING

Horseley area of Tipton at the end of the eighteenth century. The name Horseley Ironworks can still be seen in profusion on the BCN and on the northern section of the Oxford Canal. The works still exist, although the plaque outside now says 'The Horseley Bridge and Engineering Co Ltd'. They owed their initial success to James Brindley whose wandering, wavering canals might have been thought adequate for some of the less heavily used routes, but proved hopelessly inadequate on those with a very busy trade. The Birmingham Canal at the very heart of the canal system was one obvious candidate for modernisation, and the building of the Grand Junction to Braunston brought an immense increase in trade to the Northern Oxford. Both modernisation programmes – the first the work of Telford, the second that of Marc Brunel – presented the engineers with a problem. A new straight line could be driven through the meanderings of the old, but it left a series of loops across which the tow-path of the new canal had to be carried. The answer lay in standardised iron bridges, cast at Horseley. The BCN bridges came in an assortment of sizes and were pleasant and unassuming; the Oxford bridges were altogether more elegant. One can still see how they fit together. The main arches are built up of curved plates topped by ornate railings and joined together at the centre. The arches are then fixed to each other by a series of metal plates. Nothing could be simpler, but the results are quite delightful. The great advantage of casting is that once you have the pattern you can repeat it as often as you like, but there is a bonus to be had as well. You can easily choose elaborate decoration. Rennie made use of this for his bridges across the Kennet and Avon on its path through Sydney Gardens in Bath. But for the most elaborate example of all, one has to look not at a bridge but at the

continued from page 84

Peak Forest
  Whaley Bridge, canal and tramway interchange; Buxworth Basin.

Tunnels (by length)
Huddersfield Narrow
  Standedge, 5,415yd (4,951m)
Thames and Severn
  Sapperton, 3,808yd (3,482m)
Dudley
  Dudley tunnel, 3,172yd (2,900m)
Grand Union
  Blisworth, 3,056yd (2,794m)
BCN
  Netherton, 3,027yd (2,768m)
Trent and Mersey
  Harecastle, 2,926yd (2,675m)

Deep cuttings call for high bridges. This photograph taken around 1910 shows the horse having a snack while it pulls a load up the Shropshire Union Canal near Market Drayton (British Waterways Board)

A Tramroad on the Brecon and Abergavenny Canal

This rail-road is adapted to the size of the waggons, or carts, which convey the coal to the canal. On each side is an iron groove, which extends the length of the road, and on which the wheels (four or six in number) run. They are so contrived as to run downwards the whole way (sometimes for the extent of some miles) from the works; so that when laden, they require no horses to draw them down. Indeed they acquire so great a degree of velocity in their descent, that a man is forced to walk or run behind the cart, with a kind of rudder or pole affixed to the hind-wheel, which he locks up when it proceeds too fast. Should this pole break (which it sometimes does) the waggon flies away, and overturns everything it meets. Of course, any one who is coming up the road, is in imminent danger unless he can by any means get out of the way; which is very difficult, as the road is narrow, and runs along a precipice. Last year, Mr. Frere, the proprietor of the iron works, was returning from London, and going along the rail-road in a post-chaise, when about a hundred yards from him, he saw one of those waggons coming down upon him with astonishing velocity. He could not possibly get out of the way, and must have been crushed to pieces, if fortunately the waggon had not broken over the iron groove, which had hitherto kept it in the track, and run forcibly up an ash-tree by the side of the road, in the branches of which it literally stuck, and thus saved him from immediate destruction.

(The Duke of Rutland, *Journal of a Tour Through North and South Wales*, 1805)

aqueduct that carries the short Engine Arm across the Birmingham Canal at Smethwick. Here eighteenth-century classical simplicity has given way to nineteenth-century Gothic. The basic design may be a simple arch, but it is topped by a decorative device known as a blind arcade: a series of pillars joined by pointed arches. This is the exception to the rule that says that on canals form was dictated by function: the arcade is there to impress and please the onlooker. It still succeeds a century and a half after it was built.

Locks and bridges can be seen in isolation, as examples of engineering design and style, but the 'feel' of a canal, its particular character, comes just as strongly from the rhythm of its movements, its alternation of bends and straights, cuttings and embankments. A contour canal can seem as natural as a stream wandering through a meadow. Where the Oxford Canal briefly joins in with the Cherwell at Shipton, and the Trent and Mersey merges with the Trent at Alrewas, there is no sense of dramatic change in moving from artificial to natural waterway and back again. This is certainly not the case on many later canals, in particular those which make extensive use of cut and fill. It is the engineering that makes a journey on the Shropshire Union unique and unforgettable. The deep, somewhat dark cuttings are overhung by lush vegetation like some jungle backwater, an effect which is balanced by the feeling of a grand processional created by the tall bridges that rise over the cuttings like triumphal arches. The rest of the world might just as well not exist, for nothing can be seen except the narrow enclosure. The banks produce quite the opposite effect, for the boater now looks out over the countryside, enjoying wide vistas. These effects are, if anything, even more marked in town than in country. Telford's new Birmingham Canal drops into a deep cutting at Smethwick and stays in it right through to Oldbury. It is extraordinary, for the city seems scarcely to intrude into this very private world. The image of the town canal is of a greasy, mucky creek filled with supermarket trolleys and less attractive debris. No one could deny that such canals are not difficult to find on the BCN, but the main line in summer could easily pass for a nature reserve, for the steep banks of the cutting are brilliant with flowers. The banks can give almost aerial views of the town. The best known is 'The Burnley Mile' on the Leeds and Liverpool Canal, although it is not, in fact, quite a mile (1.6km) long. Once boatmen looked out over a scene of countless mill chimneys, described by L. T. C. Rolt as the finest industrial landscape in Britain, but those words were written before the great decline in the cotton industry, before the new roads and the shopping precinct had replaced the old heart of the town. Today, Rolt's accolade might more aptly be applied to Bollington on the Macclesfield Canal, a typical tight, clenched-up little mill town where streets and houses huddle down into the hollow and only the tall chimneys reach up to the sky. But whatever the scene – town or country – the bank and the cutting continue to create their own very different worlds.

While cuttings and banks are the most obviously dramatic features, canals sometimes tackle the high ground by following a route around the shoulder of a hill. This method of construction can give equally dramatic views but is one which is also liable to give considerable engineering

difficulties, as the hillsides are inevitably prone to landslip. The most famous example is the section of the Llangollen Canal to the west of Pontcysyllte, and that was closed for a time by just such a fault as recently as the 1980s. But perhaps no canal shows the technique to better effect than the Brecon and Abergavenny, which winds its way around the slopes of the Brecon Beacons, high above the valley of the Usk.

The placing of locks also affects the way in which we view a canal. Brindley's habit of spreading them out over a wide range of countryside gave way on later canals to groupings into long flights. The sight of row upon row of black-and-white balance beams marching up a hillside in orderly procession is stirring stuff for the sightseer, but is daunting for the boater who sees less of a magnificent spectacle and rather more of a promise of hard work. The wide locks of Hatton on the Grand Union and Devizes on the Kennet and Avon are unforgettable, but paradoxically, the longest flight of all, Tardebigge on the Worcester and Birmingham, is not so impressive, partly because the locks are narrow but also because they are laid out on a curving path so that only a few can be seen at any one time. Locks do at least give one ample time to look around and appreciate some of their finer points. In time, one develops a list of personal favourites. The following have been chosen because they appear on the author's list but also because they demonstrate something of the variety of lock architecture and scenery.

Tyrley Locks on the Shropshire Union begin with a wharf, warehouse and cottages in an open setting, but as you go down, the trees and the land close in until you reach the bottom, which is a narrow rock cutting. This rock itself still bears the marks of pickaxes and the drill holes that were once packed with powder for blasting. In complete contrast, Greenberfield Locks on the Leeds and Liverpool have a totally open setting in the Pennine Hills, where the stone that pokes through the thin earth of the ridges is repeated in the chambers of the lock and the drystone walls that march alongside the canal as it curves and twists through this very uneven land. The list of variations could be extended almost indefinitely to include different types of lock. There are the alarming-sounding – and somewhat alarming-looking – guillotine locks that are common in East Anglia. Here, instead of opening outwards, the gates are raised vertically like the blade of the scaffold. Boaters tend to hurry under the raised gates with fingers firmly crossed. Even more extraordinary is Thurlwood Lock on the Trent and Mersey, a vast steel box designed to withstand subsidence from brine pumping. It looks as if it could withstand a direct hit from a large bomb. There is no end to the study of locks and no end to the differences to be noted. However, other means have been used to move boats from one canal level to another.

Various alternatives to locks were tried in the canal period, of which the most common was the inclined plane. Such a device was tried in Ireland on the Tyrone Canal in the 1770s, for it was originally planned as a 'tub boat canal', one in which the boats were literally like small tubs which could be pulled up the slope over rollers or floated on to a wheeled carriage. Both methods seem to have been tried on the Tyrone, but with little success. English engineers certainly showed little early enthusiasm, as Robert Fulton, an avid enthusiast for the subject, pointed out in a book of 1796. He compared the opposition to the Bridgewater Canal with opposition to innovation at a later date:

> But as local prejudices opposed the Duke's canal, in the first instance, prejudice equally strong as firmly adhered to the principle on which it was constructed; and it was thought impossible to lead one through a country, or to work it to any advantage, unless by locks, and boats of at least twenty-five tons, till the genius of Mr William Reynolds, of Ketley, in Shropshire, stepped from the accustomed path, constructed the first inclined plane, and introduced boats of five tons.

The Ketley incline was part of a private canal serving the Reynolds ironworks and it was soon followed by other inclines on the Shropshire

The famous Foxton Incline on the Leicester Arm of the Grand Union. The Grand Junction Canal Company boat has been floated into the caisson which is at the top of the incline. Caisson and boat can run up and down the hill on a railed track (British Waterways Board)

Tub Boat Canal. Most such inclines worked in the same way. The tubs were floated on to a wooden, wheeled carriage which was then lowered down a railed track to the next section of canal at the bottom, where the tub was floated off again. Most inclines were arranged so that the load all went downhill, which meant that their weight was sufficient to act as a counterbalance to drag empty trucks back up a parallel track. Additional help could be supplied by a steam engine at the top. Remains of inclines of this type can still be seen, including the Hay incline, running down to the Severn at Coalport, and the various inclines on the Bude Canal. The latter boasted two immense structures, at Marham-church and Hobbacott Down, 800ft (244m) and 935ft (285m) long respectively, and four somewhat smaller planes. These devices certainly had their uses, but they were of comparatively minor importance when set against the many tramway inclines that served canals in hilly country. On these forerunners of the railway, trucks were pulled along level sections by horses. Because the horses needed to walk down a clear track between the rails, the lines themselves were mounted on square stone blocks instead of the more familiar wooden sleepers. The rails, too, were different from conventional railway track, being generally L-shaped to take waggons without flanged wheels. On steeper sections, inclines similar in principle to the tub-boat inclines were used. At Whaley Bridge, there is a unique canal-tramway interchange shed, where the waterway runs into one end of the building and rails come out at the other. There was a late resurgence of interest in such devices with the Foxton incline, which was completed at the beginning of this century. This worked on a quite different system from that of the simple tub-boat canals. Special caissons – watertight boxes into which narrow boats could be floated – were built, after which caisson and boat together could be lifted up the track by steam power. A pair of caissons ran on two sets of rails, but the scheme was never a great success: opened in 1900, it had closed by 1911. Boats using the Leicester Arm of the Grand Union had then, as now, to work up the Foxton Staircase of narrow locks. That is not quite the end of the story, for enthusiasts are at work on the long, slow grind of restoration.

The inclined plane was by far the commonest alternative to locks for raising and lowering boats, but there were engineers who thought in terms of vertical lifts. Fulton showed off his design in his treatise, and some devices were put into practice, of which the most bizarre must have been that at Combe Hay on the Somerset Coal Canal. A huge pit 88ft (27m) deep, 88ft (27m) long and 20ft (6m) across at its widest point was completely filled with water and into this was lowered a watertight cylinder large enough to hold a canal boat. A crew waiting to take their boat uphill went down a short tunnel and into the submarine cum caisson, when the watertight doors then clanged shut behind them. Water was pumped out and air allowed in until there was enough buoyancy for the cylinder to rise majestically to the surface where the crew could be released to continue on their way. One can only marvel at the courage of the boatmen who trusted their lives to this eighteenth-century contraption. The experiment was, not surprisingly, short-lived. Just one vertical lift has survived in Britain, at Anderton, where it links

A Fellows, Morton & Clayton motor boat leaving the Weaver and entering the Anderton lift ready to be hauled up to the Trent and Mersey Canal (Michael E. Ware)

An engraving of the castellated portal of Sapperton tunnel on the Thames and Severn Canal (Bodleian Library)

the Trent and Mersey Canal with the Weaver Navigation. It has two caissons which, when the lift opened in 1875, were counterbalanced and worked hydraulically. This was soon changed to the present system of independent caissons worked by electric motor, and the counterbalancing was achieved by weights that were liberally hung out all around the lift. It is, in its way, almost as extraordinary as the Somerset caisson lock.

Lifts and planes are fascinating simply because they display such great ingenuity, but they are of only marginal importance in terms of the canal system as a whole, although such devices, on a far grander scale, remain in use in Europe where commercial traffic still thrives. The principal devices, apart from locks, cuttings and banks, for coping with hills and river valleys were tunnels and aqueducts. Tunnels are, perhaps, the least obviously interesting features so far as boats are concerned, for you go in one end, remain in the dark for what can seem an eternity while drips fall down the back of your neck, and then thankfully emerge again into the light. A few try to impress with a show of elegance, notably Sapperton on the Thames and Severn Canal, which has a classical portico, decorated by columns and niches at one end and castellations at the other. The Brandwood tunnel on the Stratford Canal is appropriately embellished with a bust of Shakespeare. In general, the main surface signs of tunnels are the tops of air shafts which can appear in the middle of fields or even, as with Gosty tunnel on the Dudley Canal, in a suburban front garden in Old Hill. Tunnels are not always simply straight holes through the ground: some are lined with brick to form complete tubes, while others rely on the strength of the natural rock and many more use a mixture of the two. The most remarkable must be Dudley tunnel, which is not merely a mixture of lined and unlined sections, but has underground branches stretching off in different directions. It varies in width from the narrowest of bores into which a boat slips like a finger in a glove, and echoing caverns. Dudley tunnel was intended from the first to serve underground limestone mines, much as the Duke of Bridgewater's canal took boats deep into the coal workings at Worsley. An extension of this idea can be found on the little Tavistock Canal that ended in an incline above the port of Morwellham on the Tamar. Here the tunnel was driven through by the engineer John Taylor, partly as a transport route and partly to test for copper ore deposits. The experiment was successful and a new mine, Wheal Crebor, was opened to work the lodes.

Aqueducts win all canal popularity prizes. Everyone, it seems, enjoys the prospect of sailing high in the air on one stretch of water, while looking down on another stretch of water far below (well, almost everyone, for the author once had a passenger who retired to the cabin with a tranquilliser and stayed there until Pontcysyllte was safely crossed). No such fears could have afflicted even the most nervous boaters when they crossed the aqueducts that had been built for the first generation of canals. Brindley's Sow aqueduct on the Staffs and Worcester was constructed with very low arches, carrying the huge pile of masonry he felt to be necessary to take the weight of puddled clay and the outward pressure of the water. It is interesting to compare it with Brynich aqueduct that carries the Brecon and Abergavenny Canal,

*The preserved ex-Fellows, Morton
& Clayton steamer* President *at
the Black Country Museum,
Dudley* (Anthony Burton)

begun in 1793, across the River Usk. Here the arches are higher and, because they represent a greater proportion of the height of the whole structure, they make it at once lighter and more elegant. The buttresses that rise from the river to the top of the parapet, apart from being structurally useful, add to the lofty feeling. It is altogether a more confident work than Brindley's. Other engineers borrowed techniques from contemporary bridge builders. They had discovered that the load on an arch could be reduced without any weakening by piercing the spandrils – that is, by leaving holes in the space between the tops of the arches. Benjamin Outram used this method in his majestic Marple aqueduct on the Peak Forest Canal. Rennie was the acknowledged master of architectural embellishment, and had a happy knack of finding the right style for the right place. Although Dundas aqueduct on the Kennet and Avon Canal is probably his most famous work, for sheer scale it cannot begin to match that which carries the Lancaster Canal across the River Lune. Where Dundas seems to have all the lightness and grace of the best Regency architecture, the Lune has an austere dignity. Here the architectural trimmings of balustrades and pilasters make far less impact than the monumental march of the arches across the river. Dundas might be the more obviously attractive, its pale stone contrasting with the heavy darkness of Lune, but the Lancaster aqueduct seems to have found the perfect combination of form and function.

The coming of the iron aqueduct with rather insignificant Longdon and far from insignificant Pontcysyllte made it possible to economise on materials – which could also mean economies on embellishment. Edstone aqueduct on the Stratford Canal is an obvious example. For the boater, it provides the experience that is unique to this type of structure, for the iron side plates can scarcely be seen below the gunwales, giving the eerie impression of flying. But to the spectator on the ground there is simply a series of dull brick piers carrying the ironwork: it has all the visual appeal of a bridge on the M1. Hybrids, in which an iron trough replaces puddled clay as a lining for the canal, are often far more satisfying. Jessop's Chirk aqueduct is somewhat overshadowed by a neighbouring railway viaduct but is very fine, and even grander is Hugh Baird's Almond aqueduct on the Edinburgh and Glasgow Union Canal. The aqueduct story continues into modern times, for twentieth-century road building involves supplying a new concrete aqueduct to take the Grand Union Canal across London's busy North Circular Road.

None of these structures was of the least use without water. Reservoirs were only a part of the answer, for the water still had to be shifted from reservoir to canal. On the Rochdale, for example, this was no problem as gravity could be relied upon to do the work. In some cases, however, the water source was below the level of the canal and pumps had to be installed – and that, for most of the canal age, meant steam power. Engine houses can still be seen on many canals, but few still have their engines in place. Two notable exceptions are the Leawood Pumping Station on the Cromford Canal and Crofton on the Kennet and Avon. The latter boasts two massive beam engines, the elder of the two having been sent down from Boulton and Watt's canalside works at Soho in

The first iron-trough aqueduct at Longdon-upon-Tern, photographed in 1963 when it still held water. It was designed by Thomas Telford and the Shropshire ironmaster, William Reynolds (Royal Commission on the Historical Monuments of England/Michael E. Ware Collection)

The Humber keel Comrade. *She was regularly used for trading not only on the Humber but as far inland as Sheffield* (Anthony Burton)

93

Birmingham in 1812. This makes it the oldest working steam engine still able to perform the task for which it was built. To see these lovely machines at work is a great treat and an impressive one, for, working together, they sucked up water and sent it thundering into the canal feeder at the rate of 250,000gal (1,136,000 litres) an hour.

Canals need more than engineering works designed to help move the boats: they need to be kept running, and that requires maintenance and administration. Even the companies who showed no interest in grandeur in the structures on their canals, took a very different view when it came to their own offices. Classical styles predominate: rather restrained in the case of the Birmingham Canal and altogether charming in the Leeds and Liverpool office at Leeds, while the Forth & Clyde Company chose an enlarged version of the Georgian house at Port Dundas. Finest of all is Cleveland House, which strides across the Kennet and Avon on its passage through Sydney Gardens. The office block is as unofficelike as one can imagine, looking similar to a French country hotel.

One might expect maintenance yards to be severely practical places, since they are there to deal with purely practical matters: forges provided ironwork, carpentry shops could supply anything from a new front door for a lock cottage to a replacement gate for the lock alongside. There were stores and wharves, for the canal was not just there to be maintained but also provided the main transport route for the gangs as well. Hartshill on the Coventry Canal is a typical small yard, but full of pleasing details. It lies just off the main canal, and the entrance to the yard has rounded corners to make the swinging turn into and out of the yard easier for boatmen. Boats can tie up alongside the wharf with its simple hand crane, or pass through an arch into the buildings themselves to be loaded in the dry. The style is all pleasantly unassuming, and topped with an attractive little clock tower. Other yards chose more elaborate details, for example the water tower at Bulbourne on the Grand Union does its best to persuade the passerby that it is an Italian campanile, while Ellesmere yard is built in the style that can only be described as mock Tudor.

Many different buildings turn up along the way. Lock cottages are perhaps the commonest feature and although generally built in a plain vernacular, they do occasionally show variations. Telford indulged his taste for architecture in the Shropshire Union cottages, using relieving arches round the windows to add interest to the façade. The oddest buildings must be the barrel-vaulted cottages on the Stratford Canal, and an even odder story has grown up around them. It is said that the company was short of cash – which is very true – and, being unable to afford *bona fide* builders, they handed the job to the navvies. As the only structures navvies could build were tunnels, they built tunnel-shaped cottages. A rather more obvious explanation is that the design provides a living space which uses the absolute minimum of building material, and from this came the saving. The most striking exception to the general rule of unadorned plainness comes on the Gloucester and Sharpness Canal. The cottages beside the large swing-bridges, which are an essential part of the ship canal, are basically plain houses but they

Officers of the Birmingham Canal Navigations pose outside the handsome company offices on the occasion of the annual inspection of the system in 1912 (National Railway Museum, York/Michael E. Ware Collection)

A pair of British Waterways narrow boats passing Bulbourne Yard on the Grand Union Canal in the 1950s (Anthony Burton)

The port and town of Goole grew up with the development of the Aire and Calder Navigation. Here a collier is being loaded with coal at the staithes. Note the men up aloft working on the fore upper topsail (Michael E. Ware)

have been aggrandised by slightly absurd porticoes, almost as big as the houses themselves.

There were official houses alongside the canal for lock-keepers and the like, but there were other houses which played just as important a role in the life of the waterways. These were the public houses which were more than just places to slake the thirst. They were the centres where a constantly moving community could temporarily meet together. Some, such as the Greyhound at Hawkesbury Junction, were famous boating pubs, which not only supplied beer but often ran small grocery businesses as well. A canal without beer would be as unthinkable as a canal without water.

Companies needed to pay for their canals by collecting tolls, and canal toll-houses were built, many in a distinctive style, either octagonal in plan or having jutting bays. They were necessarily built at junctions and the toll collector needed to be able to look out in all directions. The best views must have been those of the BCN, where the toll offices were sat on islands in the centre of the waterway, while the most attractive must be the toll-house at the Bratch. But by far the most important buildings in terms of size and visual impact are those concerned with the prime function of the canal, carrying goods for the new industrial world. These goods needed to be kept in warehouses, and the industrialists soon came to realise that their transport costs could be reduced if they saved on trans-shipment by building their own works and factories directly alongside the canal.

Wharves and warehouses were built whenever a canal came close to a settlement, and the bigger the settlement, the bigger the development. The most significant centres, however, were those where waterways of different sizes met. From Wigan to Leeds, locks can take wide boats 62ft (19m) long, but narrow boats over 70ft (21.5m) long can travel to Wigan up the Leigh branch and carry on to Liverpool. So there had to be somewhere to store goods that started in Leeds but were intended for Birmingham and vice versa. The result was a complex of warehouses based on the famous Wigan Pier. Here one can see how the junction became a centre for development and just how the buildings were designed to make for efficient use of the canal. The earliest warehouse was the Terminal Warehouse of 1777 and it shows a basic design that was used for many such buildings throughout the system. It has two storeys and an attic, but is built directly over barrel-vaulted arches so that boats could float under the building for loading. Later buildings show a variation on the theme, with extensive canopies stretching out over the wharf and far enough over the water to provide cover. Above these are weatherboarded hoists so that cargoes could be lifted to all floors of the buildings. Industrialists also found this an attractive site. In the early days of the cotton industry, waterwheels provided the power and determined the siting of mills, but the steam-powered mills of the nineteenth century had no such constraints. A canal-side site with its own wharf for supplying cotton from Liverpool and coal from the surrounding collieries had obvious advantages. Trencherfield Mill had its own wharves, and visitors can still see the mighty steam engine whose appetite for coal kept the barges busy.

Any industry that needed bulk supplies would have found a canal-side site advantageous. The Caldon Canal was built primarily to serve the limestone quarries at Caldon Low, but the canal also runs down the valley of the Churnet. Eighteenth-century potters needed flints, and flints were brought from far away by canal and then needed to be ground using waterpower. Here, then, was an ideal opportunity, and a flint mill was built at Cheddleton which made maximum use of the canal. The first stage in production was to calcine the flints, heating them in a furnace to make them easier to grind, so the furnaces are actually built into the wharf. The flints could be unloaded from the boat, dropped straight down into the furnace and then removed from the bottom and carried off to the grinding mills on a plateway. The two water-powered mills are still there and are still able to work, if only for demonstration purposes. But, again, steam power brought change. As they did not need the river, new mills could be built nearer to the potteries, and there is another bone and flint mill, steam powered this time, at the junction of the Caldon and the Trent and Mersey at Etruria. Similar stories can be found repeated throughout the canal system for all kinds of industries, from distilleries on the banks of the Forth and Clyde to glassworks on the Stourbridge. In some cases, the effect was so marked as to have a profound effect on the pattern of development of a town. Leamington Spa is best known as a fashionable resort, but there was another aspect, a considerable industrial zone that developed around the Grand Union.

We started this short survey with a look at a single, isolated country lock and we have arrived at a major industrial complex, but for most of us who travel the canal for pleasure, it is the former that we seek out

A contrast in styles and materials: the worn cobbles and smooth parapet at Dukinfield Junction bridge in Manchester and the tall chimney and four-square brick bulk of the cotton mill (Derek Pratt)

rather than the latter. It is perhaps the ultimate irony that we go to the canals for 'peace and quiet', to 'get away from it all' and by 'all' we usually mean the pressures of the modern world which the canal system helped to build. But because it was a part of the building process rather than a product of it, the canals do look back to another world. If I could pick just one place to exemplify that special distinction, it would be Dukinfield Junction where the Peak Forest, the Huddersfield Narrow and the Ashton Canals all meet. The Ashton tow-path is carried across the Peak Forest on a fine, low, hump-backed bridge with sides of stone slabs and a cobbled roadway on top. It owes everything to local tradition, developed by generations of builders who constructed packhorse bridges throughout the Pennine hills using local materials. At the junction itself is a typical nineteenth-century steam mill with its tall chimney and its four-square main building to house the spinning machinery and engine house alongside. It has little to do directly with its location, the vivid red brick seeming to bear little or no relationship to the spot on which it stands. It, and others like it, owes its existence to the canal age, since, for the very first time, it became possible to bring new materials from all parts of the country. The canals ushered in a great age of change: happily, for those of us who love them, they themselves remain in a different, more subtly captivating world.

Canal Towns

Just as in the nineteenth century he railway gave rise to new towns, such as Swindon d Crewe, so too did the canal age, if not on quite h a large scale. In general, such towns developed a nd trans-shipment points, where one type of canal r another or a canal reached a navigable river. Cargoes ld then have to be changed between, for example, a ow canal boat and a broad river barge. Transfers cou t always be made straight away, so warehouses wou e needed to store the goods. The trans-shipment poi came a centre of growth, and the greater the trade, t eater the growth would be.

Stourport is generally taken as th sic canal town. When James Brindley decided to the Staffs and Worcester Canal down the valley c e River Stour instead of cutting across country to t tablished port of Bewdley, the junction of canal and i was made at a spot occupied by nothing but a solita nn. Here the company had to set about building small inland harbour. A complex of locks was construc to allow the passage into the basin of both the large r craft and the canal narrowboats. Warehouses and ffices were added and those who manned them need houses, so that gradually a town developed. Merchan found it a good centre at which to do business and t ew town began to grow and prosper, with ever-grand ouses and a fine new hotel. The area around the basin ill retains its essential character as a Georgian new tow A similar story was repeated at Shardlow and, later i the canal age, at Ellesmere Port. The latter no longer epends for its significance on its connection with the Ellesmere Canal, for even by the end of the last century the arrival of the Manchester Ship Canal had greatly increased its importance. But at its heart still lies the complex of warehouses and docks designed by Thomas Telford. They were sadly reduced by fire some years ago, but what remains is home to an impressive boat museum.

The grandest canal town in concept was Goole, created at the junction of the Aire and Calder and the Ouse. The navigation company decided that they needed a new port from which to send out the coal from the extensive South Yorkshire coalfield. That meant building a dock capable of taking sea-going ships as well as the river barges. Work on such a scale inevitably brought in large numbers of men, and the company set about creating a new town, not by haphazard growth but to a set plan. The port prospered, largely because the Aire and Calder prospered. Steam tugs were in use as early as 1831, and in 1862 William Bartholomew introduced trains of compartment boats, the 'Tom Puddings' which continued in use into the 1980s. They were loaded at the collieries, taken in trains of up to fifteen vessels to the docks where each 'pudding tin' was lifted out of the water on a special hoist and upended over the hold of the waiting coaster. Its trade has since declined and much of the old canal town has gone.

The canal towns may not seem very large by modern standards, but they were places of considerable importance in their day. They remain as reminders of the vital role that the waterways played in building the new industrial Britain: and they also serve as timely reminders that two centuries ago a new town could be a place of elegance and true worth.

6 THE CANALS AT WORK

The day of the grand opening has come and gone: the last speech has been read, the last patriotic air played by the military band and the final toast to the success of the venture has been drunk as the last of the celebrators is persuaded to go home. Now, you might think all that is needed is for the canal company to sit back and wait for the money to roll in as the cargoes roll out. Alas for the company, this was never so. A canal did not run itself in the eighteenth century any more than it runs itself in the twentieth century. Then, as now, there were two aspects to the working life of a canal. The first, that of keeping the canal open and hopefully profitable, fell to the canal company and involved everything from maintenance and repairs to administration and toll collection. The second involved the movement of cargo: warehousing and loading and – the principal object of the whole exercise – running boats. This part of canal life brought in many different concerns.

Canal companies were no different from many other businesses. Those who promoted them may well have been local businessmen and manufacturers whose principal interest was in acquiring an improved transport link that would increase efficiency and reduce costs, but once the canal was completed the emphasis inevitably shifted to making a profit. And they were like other businesses too, in that they employed office staff to keep ledgers, tot up figures, write letters and take notes at meetings – all very ordinary, all very dull, but it is thanks to those anonymous clerks as much as anyone that we have some idea of what canal life was like in the early years. Administration was nominally in the hands of the committee, consisting of the more important share-holders. Their meetings, however, were at best somewhat irregular, perhaps no more than annual events, in which the ceremonial dinner loomed at least as large as the approval of the accounts. In practice, the actual running of the business lay in the hands of salaried professionals, with the company secretary who had seen the administration through the often exciting days of construction staying on to supervise the calmer days of carrying. Under him would be a conventional office staff. But affairs could not just be run from a central office. Income came primarily from tolls on goods moved by a myriad of carriers, ranging from owners with no more than a single boat to large concerns with huge fleets. The boats were constantly on the move throughout the canal system, and no company was so naive as to believe that a boatman would go out of his way to visit their offices demanding to pay his dues. The canal company's front line on which the profits ultimately depended was made up of the toll collectors.

We are all fairly used to paying tolls. We pause briefly at the end of

Canal Running Costs

When setting out his proposals for building the Forth and Clyde Canal in 1767, John Smeaton also gave the following figures for the men needed to keep it going once it was completed:

16 labourers	....	1s per day
2 masons, 2 carpenters	....	1s 6d per day
2 overseers	....	£40 p.a. each
Surveyor	....	£80 p.a.
2 Toll Collectors	....	£40 p.a.
1 Toll Clerk	....	£80 p.a.

6 lock keepers 'to be a check upon the bargemen from doing damage to the works, by running against the lock-gates, leaving the cloughs running, so as to let off the water, &c.' 3s 6d per week each.

Canals made money by charging tolls, which varied according to the weight and nature of the cargo carried. Here an official is gauging a pair of Grand Union Canal Carrying Company boats, by measuring the height of the gunwales above the water line. That height will correspond to a particular weight of cargo on board (Michael E. Ware)

a bridge, pass over a few coins and drive on our way. Canal toll collection was more complex. Tolls were charged on a ton-per-mile basis and the rates varied for different types of cargo, so the toll collector had to know how much the cargo weighed, how far it had come and what the cargo was. To establish the first criterion, each boat had to be 'gauged'. It is obvious that the more cargo you load into a boat, the lower it will sink into the water, so each boat had its own list of measurements showing the height above the water line for different loadings. All the gauger had to do was measure that height, compare it with the official figures for that particular boat and he then had the weight of cargo.

Toll rates could be simple or complex. The BCN had just two basic categories of tolls, with the usual exemption for road materials. The Exeter Canal, at the opposite extreme, had over two hundred different rates, varying from anchovies at 1d a barrel to woad at 1s 6d per hogshead, and just in case anything had been left out they put in a clause at the end to say that everything else went at 2s 6d a ton and, as a final afterthought, they charged 1d for empties.

There were charges for moving the goods on the canals, but goods also had to be brought to and from the various wharves by road, by tramway or by another canal or river, so there would be a period of storage for which wharfage rates were charged. Some wharves were owned by the canal companies themselves, others belonged to private concerns. The wharf managers, or wharfingers, with their band of clerks, not only ensured that the wharf owners received their dues, but were also responsible for loading and unloading and for controlling the movements of boats. Here there could be real conflicts of interest. Boatmen were generally paid by the load: the quicker it was delivered, the quicker they were paid and the sooner they could collect the next cargo. Time spent at the wharf was not just time wasted, it was money wasted as well.

Not surprisingly, one finds the early records of the Birmingham Canal recording 'willfull disobeyance of the Company's Bye Laws at the Wharf'. The fundamentals did not change greatly over the years. A former wharf manager for Fellows, Morton & Clayton (FMC), the famous carrying company, recalled how, in the 1920s, he would demand respect from those who came to him for loads: 'If a man came to my counter for a job and he'd got a cigarette in his ear, he wouldn't get a job. And if I asked him in the office and he didn't take his cap off he didn't get the job.' The wharfinger had to rely on his own men to spot misdeeds such as pilfering. As the FMC manager pointed out, the experienced porter could lift a case of tins and know at once that although the case looked full, something was wrong – and then at the bottom he was likely to find bricks or stones where the tins should have been. In the early days it was by no means unknown for large-scale pilfering to take place with the collusion of an unscrupulous wharfinger. Early in the nineteenth century there was said to be a shop in Wigan which was entirely stocked with goods stolen from canal boats. The company usually tried to minimise this problem by ensuring that only the most respectable men were appointed and at a decent salary, with, in a few cases, a bonus in the form of a commission on goods handled. It was essential that the company could rely on their wharf managers, for the temptations were clear and the chances of being caught out slender. Loads were never weighed with great accuracy, and a certain amount of 'lightening' was more or less accepted. An 'accidental' shift or bump as one approached a busy wharf could send a few bucketfuls of coal sliding into the cut to be retrieved later to keep the boat cabin's stove going. And it was not just pilfering that created problems. It was not unknown for a boatman to dump some of his cargo to lighten the boat and speed the journey, safe in the knowledge that once it was gauged it would not be checked again.

There was a more positive side to the relationship between the wharf staff and the boatmen. When it came to the practical business of loading the boat, the boatman had the last word:

He tells you what to put in the boat, where to put it; whether you are in the middle quarter, back of the mast or the fore end. You see some boatmen will not have any stuff at all put in the fore end,

Gauging

Gauging, means of ascertaining by the draught of the vessel the weight of cargo on board for the purpose of taking tolls. The first gauging of canal boats is carried out at a weigh dock, where particulars of the boat's draught are taken when empty, and when fully loaded, and at intermediate points, such as at every ton of loading. The boat is loaded with weights kept for the purpose, which are lifted in and out by cranes; the result arrived at is then either transferred to graduated scales fixed to the boat's sides, which can be read at any time, or the particulars of each vessel are furnished to each toll office in a book, from which on gauging the immersion of the boat at any time the number of tons on board can at once be ascertained. The usual method of gauging a boat for immersion is to take what is called the 'dry inches' that is, – the freeboard – at four points, at one point each side near the bows and at one point each side near the stern. This is done by an instrument consisting of a float in a tube, having a bracket projecting from the side of the tube. The bracket is rested on the boat's gunwale, and the float indicates the number of inches between that and the level of the water in the canal. The four readings are then added together and divided by four, which gives the average for the whole boat.

(Henry Rodolph de Salis, *A Handbook of Inland Navigation*, 1928)

Tonnage Rates Set by Act of Parliament for the Grand Junction Canal

The rates give a clear idea of what were thought to be the principal goods the canal would carry.

	d.
Lime and Limestone	¼ per Ton, per Mile

Cattle, Sheep, Swine and other Beasts, Flint and other Stone, Brick, Tiles, Slate, Sand, Fuller's earth, Iron-stone, Pig-iron, Pig-lead, and all kinds of Manure, (except Lime) .... ½ ditto. ditto
Coke and Coal .... ¾ ditto. ditto
All other Goods, Wares and Merchandize whatsoever .... 1 ditto. ditto
For all Goods, Wares and Merchandize, passing from the Canal into the Thames, or *vice versa* .... ½ per Ton.
All Barges and other Vessels whatsoever, navigated on the Thames, or any part thereof Westward of Londonbridge to Strand-on-the-Green, or Brentford, by an Act of the 17th George III. pay to the Lord Mayor Alderman and Commons of the City of London.) ½ ditto

Fractions to be considered as One Mile, and all Fractions of a Ton to be taken according to the Quarters of a Ton contained therein.

Forty Cubic Feet of Oak, Ash, or Elm and Fifty Cubic Feet of Fir, Deal, Plank, Poplar, Beech or Birch, to be rated as One Ton; One hundred and Twenty Pounds, Avoirdupois, of Coal or Coke, as One Hundred Weight; and One Hundred and Twelve Pounds of any other Article. Proprietors may fix the Price of Carriage for any Parcel not exceeding Five Hundred Weight, affixing the same on every Wharf of the said Canal.

EXEMPTIONS

Officers and Soldiers on march their Horses, Arms and Baggage, Timber for his Majesty's Service and the Persons having Care thereof; Stores for ditto, on Production of Certificate from the Navy Board or Ordnance. Also Gravel, Sand, and other Materials for making or repairing any Public Roads, and Manure for Land, if the same do not pass any Lock.

(From Joseph Priestley, *Navigable Rivers and Canals, 1831*)

because the boat won't swim. Every boat has a personality, and there's no two boats alike. You can measure all your planks, you can do this and that, you can have the beam right, you can do everything but it doesn't work. No two boats are alike.

The wharf men also acted as liaison for the boating community, arranging schedules so that families could all arrive at the same place at the same time for important events such as weddings and funerals. They were the links between the ever-shifting boating population and between them and the company installed at the central offices. Out along the line there were other links in the longer chain of the canal.

Lock-keepers are a rarity on the canals these days, except on the more modern commercial waterways where they operate powered locks. The lock cottages have been largely sold off, but the regularity with which they are found along the canals is a measure of how essential they were to the smooth running of the system. The keepers were not there to work the locks, although they might be prepared to give a hand at the busiest times. Their job, basically, was to look after the locks, to see that they were used in a proper manner and to make sure that water was not needlessly wasted. It sounds almost too good to be true, but the same problems that beset the wharf manager afflicted the lock-keeper. When I go boating I do all the things that one is supposed to do: wind down paddle gear instead of letting it drop and wait patiently, never trying to force gates. But I am on holiday. The working boatman with a living to earn had only one overriding thought: to move on as quickly as possible. Possible damage to locks and water wastage were of far less concern than the urge to get moving. Byelaws might say, for example, that locks must not be used after dark, but if the boatman thought he could get away with it, he would try to get through. An old lock-keeper told the author about his predecessor who was determined to stop such shinanigans and arranged a cunning system of wires at the lock which set off alarm bells in the cottage. That scheme was short-lived. The boatmen hired a posse of small boys to come out time after time to set the alarms jangling. After many disturbed nights and no boats in sight, the lock-keeper gave up the scheme. Lock-keepers were expected to sort out orders of precedence for boats at busy times, a job which must have had a great deal in common with that of being referee in a free-for-all wrestling match. There was also a more rewarding side to the job, and the good lock-keeper took a pride in his locks which would often be on a long flight, ensuring that all the mechanisms were always in perfect working order. Anyone who regularly travels the canals will find the same is true today, and what a joy it is to find paddle gear well greased and in good condition – it can halve the work, and halve the time it takes to go through a lock.

Many lock-keepers came from boating families – as they still do on those few canals and navigations that employ them. Seeing a lock-keeper coming out of his attractive cottage by the Thames on a sunny afternoon must make many boaters sigh with envy for such an idyllic life. But at least one lock-keeper, a former Thames waterman, said that he would leave the lock and go back to the working life of the river straight away if only the work was still there to be done. There is, in any case, a good

deal of delusion in the envy. Rather like the pub drinker who sees the landlord chatting behind the bar and not the man with shirtsleeves rolled up lugging heavy barrels around and clearing up the cigarette ends, so the boater misses other aspects of the lock-keeper's life, such as river control, being out in all weathers, adjusting weirs and paddles to control the flow.

Like the wharfingers, the lock-keepers had ample opportunities to 'divert' a cetain amount of cargo, and they had other sources of revenue. One of the lock-keeper's duties was to keep traffic flowing and ensure the proper priorities were preserved – but the boat that had priority under the laws might not always get ahead of the boat whose captain had slipped a coin into the lock-keeper's hand. In spite of numerous regulations which made it absolutely clear that the keeper was to devote all his attention to his duties and was not under any circumstances to go into business on his own account, the temptation seems to have been irresistible. Many a lock-keeper operated a small grocery and chandlery

on the side, and the circumstances were ideal for both parties. The boat had to stop at the lock anyway, so what better place to buy a few essentials without wasting valuable time? It suited the lock-keepers, it suited the boat people, and, if it did not altogether suit the company, there was not very much they could do about it. It seems that as long as the locks worked well and traffic flowed smoothly, the company was prepared to turn a blind eye to such trade. A good lock-keeper was a most valuable person, so much so, in fact, that unusually for those times, they even received retirement pensions.

Wharfingers and lock-keepers looked after much of the day-to-day business of running the canal and its traffic, but their work depended on the canal being kept open, and that was the responsibility of the maintenance men. Essentially, all the jobs that were a part of canal building were also a part of canal maintenance. Carpenters built new lock gates as the old succumbed to wear and tear; bricklayers and masons repaired bridges and culverts, lock chambers and tunnels. The bulk of the work, however, fell to the labourer who cut back weeds, trimmed hedges, repuddled where necessary and kept the channel open. The latter was, at first, heavy manual work, the commonest method being a bag and spoon dredger. Basically, this was just a scoop, consisting of a bag fastened to a metal ring, on the end of a long arm. The bag scooped up the mud, but let the water dribble out. To dip it down, haul it out with its load of mud and then swing it across so that the contents could be dumped required the concerted efforts of two brawny men. The opening up of the steam world in 1800 that followed the ending of a virtual monopoly by Boulton and Watt, brought forward a rush of new ideas, which included steam dredgers. William Jessop designed an engine for use on the Caledonian Canal and it was built, inevitably, by

The canals did not just serve the industrial world. Here the newly harvested hay is being loaded directly on to a specially adapted narrow boat with side planks making a wide platform. The scene is the Bridgwater and Taunton Canal near Huntworth (Michael E. Ware)

the Butterley Ironworks. It was designed in 1805 and its appearance was greeted with great enthusiasm. The poet Robert Southey went to see it at Fort Augustus in 1819, and his account is that of a man enthralled by the wonders of technology, although his views might not be quite those of the modern environmentalist:

> The dredging machine was in action revolving round and round, and bringing up at every turn matter which had never before been brought up to the air and light. Its chimney poured forth volumes of black smoke, which there was no annoyance in beholding, because there was room enough for it in this wide clear atmosphere.

The new possibilities for the steam engine had come about with the use of high-pressure steam, whereby a small engine could do the work of its much larger older brother of the eighteenth century. The high priest of the new steam age was the Cornish engineer Richard Trevithick, who designed a variety of engines for various purposes, including a dredger, a pump which could be mounted on a boat and a 'nautical labourer', intended for use in the docks. The latter was, in fact, a floating steam crane which was pulled around by a paddle tug. It was patented but never built, partly because the dockers, seeing their livelihood threatened by the mechanical marvel, declared that they would drown the Cornishman if he ever appeared with his machine. Trevithick also designed a steam engine for a canal boat. His ideas were perhaps too far ahead of their time, for although his designs were often entirely practical, few came into use, although some Trevithick engines did appear in canal works in the early nineteenth century. In spite of all these advances, many companies still found human labour to be cheaper than steam power and stuck with the old methods for a very long time.

Summer on the canals brought its own problem – lack of water – so that the control of reservoirs and feeders was always of prime importance as well as a high standard of canal maintenance to stop water being lost. This was an area where the multitude of independent companies looked very much to their own affairs. Having obtained enough water for their own canals, they had no intention of letting it drain away, free of charge, into another company's waterway. Even today, you can see the steps taken to prevent this from happening, although the system is virtually all under control of one body. In the early years, jealousy between rivals reached almost paranoid proportions. The proprietors of the Coventry and Oxford Canal companies wrangled endlessly about where their two canals were to meet and, unable to agree on a sensible solution, they arrived at an absurd one. The two canals ran side by side for a whole mile. When they did finally see sense, they created a junction at Hawkesbury which was and is difficult to negotiate – and they then found that the Oxford was a few inches higher than the Coventry. To make the junction, a stop-lock had to be built with a fall of just 6in (15cm) – small enough, but it was with great chagrin that Oxford proprietors saw Oxford water pour into the Coventry Canal. Other companies also built stop locks, not to overcome differences in level, but simply to hold back water for their own use.

A Lock-keeper on the Oxford

Older books seldom give more than a perfunctory description of a lock-keeper's life, but change on the canals came only slowly and there are still men alive who remember the working days when horses pulled the boats into the locks. George Bloomfield's father was foreman at Claydon Yard, a small maintenance depot at the top of a flight on the Oxford Canal. George himself left school at fourteen and in 1927 at the age of fifteen he took over the lock from his stepbrother, who had left to become a bricklayer's helper, which was a better paid job than lock-keeping. Claydon was a busy spot. There was stabling for fifteen horses – in the 1920s it was still usual for nine or ten stalls to be occupied – and reeds had to be collected for bedding material for the horses. A carpenter worked at making lock gates and there was a forge, but no regular blacksmith. The standard working day for the Claydon men was eleven hours – more than sixty hours a week. In 1932 George moved to Banbury, where there was a little extra money to be had by helping to unload boats. The company was understanding, it seems, about his working extra hours for himself, but less understanding in other matters. One of George's jobs was moving the drawbridge across the locks. In 1935 he was doing this as he had done many times before when a group from the employment office decided for a joke to haul down on the high balance beam while George was on the bridge. The platform shot up and George pitched down, trapping his foot between the bridge and the stonework, breaking four toes and leaving him with a permanent disability. There was no compensation for accidents at work, nor was the company noted for flexibility. Lock-keepers could be moved about at the company's whim and George was ordered to

continued on page 106

continued from page 105

Coventry. But he had recently married a local girl who had no wish to move, so George was left without any real choice. In 1942 he left the canals for good. But the family tradition lived on: his father worked as Claydon foreman until his retirement in 1948, when he was replaced by George Bloomfield's younger brother, Arthur. When I first travelled the Oxford Canal, the memories of the working past lived on: the stable block was still there, the big hearth, blackened by countless fires, still sat in the centre of the forge and the reeds grew in profusion, for no one any longer needed to bed down working horses for the night in Claydon.

Cheating the Company

As a former wharf manager pointed out, the gauger who had to assess cargoes for toll payments had to keep his eyes open. A popular trick was for the boatman to wander casually over to the opposite side of his boat to talk to a friend, causing it to tilt over that way. To the gauger it appeared higher in the water and so he read off a light cargo. But such little ruses were nothing compared to those of disguising the nature of the cargo. The original acts, for example, often specified that stone for the repair of public roads should be carried free of charge, so it was very tempting to put a more valuable cargo in the middle of the boat and pile the stone all around it. A boatman on the Coventry Canal tried that trick in 1861, but he was discovered and fined by the magistrates. The company then issued a poster warning other boatmen that anyone trying the same device would not only be fined, but charged the maximum toll rate on the entire cargo, road stone and all.

Summer was the time for listing the jobs that would need to be done in the winter, just as it still is today. But, unlike today, the canals expected to keep carrying throughout the year, so that stoppages had to be kept as short as possible. The maintenance gangs worked flat out, and on these occasions rival canals would generally co-operate as far as possible to see that stoppages on through routes could all occur at the same time. But winter brought the biggest hold-up of them all – ice. Once the ice reached a certain thickness and the working boats could no longer get through, the ice boats were called out. These vessels were short and stout and either built of iron or reinforced with metal. Instead of the single horse of the narrow boats, a team was harnessed for extra power. The men on the boat stood up, holding on to a high central rail for support – which, as they were all too well aware, was vital. The horses set off, sending the boat speeding towards the ice. The idea was not so much to break through it as to haul the boat over it, so that the weight would carry the vessel down to the water. The job of the men on board was to rock the ice breaker to and fro to widen the cracks in the ice and create a passage. Too energetic a crew could find themselves sliding over the frozen canal or, which was far more uncomfortable, falling through into the icy water. The job was appreciated only by any small boys who could wangle a place on board. Even in latter days, the horse-drawn ice-breaker was considered far the best way of coping with the problem. The other difficulty came with freezing in the lock, when the lock-keeper had to try to break the ice into blocks which could be floated out of the open gates. Once there was a serious build-up, especially behind the lock gates, all boat movements came to a halt until the thaw. It was the worst of times for boat people: employees had reduced wages and the self-employed had no wages at all. During the great freeze in the last century, boatmen used to beg in the streets of Banbury with a narrow boat carved out of ice.

Now, sadly perhaps, memories of the working life of the canals appear as little more than structures which survive, but whose usefulness is at an end. Some aspects of canal life have gone for ever, it seems. When was a full-time mole catcher last employed on the waterways? Yet this was once an important job, for the little creatures could easily destroy a tow-path with their burrowings. The end of horse-towing has now reduced the need for tow-path maintenance, which has dropped a long way down the list of priorities. In the same way, the coming of the motor boat, the motor tug and the steam tug ended one entire occupation: professional leggers went out of business. They were the men who spent their entire working lives lying flat on their backs, 'walking' the boats along by pushing with their feet against the tunnel sides. One legger reckoned that in his working life if he could have put his trips end to end, he would have legged four times around the world. Other tasks are relatively unchanged, for maintenance still needs to be done. Stop planks can still be seen neatly tucked away by bridges, ready to be slotted into place so that a length of canal can be drained for essential work. The maintenance yards still make lock gates and still send out their boats to dredge the canal, although not, however, with bag and spoon. Other sights are rather more forlorn. A faded sign on a warehouse wall

announces that goods can be carried to all parts of the country at moderate cost, but the warehouse has not seen any goods for many a year now. Stables stand by locks, some still very grand and spruce, such as those at Bunbury on the Chester Canal, built as part of a modernisation programme by the Shropshire Union Company. At the opposite extreme, at Cookley on the Staffs and Worcester, the horse's temporary home is little more than a cave carved from the sandstone. The horses have all but vanished from the canal, and the working boats are no more than the smallest fraction of the great fleet that once carried a nation's trade. We have busy waterways still, but what we have lost is the richness and variety of a way of life that lasted well into living memory, for, in the end, all the fine engineering, all the administration and all the costly maintenance were there to serve the boats and their cargoes.

We sometimes tend to sentimentalise the working past of the canals, seeing it in terms of a romantic and colourful way of life, but by doing so we lose sight of an essential fact. For the best part of a hundred years, the canals formed the main arteries of trade in a country that was leading the world into the new industrial age. A tremendous variety of goods was carried, but at the heart of the trade lay just one basic commodity – coal. There was coal for the new engines of industry, and coal for the houses of the workers who had left the countryside where fuel could be found in the hedgerows and who were now living in the closed-up terraces of the towns; there was coal for the furnaces of the iron industry and for smelting the copper and tin that were coming from Cornwall; that coal was moved by canal. Without the canals the process of industrialisation would have been far, far slower and our history textbooks would be telling of an industrial evolution not a revolution.

Coal may have been at the heart of the system, but it was by no means the only commodity carried, and one of the ways in which the richness

Ice was the great enemy on the canals, for it could bring all traffic to a halt. The lock-keeper looking down on this wintry scene at Bingley on the Leeds and Liverpool must have known that he would be hard pressed to keep his locks open (Michael E. Ware)

107

The Bolinder

The diesel and semi-diesel engines brought change to the canals in a way that the older steamers had never done, and it began with the success of the Bolinder engine. Erik August Bolinder was born in Stockholm in 1863. He joined the family firm, which he took over in 1888. In 1893 he designed a paraffin engine, but soon began to concentrate on heavy-oil engines for marine use, at much the same time as Rudolf Diesel was working on the engine that still bears his name. In 1908, Bolinder produced a very simple two-stroke engine. It had one disadvantage, in that the fuel had to be pre-heated in vaporiser. Once running, combustion provided enough heat to vaporise the fuel, but for starting, a blow-lamp had to be used on the vaporising bulb – an alarming idea in a wooden boat.

A Bolinder was fitted to a Thames lighter, the *Travers*, in 1910, and the experiment proved a great success. By 1930, Bolinders had been fitted to 230 narrow boats. Boat owners worried by the combination of the hot bulb and diesel fuel were given a spectacular demonstration by Bolinder salesmen, who poured diesel into the hold and then dropped in a lighted match, which was at once extinguished. The distinctive 'popping' beat of the Bolinder soon became as much a feature of canal life as the ring of horseshoes on the tow-path. There was another distinctive Bolinder noise – the back-fire. By pulling a lever on the engine, the boatmen could alter the firing of the fuel injection, produce the back-fire, and so put the whole engine into reverse.

(Above right) *Restoration in the Pennines. The summit lock on the Rochdale Canal.* (Right) *The Huddersfield Canal near Marsden. On the left is the canal reservoir, on the right the pond for a woollen mill* (Anthony Burton)

of the canal scene has been diminished is the loss of the great variety of cargoes and vessels that could be found during the height of their working days. Boats might be seen moored up by a field, taking the harvest straight into their holds; they could carry sugar for Tate & Lyle or chocolate for Bournville; more up to date, there is 'Caggy' Stevens, whose old horse Mac was once as familiar a character as Mr Stevens himself, for Mac worked for many years hauling loads of metal throughout the BCN; or there were the narrow boats of T. & D. Murrell, taking lime juice from Brentford to Boxmoor. But perhaps the most famous, certainly the most dramatic, load ever carried on the canals was gunpowder. Boats are, theoretically at least, the ideal form of transport for explosives – indeed, major centres of gunpowder production, such as Faversham in Kent, had their own system of waterways for moving the powder. Iron wheels on roads can cause sparks, boats on water do not. Nevertheless, in the most famous of all canal accidents, the barge *Tilbury* blew up under Macclesfield Road-bridge on the Regent's Canal on 2 October 1874. The *Tilbury* was one of a train of six vessels being pulled by a tug. She had a mixed cargo on board, including barrels of petroleum as well as the 5 tons of gunpowder. The three men and the boy on board were all killed and one other barge was sunk. The bridge was demolished, but it retains one of the few physical reminders of the accident, for when it was rebuilt one of the supporting arches was reversed, so that the notches scored by thousands of tow-ropes now appear on the wrong side.

From the beginning, there was also another 'cargo', which has steadily grown in importance over the years: people. In the early years there was a variety of specialist craft for passengers, and although we now think of pleasure boating as a modern phenomenon, it was given due consideration from the very first. Josiah Wedgwood's partner, Bentley, who wrote the pamphlet in favour of the proposed Trent and Mersey Canal, described the delights of having a canal at the bottom of the garden, or 'a lawn terminated by water' in the more elaborate language of the eighteenth century. He then continued:

And if we add the amusements of a pleasure-boat that may enable us to change the prospect, imagination can scarcely conceive the charming variety of such a landscape. Verdant lawns, waving fields of grain, pleasant groves, sequestered woods, winding streams, regular canals to different towns, orchards whose trees are bending beneath their fruit, large towns and pleasant villages, will all together present to the eye a grateful intermixture of objects, and feast the fancy with ideas equal to the most romantic illusion.

And everything he promised to the canal traveller over two centuries ago is still there to charm and delight today. The variety of scenery is as great as it ever was, but with the passing of the hustle and excitement that marked the working life of the canal, something important has gone from the canal scene. And nowhere, perhaps, is the loss of colour more clearly seen than in the gradual disappearance of the trading craft of the waterways.

The Norfolk wherry Albion *on the waters where she began carrying cargo in 1898, the Broads*
(Anthony Burton)

The famous Wigan Pier on the Leeds and Liverpool. The fine warehouses with their canopied hoists now house a museum
(Anthony Burton)

Seals and Tokens

All canal companies had official seals which were used for important documents. They needed to be stamps of authentification, so that in purely practical terms it was necessary that there should be some degree of elaboration to make forgery difficult. Many companies also issued tokens. The period of canal building came at a time when coinage was in short supply, which meant that wage days could present real problems. So companies, in effect, issued their own coinage. The system could work well, with local traders happy to accept the tokens, secure in the knowledge that they would be exchanged by the company for coin of the realm. Equally, however, it was open to abuse. The most notorious examples are those of the 'truck' system where tokens could only be used in company stores, where prices could be kept artificially high. Other problems arose when local shop-keepers lost

confidence in the company, so refused to accept tokens from the workforce. This presented real difficulties where the tokens were paid to navvy gangs by the contractors. It takes little imagination to picture the scene of several hundred tough navvies descending on a town for a night out only to find there was no way they could spend their wages. More than one navvy riot can be traced back to just such an event.

Today, seals and tokens are of interest for their pictorial, decorative and historical associations. Tokens, in particular, have become popular with collectors, because of the scenes they depict. One of the biggest of all contractors, Pinkertons, for example, issued shilling tokens to workers on the Basingstoke Canal, showing the tools of the navvy's trade: a wheelbarrow with pick and spade. Others show canal scenes: all are of interest.

The Calder and Hebble company seal is a good example of a very straightforward design which depends for its effects on the decorative quality of the lettering.

The Grand Junction Canal Company emphasized their own importance with a suitably imposing motif.

The Staffordshire and Worcestershire seal is rather crudely designed, but very interesting. It has to be remembered that when work started on this canal no one knew what type of boat was likely to be used. It was never, however, going to be anything very much like this.

The Stourbridge Canal scene although still quite crude shows that the artist knew rather more about boats that did the designer of the Staffs and Worcester seal. The mast is set too far back, but otherwise this is easily recognisable as a simple day boat. What makes this seal particularly attractive is the view it gives of the industry served by the canal. In the background is a steam pumping engine, pumping up water from a pit, while belching clouds of smoke into the sky.

The Aire and Calder seal is a formal coat of arms, showing a fleur-de-lys, the white rose of Yorkshire and a fleece. The fourth quadrant is the most interesting, showing a splendid and accurate representation of a 'sloop', a vessel as much at home on the broad waters of the Humber as in the confines of the inland navigation.

If the Aire and Calder could accept coastal vessels, then the Caledonian could go even further, for it was built as a ship canal, able to take vessels such as this brig. This represents an impressed letterhead as opposed to the formal seal.

7 THE CRAFT OF THE INLAND WATERWAYS

Of all the varieties of craft used on British canals, the narrow boat must be given pride of place. There were vessels whose design was already so old that the origins were lost in tradition by the time the canal age began; there are vessels afloat today and trading successfully of a size and power that Brindley and his contemporaries would marvel at, yet the narrow boat retains its unique position. It was the narrow boat which plied the waterways that spread out in a complex network from Birmingham, the heart of the canal system. Where other craft evolved from a long line of barges and lighters, the narrow boat was the creature of the canals. The design would be inconceivable for a cargo boat, unless it had to meet very special requirements, and that is just what the narrow boat had to do: it had to fill with as little waste as possible one of Mr James Brindley's locks. The bigger the boat, the more cargo could be carried, so every inch was valuable, and the narrow boat was quite simply the largest vessel that would fit a narrow lock. In its earliest form, it was the simplest of craft, and although change was slow and steady rather than dramatic, the canal narrow boat developed into a craft that was ideally suited to the circumstances in which it had to work. Its demise had nothing to do with design faults of its own, and everything to do with the nature of the waterways on which it was worked. Its origins were suitably simple.

The story of the narrow boat really begins with the long, thin 'starvationers' of the Bridgewater Canal, designed to go underground to be loaded in the mines of Worsley. They were roughly 48ft (15m) long and 4½ft (1.5m) wide, and 'roughly' was also the word that could best describe how they were constructed. They were wooden boats, consisting of little more than an open cargo hold and a small space for the steerer. What does seem to be true is that they worked very well and were easy to handle. Brindley knew when he took his decision on lock dimensions that he was setting a standard for boats as well, and when he decided on his narrow locks it must have been a comfort to know that the ratio of length to beam would be approximately 70ft (21.5m) to 7ft (2m) or 10 to 1, the same proportions that had been shown to work so well with the duke's starvationers. Over the years, there were to be numerous small variations in narrow-boat sizes. Some boats were built for speed: the fly boats of the Trent and Mersey were given suitably fine lines, trimmed down to a length of 68ft (21m) and a beam of 6ft 10in (2.1m). What they lost in carrying capacity, they made up for in shorter journey times. Shropshire Union boats that had to travel on the Shrewsbury Canal had to slim down to a dainty 6ft 2in (1.8m) waist. In Wales, the canal builders saw no good reason to conform to English

The Bridgewater Canal has its beginnings in the mines of Worsley Delph. The photograph shows Coal Board officials inspecting the old workings. The boat is a 'starvationer', the vessel specially designed for the canal, which was loaded at the coal face and then floated out to be towed off along the canal to Manchester. It is seen by many as the forerunner of the narrow boat (Michael E. Ware)

standards and the narrow locks on the Glamorgan Canal, for example, could take vessels no more than 60ft (16m) long, but they could be a stout 8ft 6in (2.5m) at the midriff. But for all these changes, narrow boats remained essentially the 70 × 7ft (21.5 × 2m) craft that they started out to be.

In the early days, the boatman regarded his boat much as a carter regarded his cart. It was a means of carrying goods and that was all; there was no need for fripperies and decoration. Many early boats were very like their forerunners, the starvationers, little more than a bare hull, a post for a tow-rope to be attached and a tiller for steering. As journeys became longer, a simple cabin was added – really little more than a flimsy wooden hut in the stern; and as customers became more demanding, so more care had to be taken in providing a means of keeping cargo dry. Longer journeys, particularly those undertaken at the modest pace of a plodding horse, with frequent interruptions for locks, meant long periods away from home, during which no money reached families. By the 1790s, that great period of canal growth, there was a steady move among boatmen to take their families with them and a new type of narrow boat appeared with carefully organised living accommodation in a back cabin. The impetus for the movement of families on to the boats was the arrival of the railways. The new, aggressive competitor had to be fought, and that meant lowering costs and that, in turn, inevitably meant that many boatmen could no longer afford the luxury of a house on the land, so they joined the floating population of boating families. The narrow boats were home to a community, the community developing its own traditions and way of life, and part of those traditions became expressed in the boats themselves. When we talk today of a 'traditional' narrow boat, we are certainly not thinking of the crude craft of the 1760s, nor even the more sophisticated vessel of the 1830s, but of the highly decorated family boat of the end of the nineteenth century which continued into modern times. This is the boat we can now look at in more detail.

This unlikely looking vessel, Bournville 1 was built for Cadbury's in 1911 and it has a special place in canal history as the very first narrow boat to be fitted with the Swedish Bolinder diesel engine (Cadbury Schweppes)

The first basic design was that of the wooden, horse-drawn boat; in time, there would be boats with hulls using iron and wood, boats with all-iron hulls and even, for a short time, concrete boats. The material used for building made comparatively little difference to the arrangement of the vessels. Starting at the high bow, protected by a rope fender, the vessel widens out until it reaches its full beam at about 7ft (2m) from the stem. This forward area is decked over to provide a useful storage space, and on family boats a tiny fore-cabin could be included to accommodate small children. The next section of the boat looking aft is essentially a flat-bottomed topless box. Its beginning is marked by a triangular board rising up above the fore-deck, the cratch. Behind it is a simple wooden frame supporting the top planks, which are just what the name suggests, a line of planks running right down the boat to the cabin at the back. They make a convenient walkway and mark the top of the hold. When a cargo needs to be protected, it can be 'sheeted up'. Side cloths are unrolled from the gunwales and are then fixed and laced together by ropes passing over the top planks. Extra tarpaulins can also be fastened over the top planks. There is a little more to see, for a variety of objects – a lamp at the front, and various poles and knobs sticking up (of which more later) – might be attached to the cratch and its top planks.

Beyond the hold is the back cabin, the family home, a masterpiece of economical design. It needs to be, for an entire family may have to fit into a low-ceilinged space, perhaps 10 × 7ft (3 × 2m). The cabin has a sliding hatch and a pair of doors, opening out into a small well or cockpit for the steerer. The steering position has great advantages in cold weather, when the steerer can enjoy some of the warmth from the cabin stove. Overhanging the well is a massive, curved wooden tiller that slots into the stern post. The tiller is used turned down, but can be taken out, reversed and left pointing upwards to provide easy access to the cabin when the boat is moored. At the very stern is the rudder and at the back of that the tipcat or stern fender. Such, at its very simplest, is the wooden narrow boat.

The boats were generally built in small boatyards, often family run, and the techniques and tools were those of traditional boatbuilders everywhere. Plans and blueprints were virtually unknown, for designs were carried in the craftsmen's heads and passed on by experience, not by the book. First, a cradle or platform was erected on which the boat was to be built, and on this the planks were laid out for the bottom. These were invariably elm, and untreated elm at that, for one of the properties of that wood is that when it is immersed in water it simply soaks up the liquid, and once it is saturated, it will last for years. In fact, most repairs were due to damage caused by rubbing along the bottom of shallow canals rather than by faults in the wood. The planks were then cut and shaped to give the boat its shape in plan. A keelson – a huge baulk of timber – was set in place to run right down the centre of the boat. The keelson is actually made up of individual timbers jointed by scarf joints, that so elegant example of the shipwright's craft, in which timbers the width of small trees fasten together like pieces of a jigsaw. I once had the opportunity to go down to the bottom of Nelson's flagship

Where to See the Boats

Happily, there are still working boats to be seen on British waterways, but the best preserved examples can often be found in museums. The following list gives brief details of these museums, and also lists the surviving sailing barges and river craft which can be visited or in some cases, chartered.

Museums

The Black Country Museum, Tipton Road, Dudley, West Midlands
A collection of narrow boats, including the restored Fellows, Morton & Clayton steamer *President*.

The Boat Museum, Dockyard Road, Ellesmere Port, Cheshire
A splendid collection housed in and around Telford's terminal complex on the Shropshire Union: everything from the Skinners' old narrow boat *Friendship* to a 300-ton weaver packet.

The Canal Museum, Canal Street, Nottingham
A small museum housed at the old Fellows, Morton & Clayton wharf and featuring their boats.

Cotehele Quay, Cotehele, Cornwall
The small maritime museum is home to the Tamar sailing barge *Shamrock*.

Dolphin Yard Sailing Barge Museum, Crown Quay Lane, Sittingbourne, Kent
An old barge repair yard, where Thames barges moor and restoration work goes on.

National Waterways Museum, Llanthony Warehouse, Gloucester Docks, Gloucester
Opened in 1988, the museum has a number of craft ranging from a mahogany river launch to a steam dredger.

continued on page 117

HMS *Victory* and there, too, the massive keelson was fastened together by scarf joints. Somehow it helps to place the narrow boat not as something special, unique even, but just as part of a long tradition of shipbuilding that stretches back through the centuries.

With the bottom in place, two suitably large hunks of oak were chosen and shaped to be set in place as stem and stern posts. Now the planks could be added and the hull could begin to take shape. The bottom planks or strakes had to take a double curve, bending both inwards and upwards. You can bend the plank one way with ease, but a double bend risks splitting, so a timber where the grain itself provides a part of the curve quite naturally was required. One wood where this can be found is the English oak – which gives the oak its unique role in the days of the great wooden ships. L. T. C. Rolt in his book *Narrow Boat* tells of visiting that most traditional of traditional boatyards, Tooley's of Banbury, and how old Mr Tooley understood the special qualities of timber almost as a sixth sense:

Mr Tooley must have carried this natural curve in his mind's eye, for he related how, years ago, he had spotted a suitable oak tree growing on the outskirts of the town, and when at last he heard that it was to be felled to make way for housing development, he bought it. Now it lay in the yard sawn into timbers ready to use, and I can think of no better fate that could befall an English oak.

There were two basic methods used in the yard for shaping timbers. The shape of the posts, for example, was provided by cutting with the adze, a tool rather like a long-handled axe with the blade turned through 90°, so that if it is swung down on to a piece of timber it does not slice into it like an axe, but scoops a piece of wood out of the surface. The other method was steaming: if wood is heated in a steam chest it becomes pliable, so boatbuilders could bend a plank to the required shape. Once the bottom strakes were in place, a series of knees were put in. These were L-shaped, originally made of wood and later of iron, with the bottom of the 'L' on the bottom of the boat and the vertical providing the frame to which the side planks were fastened. Gradually, the boat took shape and the cabin frame was fitted. A boat, however, is not much use if it leaks, so it was made watertight by the age-old method of caulking, which involved cramming a roll of oakum in between the planks using a caulking iron, a chisel-like tool that was held against the oakum and driven in with a mallet. Once that was done, the seams were coated with pitch. This was the basic pattern, but there were all the special features to be added – the lining of the hold, posts and decking, and cabins to be completed and fitted out. Each yard had its own ways of building and there were further variations because each customer had his own particular requirements. It is doubtful if two boats were ever exactly the same, even from the same yard. But for all yards, the great moment came when the new boat was launched – always sideways on. Alex Waterson, writing of boatbuilding days at the Ladyshore yard on the Manchester, Bolton and Bury Canal, remembered what it was like when a boat was finished:

The fire under the pitch was raked out, and a pot of strong sweet tea on the boil. Soon the lingering smell of pitch which filled the cabin was joined by the tang of cigarettes and pipe smoke. There is nothing so satisfying as a mug of hot sweet tea and seeing the result of six months work riding at her moorings outside the cabin window . . . and it was almost time to go home!

Many of the details of the finished boat depended on the work it was required to do, and the life of those to whom it was home. The original boats all had to be towed, generally by a horse, although some boatmen, such as the late Joe Skinner, preferred mules. Whatever the animal, there had to be a means of attaching the tow-rope to the boat. Most of us would probably tie a line to the bows – and most of us would be wrong since, as any engineer with a knowledge of theoretical mechanics will tell you, the net result would be to pull the boat inexorably towards the bank. So the mast to which the rope was attached was set approximately 20ft (6m) back from the bows. It is surprisingly easy to pull even a 70ft (21.5m) boat through the water, once it is under way. Starting it going is quite another matter, and there was a real risk that the horse would suffer a dislocated shoulder as it leaned into its collar to take the jarring pull of the full weight of the boat. Incidentally, in the absence of veterinary care, the boatmen's only cure was to force the horse into the canal where swimming would, with luck, set the shoulder back in again. Prevention, however, is always preferable to cure. A device commonly used was a long tow-line, with an eye at one end and a toggle set about 10–15ft (3–4.5m) from the eye. The boatman would drop the eye over a bollard ahead of the lock, then pass the line through a pulley on the mast from where it went on, as usual, to the horse. When starting off, the system gave the horse a mechanical advantage – just as any pulley system does – but once it was well under way, the toggle would jam at the pulley, the horse would take up the full load and the eye could be slipped off the bollard. As with so many techniques on the canal, it was a device of great simplicity and great effectiveness.

The golden age of the canal coincided with the great age of steam, and it was inevitable that engineers would begin to look for ways to move boats by these new-fangled devices. Although Britain led the world in steam-engine design, the first successful experiments came in France and were then taken up in America. Britain got into the act in 1788 when William Symington tried out a paddle-steamer on Dalswinton Lake in Scotland, where the enthusiastic passengers included the poet Robert Burns. Symington went on to build a steamer, the *Charlotte Dundas*, for the Forth and Clyde Canal. There was nothing wrong with the vessel itself which successfully towed two laden barges. The proprietors of the canal, however, were concerned about the wash damaging the banks and the vessel was simply abandoned to rot away. Various attempts were made to arouse interest in the steam tug for use on broad canals, although no one seriously contemplated a narrow paddle-steamer.

The biggest advance came in the 1830s, when Francis Pettit Smith patented his screw propeller. The argument over which was the more efficient, screw or propeller, was settled by a nautical tug-of-war between

continued from page 116

The Waterways Museum, Stoke Bruerne, near Towcester, Northamptonshire
Inside the museum are examples of engines and a back cabin, and narrow boats are usually moored outside.

Preserved Craft

Albion
The Norfolk Wherry Trust. Lettings secretary: Mrs Jill Brough, 62 Witney Green, Pakefield, Lowestoft, Suffolk NR33 7AP.

Amy Howson and *Comrade*
Humber Keel and Sloop Preservation Society Ltd. Ships's agent: J.W. Thompson, 218 Victoria Avenue, Hull HU5 2DZ.

VIC 32
Highland Steamboat Holidays Ltd, The Change House, Crinan Ferry, Lochgilphead, Argyll PA31 8QH.

two identical frigates, the screw-propelled *Rattler* and the paddler *Alecto*. When the order 'full ahead' was given, *Alecto* was towed backwards at a rate of 3 knots. Greater efficiency meant that the same work-load could now be carried by a smaller engine. The first steam tugs appeared on the canal, where they were to prove particularly useful for towing through long tunnels. But the notion of a steam-powered, cargo-carrying narrow boat was to be delayed until the 1860s, when steam narrow boats appeared on the Grand Junction Canal. The idea was enthusiastically adopted by the carrying company of Fellows, Morton & Clayton. Their steamers were very sophisticated, with twin cylinders run off steam at the comparatively high pressure of 140psi. They were the company's pride and joy. Their crews were a highly paid élite who needed to be paid well, for they had to be wooed away initially from the ranks of railway drivers and firemen. One disadvantage, however, with the steamers was that a great deal of space was taken up by boiler, engine and coal bunker. But the company could tolerate that because the steamer could work as the front end of a pair, towing one of the old horse boats behind it. The working pair was soon to become a common sight on the canals and even more common when diesels first appeared in the early twentieth century. From then on the pair would be a diesel motor boat, pulling an unpowered narrow boat behind it – the now familiar motor boat and butty.

Although essentially similar in design, motor boat and butty can be easily distinguished. The butty remained the old horse boat with its sweeping wooden tiller, but the motor has a longer 'cabin' because it includes the engine-room and there is a rounded counter stern overhanging the propeller. A Z-shaped metal rudder-head replaces the ram's head that tops the wooden rudder of the butty, and the tiller is a detachable brass tube held in place by an ornate brass pin. With this pairing, the canal narrow boat reached the final stage of its development. But to describe the outline of the craft gives little idea of how it was used in practice nor does it give any idea of what it was like to live with a boat as your only home.

A changing life for the narrow boats. The first picture shows the Willow Wren pair Avocet *and* Dabchick *on the Thames near Medmenham in 1958. The motor is steering both vessels, and the butty's tiller has been removed. The second picture shows them converted into hotel boats, cruising on the Shropshire Union Canal near Brewood* (Anthony Burton and Derek Pratt)

It would be the simplest thing imaginable to devote this entire chapter to narrow boats, for within this category there are many variations. Just to take the fleet of one carrying company, the Grand Union Canal Carrying Company ordered vessels from three yards, and each yard provided motor boats and butties in two sizes. So Harland & Wolfe produced large and small Woolwiches, Yarwood's turned out North-wiches and Walker's of Rickmansworth built Rickies. But narrow boats were by no means the only vessels trading on inland waterways. The rest can be said, as a very rough generalisation, to have developed out of the sailing barges that had been used for centuries on rivers and estuaries and out of a mixture of flats and lighters, and a few special craft built for special circumstances. It is difficult now to appreciate the wealth of vessels that once traded all around Britain's coast and worked inland through the rivers and canals. Whole categories of vessels have quite simply passed into oblivion, surviving at best as bleached skeletons

in the shining mud of a lonely creek. Yet some survive, in museums, worked by amateurs and even, in a few rare instances, still in trade. The descriptions that follow are not by any means intended to be comprehensive, but concentrate on the survivors.

The nearest equivalent to the narrow boat was, paradoxically perhaps, the wide boat, but this is not too surprising for it developed to meet the same basic needs. It was a horse-drawn barge, its size determined by the size of locks it had to go through. So, the Kennet and Avon could accept vessels 73ft (22m) long by 13ft 10in (4m) beam and Rochdale Canal boats could grow a few more inches in all directions and still get through, so that both canals could happily accept narrow boats into their waters. The Leeds and Liverpool, on the other hand, while it allowed a generous 14ft 4in (4.5m) beam, was limited for most of its length to vessels 62ft (19m) long. This was one of the curses of the system, analogous to the railway battle between Stephenson's standard gauge and Brunel's broad gauge. But where the railway battle ended with a decisive victory for the Stephenson gauge, the canal conflict has never been resolved. So, throughout its history, trade on the Leeds and Liverpool has been carried out in short boats. Their development has followed similar, if by no means identical, lines to those of the narrow boat.

The short boat began as something half way between the barges that had traditionally plied the rivers and the new narrow boat of the Midlands canals. The square, transom stern, the long wooden tiller and sweeping lines are all reminiscent of the river; but the sheeted cargo hold seems very much in the narrow-boat style. The Leeds & Liverpool Canal Company's own vessels were slightly different, with rounded sterns. Like the narrow boat, they were pulled by horses but were very economical, with a load twice that of the Midland craft. When railway competition began, there was not the same pressure on families to cut their costs by moving permanently on board. There were stern cabins

Leeds and Liverpool wide boats loading at Burnley wharf at the beginning of the century. Note the huge sweeping tiller and large rudder of the horse boat, Jay *(Lancashire Library)*

but there was never quite the same riot of decoration, although the sterns were always very colourful, with ornate lettering and all kinds of painted scenes and flowers. The arrival of motors reduced cabin space to an uncomfortable minimum, and the slight amount of family boating that had existed dwindled away. The differences between short boats and long, wide and narrow ones, were considerable, but nowhere near as great as the differences between them and the vessels that traded up the canals and rivers under sail.

No one knows when the vessels first began to trade on rivers, but old pictures give us some notion of what such craft looked like by the end of the Middle Ages. By an odd quirk, the nearest thing we now have to these medieval craft is a child of the canal age, designed like its fellows to fit the locks it would have to pass through on the new navigations. The Humber keel could have sailed straight out of the pages of an illuminated manuscript, yet when one looks at the vessel in more detail, one soon realises that it is a vessel beautifully adapted to very special circumstances. There was not strictly a keel, but several keels depending on which waterways they were to use: vessels trading right up the Sheffield and South Yorkshire Navigation were 60ft (18m) long by 15ft 3in (4.5m) beam and capable of carrying loads of 100 tons, but vessels intended for the Trent could be built right up to 75ft (23m) in length. What they had in common, however, was more important than their differences. They had to cope with the wide expanses of the Humber which, if it is not officially open sea, can feel remarkably like it on a stormy day. But they also had to work on tree-shaded canals and rivers. The design was developed to meet these different needs.

The hull looks not unlike an overgrown date box, with rounded stern and bluff bows, providing maximum cargo space in a vessel that has to fit an oblong lock. As a sea-going sailing ship, it needs some device to stop it skittering sideways over the water in a cross-wind, but the normal sailing ship answer of a deep keel is not a practical choice for a canal vessel. Instead, the vessel is fitted with lee boards like massive wooden tabletops which can be lowered into the water on either side of the ship, depending on which side the wind is blowing. Driving power comes from a large mainsail and a smaller topsail set on a mast set slightly forward of the midline. Where a modern yacht is set with triangular sails, the keel has square sails – much as one might have seen on the Viking ships that came to this country many centuries ago. The square rig has many advantages: it is easy to raise and lower – no small matter where there are numerous bridges to negotiate – and the high sails can stand proud above the shelter of trees and buildings when travelling inland. Even at sea, the rig is efficient, for the sails can be pulled round so that they almost point in a line from bow to stern, giving all the sailing advantages of today's more common 'fore and aft' rig. Those unfamiliar with sails sometimes think that they work by the force of the wind blowing into them from behind. If that was the only way in which they worked, ships would probably spend most of their lives in harbour waiting for the wind to reach just the right quarter. But ships can also sail by using the sail rather as the wing of an aircraft is used, by the effect of the wind slipping past the front of the sail reducing the

Loading a Narrow Boat

Norman Harrison, a former wharf manager for Fellows, Morton & Clayton, described how he used to have to leave the actual management of the loading to the boatmen themselves:

He tells you what to put in the boat, where to put it, whether you are in the middle quarter, back of the mast or the fore end you see some boatmen will not have any stuff at all put in the fore end because the boats won't swim. And there's no two boats, irrespective every boat has a personality and there's no two boats alike. You can measure all your planks you can do this and you can have the beam right and you can do everything and that but it doesn't work, no two boats work alike and the dry boat is considered to be an evil. If you get a wooden boat and it is dead dry they don't like it – it must weep a little because if it doesn't, during the summer months it will open out one of the days and let you down. It must have a little amount of bilge.

pressure. Again, to draw an analogy with the aeroplane, it is not the air pushing up under a wing that causes lift, but the reduced pressure above it. The more that a vessel can use this technique, the closer to the wind it can sail – that is, it can go more nearly towards the direction from which the wind blows. The whole complex of rigging, the sheets and the tacks that pull the sails across, is operated through winches so efficiently that the keel can comfortably be sailed with a two-man crew. It was by no means unknown, however, for families to live aboard, and the cabin was quite spacious by narrow-boat standards.

Even the best sailing vessel cannot move straight into a headwind. Adverse wind conditions can be dealt with by tacking, but this involves sailing a zigzag course – not a very practical solution on a canal. And no vessel can sail when there is no wind at all. So, even more than at sea, there were occasions when sails were of no use to the keel men. Horses could be hired together with a 'horse marine' for towing, or, if cash was a little short, bow-hauling became the order of the day. Matters were much improved with the arrival of tugs on the scene, and, in time, the sailing keel eventually gave up its canvas in favour of the motor. Now out of all that fleet, just one Humber keel, *Comrade*, remains in sail, safe from scrap and sailing with an amateur crew who have the benefit of instruction from her old master, Fred Schofield. Those who have been fortunate enough to sail with Fred Schofield come back realising, if nothing else, just how ignorant they are, for everything he does is performed with the ease of long-acquired, deep-seated knowledge. The seemingly featureless waters of the Humber are for him as easy to read as I should find a path through the hills. Each shift of the wind seems not so much to be sensed as to be foreseen. To sail *Comrade* in his company can seem like returning to the grand days of the sailing cargo vessel. But that is a delusion. Those of us who go out for fun, choose our weather conditions and stay in harbour if there is any doubt. There are always hands in plenty to haul on lines and turn winches and the vessel rides high in the water, not loaded down to the gunwales so that the waves break over the decking. And no one asks to bow-haul *Comrade* all the way to Sheffield.

Sometimes a second vessel joins *Comrade* on her regular weekend sailings: a similar hull, but a different sailing rig, the Humber sloop *Amy Howson*. The sloop is fore and aft rigged, in other words with a triangular foresail and a gaff mainsail. The mainsail is set so that it lies on the fore and aft axis, always stands behind the mast and has only a limited amount of travel from side to side – just as in an old-fashioned sailing dinghy. This rig was much favoured by the boat-builders on the southern bank of the Humber, while the square rig was the first choice of the North. In the days before Whitehall decided to erase centuries of local history, this was a contest between Lincolnshire and Yorkshire. Each vessel, in fact, has its virtues and defects, but they do represent two extremes of the sailing barge rig. Between them is a host of variations.

The oldest recorded sailing barges were the Severn trows, but there is a problem in describing them. The name itself is ancient and has been applied, more or less indiscriminately, to any sailing vessel on the Severn. The trow in use on the Severn in the fifteenth century was little

more than its name suggests, a trough, rounded at the stern, open to the elements and square rigged. Soon, however, a characteristic shape emerged: flat bottomed like all river barges, but very rounded in the bilges with a D-shaped transom stern, the characteristic trademark of the trow. They developed and grew in size and some became large sea-going vessels with a bowsprit and two masts. Some added even more sails and developed into genuine deep-sea vessels. To see a Humber keel and a big Severn trow side by side, one would scarcely believe that they were both inland waterways craft.

Each major waterway system had its own variety of sailing barge. The flats of the Mersey and the Weaver, for example, looked on the water to bear more than a passing resemblance to the Humber sloop with a very similar rig. But the hulls were, in fact, far more rounded, so that both the big Mersey vessels and their smaller sisters from the Weaver were quite seaworthy, more than capable of voyaging to North Wales and across to the Isle of Man. In later years, all these vessels were able to make use of steam tugs, so that in adverse conditions they could be towed. This made them much more versatile, although sailing was always preferred as the wind is free and steam coal costs money. The big change came in the 1870s with the improvement of the Weaver to meet the demands of a thriving salt trade. Locks were more than trebled in size to measure 229 × 42ft 6in (70 × 13m) and there was a rapid movement away from the small flats to big new steam packets. There was certainly nothing fancy about the packets: everything about them declared that they were working boats. Above a plain hull, its cargo hold covered by hatches, rose up a tall steam derrick at the bows and a thin smoke-stack above the engine-room at the stern. The steering wheel was generally out in the open, although some old photographs show an occasional rough shelter scarcely grand enough to be dignified by the name of wheelhouse. The Weaver steam packet could never be described as elegant, but it was never short on character.

Old and new on the Trent. The two sailing keels belong to a ship-building tradition that goes back to medieval times, but they are enjoying the benefit of a tow from the steam tug Little John. *The photograph was taken near Fiskerton, c1905* (Newark Museum)

A busy scene on the Weaver as a typical ICI weaver flat steams up the river (ICI)

In complete contrast to this are the sailing vessels of the rivers and lakes that make up the Broads, the Norfolk wherries. These were among the smallest of the breed, and the last survivor *Albion* is a mere 48ft (14.5m) long by 15ft (4.5m) beam and 4ft 6in (1.5m) draught with a carrying capacity of only 23 tons; yet she carries a single sail with the immense area of 1,400sq ft (130m^2). In appearance, the wherry is unique with her tall mast set well forward, the great sail spread out behind it skimming the tops of the hatches. She is ideally suited to the conditions on the Broads, with the long winding rivers and wide expanses of water. The tall sail catches the least breath of wind, yet can easily be managed by the helmsman at the tiller. Lack of wind, however, produces an interesting problem, for where most navigable rivers have tow-paths, the Broadland rivers have mud and reeds. The wherry is quanted. Crew members stand at each side of the vessel with long quant poles which are thrust down to the river bed. The crew lean their shoulders to the poles and walk from the bow to the stern, where they pull out the poles and start all over again. It is hard work, as the author can testify, but in a stiff breeze, the vessel comes into her own and it is one of the great delights of life to be out on the *Albion*, built in 1898 and virtually unchanged from her working days, sailing smoothly past a modern motor cruiser.

Grandest of all the sailing barges are the spritsail barges of the South East, the famous Thames barges, the largest of their kind ever to be worked by a two-man crew, and even in their latter days single-handed, when economies were forced on to barge skippers. Strictly speaking, these scarcely fall within the bounds of the inland waterways, for their territory was very much the estuaries, the tideways and the open sea, but no survey, however brief, could omit these splendid craft. Happily, many survive, if not in trade at least still in sail, and there are few finer sights to be seen around the British coast than one of the annual barge matches, when twenty or more of these grand vessels can be seen racing each other. Sailed flat out, they can generate real speed and power, a fact which was startlingly demonstrated during a match a few years ago. One of the biggest class, a bowsprit barge, was heading out to sea. Inevitably on these occasions there is an accompanying fleet of small yachts and dinghies along for the fun of it. One got a little too adventurous and decided to tack across the bows of the barge. The yachtsman had made no allowance for the huge sail area of the barge which blanketed the wind. He slowed almost to a standstill and the result was inevitable: the barge bowsprit went through the sail of the dinghy like a jousting lance, and sail, dinghy and occupant were carried on suspended until everything came to a halt. The origin of the once common expression 'swearing like a bargee' became clear that day.

The age of sail eventually gave way to the age of steam and then to the age of diesel. Some of these later developments will be looked at in Chapter 15. Often the new age meant little more than putting engines in existing craft, or converting the old sailing barges to lighters which could then be towed by tug. There were, however, a few craft specially built for the new age. The compartment boat, the Tom Pudding, designed to take coals from the mines of South Yorkshire to the port of

Goole, has already been mentioned (see p98), and these remarkably successful craft continued in use into the 1980s. These simple metal boxes, each able to carry up to 35 tons, were assembled in trains with a wedge-shaped box in front to act as a dummy bow. The trains, like long black sea serpents, were too long for the locks and it was always an intriguing sight to see the full vessels going down. If there was a train of one tug and fifteen Tom Puddings, the tug and seven compartment boats would go down in the conventional way, but that left eight heavily laden vessels with no power. So the lock was refilled, the top gates opened and the bottom paddles raised. The resulting flow of water sucked the rest of the train into the lock and once down, the whole set could be reunited and continue on its way.

Everyone has their favourites among these vessels, and I have saved one of my own for the last – the Clyde puffer, which worked the whole of the west coast of Scotland as well as the Clyde itself, and the Forth and Clyde and Crinan canals. The name comes from the way in which the engine was first used. The two-cylinder engine took steam from the boiler and then passed it from high-pressure cylinder to low-pressure cylinder, after which the exhaust steam went up out of the funnel in a series of puffs. Later, puffers spent more time at sea and the exhaust steam was condensed so that it could be fed back to the boiler. Like the Weaver packet, there is nothing glamorous about the puffer – it is everybody's favourite bath-tub steamer grown up – steam derrick in the bows, hatches over the hold, funnel and wheelhouse. The steering position, directly behind the stack, tends to bemuse novice helmsmen and helmswomen. The vessels are flat bottomed so that where no harbour was available, they could simply run up a beach to refloat at high tide. What is the appeal? Why do I go back year after year to spend a summer holiday shovelling coal in the hot and steamy engine-room of the old *VIC 32*, when for all my efforts the ship never seems to exceed a steady, stately 6 knots? It is hard to say, but the appeal of the puffer *VIC 32* is perhaps no different from that of the wherry *Albion* or the keel *Comrade*, or indeed of the more familiar canal narrow boat. Each is a working craft, perfectly adapted to its particular job and the waters on which it plied its trade.

Loading Tom Puddings with coal. Trains of compartment boats are being made up, while the tug approaches ready to take more boats in tow ready for the journey to Goole (British Waterways Board)

8 THE CARRIERS

A Wealthy Number One

In the 1920s, an elderly boatman, known as 'Old Crompton' who travelled with his sister working as mate, was loading with copper from a ship berthed in the docks at Manchester. The metal was in 1-ton pieces, and one slipped out of its sling and dropped straight through the bottom of the boat, which sank in 80ft (24m) of water. Divers were sent down to see what could be retrieved. Old Crompton was assumed to be in a state of shock, as he kept muttering 'bed, bed', yet refused to be taken away to bed. His agitation was easily explained, however, when the bed was dragged up from the cabin: there were one hundred gold sovereigns in the drawer. Very, very few boatmen possessed anything like that amount of cash.

The roll-call of famous canal-carrying companies sounds as music to the enthusiast's ears, and each carries its own special resonance: FMC, GUCCC, Clayton of Oldbury, Willow Wren, Barlow, Severn and Canal – the list is endless. To the uninitiated, such names mean nothing, but other carriers might seem rather more familiar. Pickford's were moving goods by canal long before they thought of taking furniture by road, and many a well-known company ran their own fleets, companies as varied as Cadbury's and ICI. Each concern had its own territory, its own favourite cargo, often its own special boat and its own way of doing things.

In the first heady days when a new canal was opened to traffic for the first time, the owners tended, not unnaturally, to want to start recouping their construction costs as quickly as possible. One obvious answer seemed to be to buy boats and start trading, but there was never any serious consideration given to the idea of going in the direction taken by the later railways, of the proprietor having a monopoly of the carrying trade. The railways had little choice – a free-for-all of fast-moving trains all on the same track scarcely bears thinking about – but the canals could take as many boat owners as there were boats. In any case, most companies soon found their true interest lay with keeping and maintaining the canals, and letting others run the boats and pay for the privilege. So who did run the boats in those early days?

There is a popular mythology surrounding the heyday of canals that it was all a triumph for individual initiative, men saving up for a boat and setting off into the unknown world of the carrying trade. Myth is just what it is, for from the very first the trade went to the big man: the companies running large fleets took the lion's share, closely followed by the smaller businessman with fleets of perhaps half-a-dozen boats. There was little room left for the cheery 'water gypsy' – and the big men did their best to see that the smaller men stayed that way. One boatman trying to make his solitary way on the Oxford Canal in 1794 found that the trader using Fenny Compton wharf claimed an exclusive right to it, and flatly refused to let the boatman unload there. The boatman was trading in cheap coal which would have kept his customers happy and given him a small profit, but not for the first time in the history of trading the independent fell prey to the power of the monopoly. Not that all customers favoured the one-man independent. Canal carrying was still an uncertain, untested business in the eighteenth century, and there was a certain comfort in dealing with the visibly prosperous. The merchant entrusting his valuable cargo to a wealthy carrier had at least the reassuring thought that if the worst came to the worst there would be someone there to sue other than an assetless pauper.

There is still commercial traffic on Britain's waterways – a crowded scene on the River Hull (Anthony Burton)

*A narrow boat and trow on the
River Severn at Coalport from a
painting by H. Clements, 1884*
(Ironbridge Gorge Museum
Trust)

The bigger companies soon came to build up special advantages. They could offer both a guarantee and a varied service backed up by an often impressive organisation. No one exemplified this better than the greatest of all the early canal traders, Pickford's. The family business started at Poynton, close to the eventual line of the Peak Forest Canal, and very strategically situated on one of the main routes between London and Manchester. By the middle of the eighteenth century, the business was well established. An advertisement in the *Manchester Mercury* for 1756 advised customers that James Pickford 'The London and Manchester Waggoner' had moved his London base from Blossom's Inn to the Bell Inn. He offered a regular service twice a week, from both London and Manchester, which, given the time taken for the journey, could only have been operated with a minimum of six waggons. This represented a considerable investment. One has to forget images of a horse and cart bounding cheerily off down the highway, and think instead of a heavy, lumbering, broad-wheeled waggon pulled by a team of eight horses with a ninth taken along as a reserve. Pickford, then, must have owned more than fifty heavy draught horses, and they were far from cheap.

James Pickford died in 1768 and his wife Martha carried on the business for a while, until their son Matthew was ready to take over in 1772. This was a time when canal operations were just beginning to pose a threat to the road carriers: the Bridgewater, the Birmingham and the Staffs and Worcester were open and trading, and work was under way on other routes. Pickford's decided to adopt an 'if you can't beat them join them' policy. They bought their first boat, and it looks to have been rather more an insurance than a wholehearted shot at the canal trade. Even in the 1790s when Pickford's were thriving, their stock ran to 28 waggons, 252 horses and only 10 boats. The main impetus towards increased canal trade came in 1785, when it seemed that after the long years of inactivity, work was likely to restart on the Oxford Canal, offering Pickford's a through route from Manchester to London. The competition consisted mainly of Hugh Henshall & Company, named after the engineer, but really the thinly disguised trading arm of the Trent & Mersey Canal Company. Pickford's realised that the time to strike a bargain was when the Oxford was in the doldrums and not when it had picked up momentum and was moving to a conclusion. So they negotiated a good lease for wharf and warehouses at Braunston, and even managed to get reduced tolls for as long as they needed to cart goods around incomplete sections. It was all useful experience, but they found that the meandering Oxford route was offering few advantages over their successful road-haulage business. The start of work on the Grand Junction Canal, however, promised dramatic improvements, and as with the Oxford Canal, Pickford's were quick to establish their presence, acquiring a base at Paddington long before the canal was complete.

In the early nineteenth century, the canal trade began to bite deep into the road business, and Pickford's 'insurance policy' proved to have been worth the premium. Their canal trade expanded rapidly. In 1801 they had shipped their first load of cotton to Lancashire and established a regular carting service between Paddington and central London. Soon they were extending their wharves and building yet more warehouses.

Tyseley

Of the more recently formed companies, the best known is the Grand Union Canal Carrying Company which started in 1934, and their boats are probably the ones most commonly met with on the system today. Some can be found carrying bagged coal in winter, or with the holds scrubbed out and filled with bunk beds, running as camping boats in the summer. One boat even has the unique distinction of being the star of a musical play. The name *Tyseley* tells you that this one was built at Yarwood's in Northwich. GUCCC called all the small boats by the names of stars and planets and their larger vessels by town names. They followed a simple alphabetical order: from A to H, with the exception of Halsall, they came from Harland & Wolfe at Woolwich, and the rest, up to Yeoford, came from Northwich. As carrying died away, *Tyseley* embarked on a somewhat chequered career, which included a spell as one of a pair of restaurant boats working out of Thrupp. But *Tyseley* was intended for a rather more glamorous role. The old vessel had the first whiff of grease-paint during a brief appearance in the film *Painted Boats*, but now she has achieved far greater fame as the floating home of the Mikron Theatre Company. The vessel which began her working life more than half a century ago with the GUCCC, still has a working life, running to tight schedules to take the company about 1,000 miles (1,600km) each year as they tour their shows around the canals. Fifty years of work always deserves recognition, and that is just what *Tyseley* received in 1984, a show of her own, *Still Carrying*, which told the story of that working life from GUCCC days to Mikron. And, as the title suggests, *Tyseley* is indeed still carrying.

But the Pickford family had over-extended itself. By 1815, they were owing vast sums in tolls, especially to the Grand Junction. Two of the family cut and run, selling their shares and leaving Thomas II and Matthew II to try to carry on. They failed, and although Pickford's recovered and prospered, it was no longer with the Pickford family at the helm.

At the peak of the canal trade, Pickford's worked between two main bases: at Great Bridgewater Street in Manchester, near the junction of the Bridgewater and Rochdale canals, while their London business was moved to City Road Basin on the Regent's Canal at Islington. Their success was based on efficiency, and their speciality was the fly boat. These vessels ran to a fixed timetable, empty or full. They travelled day and night using relays of horses and change crews, and they had priorities over the other craft on the canal. If an ordinary trading vessel, loading cargo when cargo was ready and then heading off to a destination to be reached as and when possible, met a fly boat, then the company law decreed that the fly boat should always have right of way. Making regulations and enforcing them are not always quite the same thing: one can imagine the scene at a busy lock when a fly boat arrived demanding priority. It is not so easy to see the skipper of a big, heavily laden boat smiling politely, touching his cap and saying 'Carry on old man, I'm in no particular hurry.' Nevertheless, the fly boats had their schedules to keep, and it was reckoned that they could average 2mph (3kph) day and night, and that included coping with all the obstacles presented by locks and tunnels. It may not sound very fast in the age of container lorries, but think of boating holidays and then imagine leaving Braunston early one day and reaching Leicester the next morning, having travelled 46½ miles (75km) negotiated 47 locks and 3 tunnels – and all without the benefit of an engine. Inevitably, the fly boats charged higher rates than the slower stage boats, and were mainly used for perishable cargoes. It only worked because Pickford's were efficient. There was no point in having fly boats dashing around the country if the goods finished up waiting to be sorted at the warehouse. Pickford's office work had to be as good as their boating work.

The idea of Pickford's as a super-efficient express service is perhaps not altogether accurate. Charges tended to be a little on the haphazard side, based less on an agreed tariff and rather more on an assessment of what the sender could afford. 'Nobility,' as one carrier remarked, 'must expect to pay for their titles.' Nor should the notion of fly boats suggest that they were hauled by potential Derby winners. It was the system of relays and priorities that was first rate and not the nags: all that was required of them was that they should maintain a steady, even pace. Pickford's did not even own boat horses at first, preferring to hire them. Although they owned eighty boats in 1820, they had no horses, but by the end of their carrying days they had four hundred canal horses of their own. Often they were pensioned-off road horses, no longer quite fast enough for the vans and light carts of the city trade, but good enough for a tow-path plod.

Pickford's canal success had been due in the first place to the speed with which as road carriers they had reacted to the threat from the new

The popular image of the canal carrier is of the 'Number Ones', the owners with just one horse – or, as here, a mule – and his own boat. This picture was taken on the Trent and Mersey near Northwich in the 1930s (Fred H. Done/Michael E. Ware Collection)

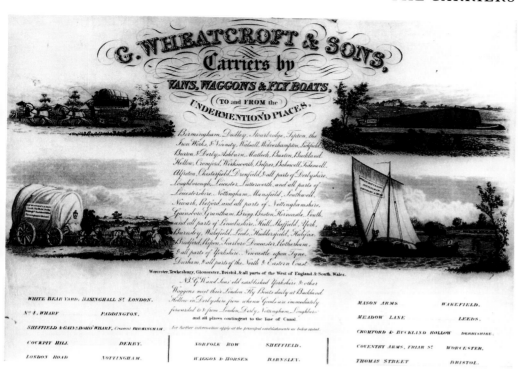

waterways. They were no slower to appreciate what the railway age would mean as the London to Manchester routes started to develop in the 1830s. They began steadily to reduce the numbers of their boats until, in 1847, they announced that they would end canal carrying the following year. After that, there was a brief flirtation with the railways but eventually they returned to the trade with which they had begun: carrying goods by road.

Pickford's were by no means the only carriers to see the writing on the station wall and a number of canal companies, faced by rapidly falling revenues, saw little option but to take to the trade themselves. They were empowered to do so by an act of 1845 and then tried, with varying degrees of success, to keep a monopoly of the business in their own areas. The Leeds & Liverpool Canal Company had a large fleet of boats trading over the whole canal, and although they were willing to accept local efforts for short hauls, they were far less tolerant of genuine competition. By far the most successful of such enterprises was the Shropshire Union, formed by an amalgamation which eventually drew together the old Birmingham and Liverpool Junction, the Shrewsbury, the Ellesmere and the Montgomery. It was to succumb, as did many others, to railway influence, but where, for example, the Kennet and Avon ran on a parallel course to the lines of the GWR, the Shropshire Union Canal reached only the parts that the railways did not. There was also the great advantage of having a canal connecting into a major port on the busy Mersey. It was a powerful position, but even so they made short shrift of rivals. Most were simply bought out and the rest were forced out. The company made no pretence about what it was doing, and the minute book for 1855 baldly records that 'the rates of tonnage are to be raised so as to exclude the private Trader'.

Pickford's At Work

At the wharf of Messrs. Pickford and Co., in the City Road, can be witnessed, on a larger scale than at any other part of the kingdom, the general operations connected with canal traffic.

This large establishment nearly surrounds the southern extremity of the City Road Basin. From the coach-road we can see little of the premises; but on passing to a street in the rear we come to a pair of large folding gates opening into an area or court, and we cannot remain here many minutes, especially in the morning or evening, without witnessing a scene of astonishing activity. From about five or six o'clock in the evening waggons are pouring in from various parts of town, laden with goods intended to be sent into the country per canal. In the morning, on the other hand, laden waggons are leaving the establishment, conveying to different parts of the metropolis goods which have arrived per canal during the night.

On entering the open area we find the eastern side bounded by stabling, where a large

continued on page 132

continued from page 131

number of horses are kept during the intervals of business. In the centre of the area is the general warehouse, an enormous roofed building with open sides; and on the left are ranged offices and counting-houses.

To one who is permitted to visit these premises there is perhaps nothing more astonishing than to see upwards of a hundred clerks engaged in managing the business of the establishment; exhibiting a system of classification and sub-division most complete. In order to show the necessity for such an amount of mental labour, we may mention that the firm have establishments in nearly every part of England, conducted by their own servants, for the general management of canal traffic.

Let us now suppose that a London merchant wishes to send a cargo of goods to Manchester per canal, and that it is through the machinery of Messrs. Pickford's establishment that the transaction is to be effected. There are, in addition to receiving-houses in different parts of town, two offices, one at the east, and the other at the west end of London, where merchandize is collected for canal transit . . . One of the two town-offices, the 'Castle', in Wood-street, presents an animated and bustling scene towards evening, when waggons, laden with packages during the day, are about to be dispatched to City Road wharf. On arriving at the wharf, each waggon draws up by the side of an elevated platform, provided with conveniences for unloading waggons and loading boats. From the southern extremity of the basin a branch turns to the east, nearly separating the yard into two portions. The portion on the southern side of this branch is called 'the dis-
continued on page 134

The Shropshire Union carrying trade grew and developed until, by the end of the nineteenth century, they were the biggest in the business, with over four hundred narrow boats of their own. There were very few that could even try to match them for size, but one private company came very close to it, and even if there was a time when the Shropshire Union could boast a greater number of boats, the private company could claim to trade over a greater part of the canal network. That company was FMC – Fellows, Morton & Clayton – although the trilogy took some time to assemble. James Fellows went into business on the BCN in 1837, and when he died, his thriving trade was taken over by his son Joshua. In the hectic years that followed, which saw the decline of many carrying companies, Fellows kept on trading – long enough to see trends beginning to reverse. The Grand Junction Company soon abandoned carrying and Fellows bought up part of their fleet, taking Frederick Morton as a partner to help run the growing empire. Fellows, however, was not the only successful carrier in the Birmingham area. William Clayton set up business in 1842 and by 1852 he had prospered so far as to establish his own boatyard at Saltley on the Birmingham and Warwick Canal. He had a general trade like many other carriers, but he soon saw that he could do even better by specialisation. Gasworks were appearing all around the country and they had valuable waste products, including tar and the liquid waste, gas-water. He was in the right place to take on the trade, and he even found one of his best customers in everyone else's chief rivals: the railways. Timber for sleepers for the Great Western Railway came by water to Bull's Bridge, and down from Birmingham came Clayton's boats loaded with creosote to treat them. In 1882, William Clayton died and the company passed to his son Thomas. Soon afterwards, in 1889, came the merger with Fellows and Morton. Clayton brought his general carrying business to the partnership and his valuable boatyard at Saltley, but the gas boat went on running from a new base at Oldbury as Thomas Clayton Limited. They were still adding new boats to the fleet right up to the 1950s, and their specially designed flat-decked boats, which can best be described as narrow-boat tankers, were a notable feature of the BCN for many years.

With the addition of Thomas Clayton's boats and facilities, Fellows, Morton & Clayton were set fair to become one of the most important carriers in Britain. Soon no one bothered with the full name – FMC was quite enough for anyone in the canal world, although the name of Joshua Fellows was to live on as the nickname for all FMC boatmen – Joshers or Jossers. In the years before World War I, FMC had a fleet of over two hundred boats, of which twenty were their famous steamers. They had their head offices in Fazeley Street, Birmingham, but they could also be found in London, Manchester, Liverpool, Leicester, Nottingham, Derby, Uxbridge, Dudley and Wolverhampton. They also acquired a notable chairman, Henry Rodolph de Salis, who took it upon himself to travel throughout the canal system of England and Wales to produce what was to become the canal Bradshaw, *A Handbook of Inland Navigation*. Even now, when I want to check on a distance or a lock size, the first thing I do is reach for my copy of de Salis.

Like Pickford's before them, FMC depended on having a good fleet,

Boatman's Strike, Braunston.

Fellows, Morton & Clayton were among the most famous of all canal carriers, but when they tried to cut pay in 1923 they were faced by that rare action, a boatman's strike. The photograph shows management and boaters separated by a line of police at Braunston (British Waterways Board)

Thomas Clayton of Oldbury concentrated on carrying the waste products of the gas industry in narrow boats specially built as tankers, easily recognised by the flat decking. The horse has stopped and the tow-rope has gone slack as the boat glides into the lock (Michael E. Ware)

continued from page 132

charging warehouse', and that in the northern the 'shipping warehouse'. The waggons, coming in laden with goods, proceed to the shipping-warehouse, where they are unladen, and the goods placed temporarily in groups on the platform of the warehouse. Each group is to form the cargo for one boat, so that there are as many groups as there are to be cargoes. The boats are drawn up at the side of the 'shipping warehouse', and are there laden. We will suppose that one is to start for Manchester that evening: into this one, therefore, are consigned all the goods brought by the various waggons from the receiving offices destined for the Manchester district; each package being weighed, checked, and properly registered before being placed in the boat . . . At the hour of six or seven in the evening the scene which we have just described is presented in its busiest phase. As a general rule, all merchandize received during the day is dispatched by boat the same night; and as the goods are not brought to the wharf until toward evening, all the operations of loading and unloading are then carried on with great celerity. Each waggon as it arrives, draws up by the side of the raised platform; the crane is set to work, the packages and boxes are taken out; the clerks and warehouse-keepers prepare the requisite entries and invoices; the goods are wheeled across the platfrom to the edge of the canal; and the boatmen assist in stowing them away in the boats. There may be half-a-dozen boats dispatched in the same evening, all to be filled subsequent to the arrival of the laden waggons at the wharf at five or six o'clock.

(*The Penny Magazine*, August 1842)

run by good men and backed by an efficient organisation. A former wharf manager reminisced about the workings of the company in the 1920s. Boats were worked in many different ways, with pride of place still going as it had always done to the fly boats, even though now there were motor boats and butties as well as horse boats. To ensure maximum flexibility they set up the 'ockers'. The motor had a captain and the butty had its own captain, and they worked as a pair with the motor towing and the butty crew managing the locks. However, they were not necessarily heading for the same final destination. They could part at any time if the butty captain felt like changing the motor for one of the company's horses, stabled at one of the many horse stations. The problem was how head office could keep track of these meanderings. The answer was the GPO. Each steerer was given a set of stamped postcards with a star against a particular address. When he reached that address he posted the card in the pillar box. This was in the far-off days before the introduction of super efficient post codes and computers, when a postcard with a halfpenny stamp posted in London in the morning would reach Birmingham in the afternoon.

Flexibility was taken a long way at FMC. A boatman had to be prepared to leave the boat to work on the wharf if told to do so, which was not necessarily to his disadvantage, for it meant that rather than simply waiting for a space at the docks he could be earning extra pay. It meant smoother running all round, but it was the company who took the decision on who should work where and for how much. It was the latter which led to what turned out to be a major strike, known to the men involved as 'the battle of the canals'. The background was a price-cutting war that was forced on the canal carriers by road competition, at a time when the cards were heavily stacked against the canal men. The sugar trade which FMC had monopolised was threatened and FMC responded by cutting their rates and passing on the cuts to the boat people. A captain loading 48 tons on a pair in London for Birmingham, found himself losing 16s a week. At the same time, various bonus schemes that had operated during World War I were also ended. In 1923 the strike, backed by the TGWU, was official.

The boat crews gathered at Braunston, where they chained their boats together to prevent them from being used. The company response was, to say the least, firm. The manager and clerks were called to the Fazeley Street office and sent in a lorry to Braunston with a police escort, with orders to cut the boats free. The boatmen had other ideas, and a fight soon started from which the FMC contingent emerged ruffled, unhurt, but unquestionably defeated. There was little harm done. The same could not be said when private police were brought in to try to break the strike. Their tactics were violent and they were as liable to attack the boatwomen as the men. The strike lasted for seventeen weeks and at the end the union claimed a victory: 'We won recognition, we won arbitration and we won a revision of the employers' claims.' In the long term, however, neither FMC nor the boatmen were to win the battle against the competition from the roads.

If FMC were the grandest of the private carriers, with a huge fleet carrying any cargo over a wide area, there were others who made a considerable success out of trading over a smaller area and in specialisation. If Clayton's of Oldbury were the undisputed lords of the gas trade, then Barlow's could claim as much for the colliery trade of the Midlands. Samuel Barlow was born in 1847 and soon followed his father into the boating business, married and set up on his own account at Bedworth with two boats. It was a good position, but he soon found a better one at Tamworth, where new collieries were being opened up. He saw this as a great opportunity and started a dual business as both coal carrier and coal merchant, so successfully that there was soon a whole collection of Barlow relations employed in the business. And that, one could say, was that, a well-run family concern that went on to grow and prosper, running day boats, or joeys as they were known on the Birmingham Canal system, and a fleet of conventional narrow boats for longer runs. There were inevitably fluctuating fortunes, and in time, although the name Barlow remained, the company was managed by others. It reached a very respectable size: there were fifty boats in the fleet at the start of World War I, but it was hardly in the same class as FMC. So why is Barlow still remembered with affection?

One reason was the boats. Many in the latter days were bought second-hand, but in 1941 Barlow's bought up the small, very traditional yard of Nurser of Braunston, the very last builder of wooden narrow boats. Nurser's built boats for Barlow but, just as importantly, they took in the sparrows and sent them out again as proud peacocks. The standard of painting was always superb, from the shadow lettering to the roses and castles. And Barlow's linked two worlds. Unlike many carriers, they did not merely fade away to the point where they simply disappeared, for they were bought up by Blue Line Cruisers. So they continued working, carrying coal on runs which included a regular shipment to a jam factory in Southall. But when that ended in October 1970, the Barlow carrying trade ended with it. But through the last years, the still traditional Barlow–Blue Line boats shared the canal with the Blue Line holiday cruisers that marked the arrival of a new canal age.

Looking through the records, it is surprising how often familiar names turn up in unfamiliar contexts. Mention the name Fellows and one immediately thinks of FMC, but before that company was formed, Joshua Fellows had already entered into another partnership. The other half started out in life as Samuel Danks & Company in 1804, trading on the Staffs and Worcester out of Stourport, but based on an older business of running trows on the Severn. The business expanded, drawing in new partners ending in Danks and Sanders, the Danks half of the equation representing the narrow-boat world of the Staffs and Worcester and the Worcester and Birmingham, while John Owen Sanders ran river barges out of Bristol. Danks and Sanders ran their fleet in direct competition with Fellows until they agreed on a merger in 1873. The new name, if cumbersome, at least could be said accurately to reflect the various lines of operation: The Severn & Canal Carrying, Shipping & Steam Towing Company Limited. They were general carriers, by no means limited to the canals and rivers, for they took goods out into the Bristol Channel and even across the Irish Sea to Cork. They were later to be known simply as the Severn & Canal Carrying Company Limited.

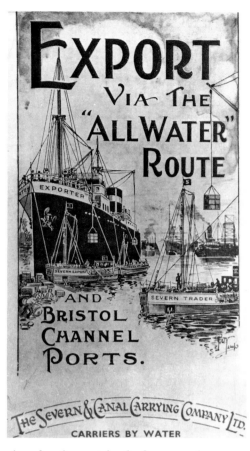

An advertisement for the Severn and Canal Carrying Company which as the illustration suggests ran a great variety of craft from big, motorised barges to narrow boats (British Waterways Board)

THE CARRIERS

They suffered the now familiar fate of the canal carriers, of profitable days followed by a steady decline. The canal trade was the first to go, but the river traffic continued, eventually to be monopolised by petrol tankers. When in 1948 the company came to concentrate entirely on this trade, the rest of the craft were sold off, and the list indicates how affairs had been developing. Seven river barges were sold, five trows and five tugs, but by then the narrow-boat fleet was down to five, where at the beginning of the century there had been about eighty.

It was the river that separated the Severn and Canal operations from those of rivals. Many of their narrow boats simply made conventional runs between Stourport or Worcester and Gloucester, but quite often they were collected together, a dozen or more at a time, to be towed by a steam tug. This was a very specialised and skilled job, for a mistake could have disastrous consequences. With a large tow, of perhaps twenty boats, hauled in two strings of ten, the steerer of the last boat would be nearly ¼ mile (0.4km) behind the tug. If the tow-rope was not properly managed, it might snap, leaving the non-motorised butty adrift on a fast-moving river with unprotected weirs – not a cheerful prospect. It must have been something of a relief to return to the more familiar, decidedly safer world of the canals – even if the regular service included negotiating the longest flight of locks in Britain.

Among the regular customers of the narrow-boat trade, in later days, was Cadbury's. When they established their new works at Bournville in 1879, they deliberately chose a site on the Worcester and Birmingham Canal where they could build their extensive, canopy-covered wharves. There was a complex movement of raw material over the waterways network. Evaporated milk came from factories at Knighton on the

Some canal companies ran their own fleet of boats. These are Leeds and Liverpool wide boats unloading bales of cotton at Church Wharf, Accrington (The Lancashire Library: Hyndburn District)

Shropshire Union and from Frampton on the Gloucester and Sharpness. Solid blocks of chocolate were sent up to Knighton, where it was mixed with sugar and milk to make chocolate crumb which was then brought back to Bournville. At first, this busy trade was carried on in the company's own boats, the fleet which had the distinction of including the first boat with a Bolinder engine. But they also used other carriers, particularly Severn and Canal and FMC. Chocolate crumb was being brought by canal from Knighton as late as 1961, although it was reduced to single motors run by British Waterways. One vessel in particular, *Mendip*, continued on that same run right through from canal nationalisation to the end of the trade. Its steerer, Mr Atkins, inevitably earned himself the nickname 'Chocolate Charlie'.

After nationalisation, British Waterways proved to be, at best, somewhat reluctant narrow-boat carriers, and when Willow Wren took over the greatest part of the trade in 1963, there was many a sigh of relief among the BWB managers. Willow Wren had, in some ways, a more favourable climate in which to work. The old system of paying a complex of tolls was ended in favour of one standard licence fee, covering all the system run by British Waterways. Willow Wren leased the boats from BWB and then hired them out again to the individual boaters. The winter of 1962–3 had been desperately hard, and at least Willow Wren were not to be liable for wages during any subsequent long winter stoppages. It was to prove the last major effort of continuing the narrow-boat trade of the canals, and ultimately when they and Blue Line stopped trading, the end of the narrow-boat carrying story had effectively been written. But among all the famous names, with their impressive fleets, there was one group that had been there at the beginning and was still there at the end, the Number Ones, the owner boatmen.

Look at a modern pleasure boater, chugging along in a narrow boat, still recognisable from the lines of its hull as a descendant of the working boat and probably decorated with roses and castles, put on by transfer rather than paint, and what you are seeing is a deliberate exercise in nostalgia. We are probably all secretly thinking that just as the boats have derived from a long working tradition, so too we are following in the wake of the working boatmen. And the often hopelessly romanticised image we have before our eyes is of the Number Ones, the independents, the free spirits, the proud owners of proud craft, able to travel anywhere and everywhere in the canal world. It is an image that has little foundation in reality. The life of the Number Ones could be desperately hard: no salary in freeze-ups, no sick pay, no one else to pay repair bills or hand out cash when a new boat was needed. The horse or mule had priority over the family when the situation became very difficult. The family could always pull their belts in another notch, but without a working animal all income came to a stop. The freedom, too, was largely illusory. Often the Number Ones worked on a regular contract, tied to a particular run. The Skinners carried to Morris Radiators on the Oxford Canal for twenty years, while others spent their whole lives trundling up and down between the collieries grouped round Coventry and the paper mills above Rickmansworth. Such regular work was obviously welcome,

A handsome pair of Ovaltine boats, William *and* Enid *at Marsworth on the Grand Union in 1954* (Anthony Burton)

137

but much of the time the boats ran back empty and no load meant no pay. The romantic image of a painted boat gliding behind a gently lumbering horse has its truth. The Number Ones were slow to move from horse boat to motor boat: the Skinners never made the change. The reason was partly innate conservatism, a stubborn clinging to tradition; but far more it was a matter of cost. The motor boat was simply beyond their means, and that is the other side of the story: low pay, long hours and sometimes atrocious working conditions. Yet somehow we all still yearn for even a glimpse of those days and dream of a way of life that has left the cut. But when it came to the actual business of working on the canal, it made no difference whether you were part of a fleet of a hundred boats or whether the boat you were on and its single horse represented the sum total of your worldly goods. You were one of the boat people and you had far more in common with each other than with anyone in that other, wider community on the land.

138

9 LIFE ON THE BOATS

A former boatman, John Saxon, wrote in a song for the Mikron Theatre:

> They call me 'water Gypsy'
> They call be 'bargee'
> But they've got it wrong my friend,
> 'Cos I'm a boatie
> Yes I'm a boatie.

The song expresses something of the mutual suspicion and incomprehension that divided the boat families from the rest of the community through which they passed. It was so in the days when the canals were just beginning. A German tourist, Charles P. Moritz, had this encounter in 1782:

> At last I came to another inn, where there was written on the sign: 'The Navigation Inn', because it is the depot, or store-house, of the colliers of the Trent.
>
> A rougher or ruder kind of people I never saw than these colliers, whom I here met assembled in the kitchen, and in whose company I was obliged to spend the evening.
>
> Their language, their dress, their manners, were all of them singularly vulgar and disagreeable; and their expressions still more so; for they hardly spoke a word without an oath, and thus cursing, quarrelling, drinking, singing, and fighting, they seemed to be pleased, and to enjoy the evening.

Having painted a picture of terrifying villainy, he continued: 'I must do them the justice to add, that none of them, however, at all molested me. On the contrary, every one again and again drank my health.' Over a hundred years later the canals were still seen by many as a scene of filth and human degradation. Arnold Bennett in his novel *Clayhanger* paints this picture of the Trent and Mersey in 1872:

> Towards the bridge from the north came a long narrow canal-boat roofed with tarpaulin; and towards the bridge from the south came a similar craft, sluggishly creeping. The towing-path was a morass of sticky brown mud, for in the way of rain that year was breaking the records of a century and a half. Thirty yards in front of each boat an unhappy skeleton of a horse floundered its best in the quagmire. The honest endeavour of one of the animals received a

frequent tonic from a bare-legged girl of seven who heartily curled a whip about its crooked large-jointed legs. The ragged and filthy child danced in the rich mud round the horse's flanks with the simple joy of one who had been rewarded for good behaviour by the unrestricted use of a whip for the first time.

It is not an agreeable portrait, nor were most of the other descriptions of canal life that were written until very recently. But what both the eighteenth-century German traveller and the twentieth-century English novelist have in common is that they viewed the boating community from the outside and were quite content to do so. In trying to see the pattern of life of boat people in the past, one has to rely on fragmentary pieces of evidence. But happily what one finds suggests a certain continuity in both the way of life and the way of working of the boating families – and neither has yet slipped beyond the reach of living memory.

The further one goes back in time, the vaguer the pattern becomes. There is no reason to think, however, that in the early years which saw the canals as extensions of river navigations, boating on the canal was other than a straightforward development from the earlier age. But as the canal system spread and the numbers of boats steadily increased, so more and more people began to be drawn to the waterways. Who were they? Where did they come from? What kind of people were they and what sort of life did they lead? The answers remain infuriatingly elusive. Harry Hanson in his detailed study *The Canal Boatmen 1760–1914* has done a great deal to dispel one popular theory. By carefully studying canal registers he has shown that there is very little evidence to support the notion of water gypsies, for covering an area from Paddington to Wigan he found few gypsy names, and some of those, such as the Jones and the Roberts, are common enough names anyway. He suggests that many boatmen came from the land much as the carters did and there is a certain amount of evidence to support that view. Others may have been

Three views of boatwomen. The studio photograph (below right) taken around 1910 shows the traditional dress with its big bonnet and full length skirt and apron. (British Waterways Board). A boatwoman at work (left) in similar costume, handling the tow line on a heavily laden boat on the Coventry Canal (Miss M. E. Waine) This photograph, taken in 1956 at Juxon Street wharf, Oxford (below left) shows the less romantic side of the boatwoman's life. Rose Skinner is shovelling coal into Jean Humphries' barrow (Oxfordshire County Newspapers)

navvies, recruited during construction when the company used boats to help shift spoil from the workings and to carry stone and brick. It seems just as likely that by the 1790s, canal companies were employing men to steer boats just as they employed them to man the locks or load the cargo. The men, in turn, employed lads to lead the horses.

In those early years, the boatman's life was little different from that of others who travelled long distances, the carters and drovers. When change came it was success that brought it. The burgeoning industrial society was demanding more and more raw material, and the demand for coal seemed inexhaustible. Villages were growing into towns and towns into cities, and everywhere there was a call for more goods. The canal world began to divide between the big, successful carriers running their fly-boat services and the steady stream of slow, regular boats

A Child's Life

Nell Cartwright began her boating days before World War I, and from the very first she fell in love with the horses. As soon as she was entrusted with leading the animal, she was up on its back and riding, and that for her remained the brightest memory of her early days. Her working day began at four or five in the morning, when the kettle was put on the stove and she set off for the locks. By the time the boat arrived, the kettle had boiled and the tea was made. After that, it was the steady plod of the horse and the regular interruption of the locks. She was unusual in that hers was not a boating family; she was eight years old when her family took to the water and her working life began in earnest. The work was hard and occasionally frightening. She remembers as a thirteen-year-old having to lead the horse over Braunston tunnel at 1am because they were due to hitch up to an FMC steamer at first light. She was cold and terrified, but the horse kept nuzzling against her. 'I thought to myself, "He's telling me not to be afraid", and when I got to the end of the tunnel, I was as brave as brave.' As always, it was the life of the horses that provided the greatest reward, although she also looked back on those few happy days when she and the other children had time off to make up their own games. Food was plain but plentiful and sweet tinned milk in the tea kept her going through the day, while family meals tended to be dominated by 'the three Bs' – bacon, beef and beer. For all this hard work which, as she grew older, included legging the tunnels with her brother, she received no pay. Her brother was paid cash and she received pocket money, a farthing a fortnight, a coin which at decimalisation was worth one tenth of the new penny. She worked in this way until she was eighteen, when after ten years she was finally paid, slightly less than £1 a fortnight.

carrying the bulk supplies. Slow or fast, however, the call was for more boats and for boats that would travel on ever-longer journeys. The man and the boy out for a short trip began to disappear everywhere except in the special world of the day boats that plied the complex network of the Birmingham canals. Recruitment might still be on a local basis, but the way of life was changing very rapidly.

When George Borrow toured Wales in 1854 he started his travels in Llangollen where he took time to talk to a boatman loading slate on the canal. He told Borrow that they were all local men on the boats, but they travelled long distances, often as far as Paddington, and that they and their families all lived in back cabins. Interestingly, although he said that most of the boatmen could read, they could only read in English despite the fact that they all spoke in Welsh. So on the Llangollen Canal at least the boating family had arrived. One result of this gradual movement of families on to boats was that they tended more and more to form a closed community. Children helped with the work as soon as they were old enough and it seemed the most natural progression that they should continue in the life to which they were born. As families began to grow up, the older boys would start looking for a chance to take boats of their own, and the families were equally relieved to gain a little extra space. The girls were generally less fortunate than the boys.

The new tradition of family boating meant that there was no longer any need to recruit outsiders, for the boat families provided the new boaters from within their own ranks. There was, however, always more work for boys than girls, simply because some types of boating remained exclusive male preserves. Fly boats used a male-only crew and at a later date the steamers also barred women. One result was that in large families some of the girls would be sent off into service, although not all stayed on the land and many found a way of returning to boats. The change had another effect, for contacts between the boat families and the rest of the community became less and less frequent, and as they moved further apart, inevitably, suspicions developed. The boaters were outsiders, dirty, not to be trusted, and were probably dangerous as well. The boaters' reputation reached its nadir in 1839 with the murder of Christina Collins. She had paid Pickford's to take her from Preston Brook to join her husband at Liverpool. She was the only passenger in the care of three fly boatmen. Along the way she was raped, murdered and her body left in the canal. Opinion was understandably outraged, not merely by the act itself, but by the fact that this could happen to an innocent passenger travelling on a public canal in the care of one of the most respected of carrying companies. It confirmed all the worst suspicions of the community at large. The press proclaimed loudly that the three men responsible were typical of their class. As one defender of the boat people as a whole wrote, one would imagine from the press reports

that the inland watermen of England, without exception, were individually addicted to murder, lust and rapine; that they were never to be approached but with feelings of horror and never to have anything entrusted to their care but with a certainty of being plundered.

What was the reality?

There seems to be a strong similarity to the case of the canal navvy. A sensational murder receives wide publicity, while the quiet everyday working receives none, just as the navvy riots coloured the view of all navvy life. No one would pretend that the canal boatmen were especially saintly characters. They led a hard, rough life. Their general language was not that of a Sunday school outing, the pub was the one meeting place where families and friends could get together, and it is not entirely unknown for those who go to pubs to take the occasional drink. And there was a steady thread of violence that ran through the life right to the end, although it seldom involved more than a fist fight. The men might be the best of friends in the pub, but once outside and at work it was everyone for himself. Few looked for a fight, but if it came to it you could not back down and keep your self-respect. It was time that counted on a canal, and the boatman who was too timid to claim his rights would find himself forever at the back of the queue. Occasionally there was another solution to that problem. One rather undersize and not notably brave boatmen had a rough, tough, brawny wife who could more than hold her own against any opposition. As in many communities, there were always a few who were fighting men, proud of their prowess, and the great majority who simply stayed out of trouble.

The other charge laid against the boat families was dishonesty. There was some pilfering, no doubt, especially where goods were unloaded on to open wharves to await trans-shipment, but there is little evidence of whole-sale theft. However, one early writer, Thomas Boyle, in a book mainly concerned with railway competition *Hope for the Canal!* (1848) wrote:

> The steerers with their assistants pursue a systematic course of pillage of the goods committed to their charge, and such is the extent of the depradations carried on upon wines, groceries, provisions, &c. that there is much reason to suspect the families of such persons, as nearly, if not altogether supported in this way.

One form of 'theft' to which boatmen were quite willing to admit was poaching, but that had always been a source of contention between landowners and countrymen. The Game Act of 1831 set up heavy fines for anyone caught poaching in daylight, while the night-time poacher was automatically either imprisoned or transported. The penalties made no sense to country people, who could not understand how a free-running hare or rabbit could become a landowner's property as soon as it crossed into one of his fields any more than they could see how he could own a pigeon that happened to find a temporary roost among his trees. In this, the boatmen were no different from the rest. One notably able boatman had been known to go out with twelve snares and come back in the morning with eleven rabbits. And you would have been hard pressed to find anyone on the boats who thought of him as a thief. In spite of regulations to the contrary, it was by no means unknown for a shotgun to be kept on board and fishing was always considered open to all. Anything that could go in the pot did so – even moorhens were netted, swept out of the water by passing boatmen.

The painted Buckby can is now seen as a largely ornamental object, but in the working days it held the boaters' drinking water. Charlie Carter is seen filling his can at Hawkesbury Junction, known to the boatmen as Sutton Stop (British Waterways Board)

143

There was also a certain casualness about private property. One boatman remarked that his garden stretched from London to Birmingham, and he freely admitted to lifting the occasional potato. A boatman on the Bournville run said it was common practice to exchange a portion of chocolate crumb from the cargo for a few apples from a Worcestershire orchard, and noted that the occasional block of salt might find its way to a farmer who had just killed a pig – and the boatman would expect to have some tasty cured ham on a later trip. None of this, however, can really qualify as a major crime-wave. The principal charges laid against the boatmen were that their language was not that of polite society, they were not averse to occasional brawling, and that, on the rare occasions when they had time off, they were liable to spend it in the pub – to all of which the boat people would cheerfully have pleaded guilty. But to the prim Victorian middle class, this amounted to an indictment of wickedness. The reformer George Smith wrote of them in his famous book *Our Canal Population* (1878):

> Utterly ignorant as a large proportion of them undoubtedly are, of all religious knowledge, wholly without instruction, coarse and brutal in manner and entirely given up to the vilest debauchery and the grossest passions, can we expect, without extraneous assistance, that the children of such parents are ever likely to grow into anything better?

Smith was a zealot, much given to gross exaggeration in the cause to which he devoted so much passion – the improvement of the life of the canal children. He argued that they were being brought up in deplorably overcrowded conditions, which was undeniably true. The family on a single boat, confined to a minute area, could manage to sleep only by

Boatmen were either on reduced pay or no pay when the canal froze. Sometimes, as with this Birmingham group of 1895, they were reduced to collecting on the streets with a boat on a cart, and a somewhat chilly boatman packed round with ice (British Waterways Board)

using a Chinese puzzle-box of beds, slotted in wherever there was space, so that a double bed was opened out across the width of the cabin, with a second bunk down the side, while the cabin table was folded up to serve as a cupboard door. Children shared this confined space with their parents, which Smith regarded as an open invitation to immorality which, at its best, exposed the children to sights they could have been spared and at worst laid them open to abuse. But one has to be wary of Smith's claims. He stated as bald fact that two-thirds of the boat people were unmarried and their children illegitimate. He provided no real evidence to support the statement, and there is ample evidence to show that it was untrue. His claims of indecency might seem irrefutable by modern standards, but were they any worse than the conditions in the industrial slums? The boat people were often, as he claimed, unhealthy – their mortality rate was comparatively high – but they still compared favourably with many industrial workers. It should be remembered that in the Victorian age a Sheffield fork grinder could consider himself lucky if his dust-choked lungs lasted him much beyond his thirtieth birthday. The boat people lived a life where sanitation standards were scarcely of the highest: water was as liable to come from the cut as from a tap, and the public lavatory ran the full length of the canal in the shape of the tow-path hedge. But Smith began a movement which was to lead to inspection of boats for overcrowding and education for the boat children.

The first law empowered local authorities to inspect boats to check for disease risks and to look at education records. This proved too much for *The Times*, which declared: 'The floating home of the "bargee" is to be invaded. Its privacy is attacked. Its liberty appears doomed to pass away . . . with a display of inquisitorial powers such as was never before dreamt of.' But Smith wrote in his diary 'Thank God! Thank God! Oh, how wonderful I feel.' The act, in fact, brought neither the benefits expected by Smith nor the calamities foretold by *The Times*. The local authorities scarcely bothered to attempt any inspections, so a new act was passed in 1884 setting up a canal inspectorate. The first man in charge, John Brydone, was a successful choice. His reports show an admirable fairness and he preferred persuasion to the harsh enactment of a law. He deserved and earned the respect and affection of the boating community. But how effective was legislation in improving the fate of the boat children?

The two principal aims were to reduce overcrowding and to ensure at least a minimum education for the children. The problem with enforcing the laws on overcrowding lay in keeping track of a constantly shifting population, which, when it did stop long enough to be counted, was a hopeless intermingling of scores of families from scores of boats. An inspector visiting a crowded boat would be told that little Jimmy was from the *Lily* and young Harriet was Bill and Bess's girl from Braunston. The personnel of a boat might change at any time. A boatman with a large family might hire out the children to another family who were short of hands, and then fetch them back again if needed. But the worst excesses were stopped and a check was kept on cleanliness – not that this was necessary on many boats. The families prided themselves on the conditions in which the boats were kept. The cabins were all highly

George Smith of Coalville (1831–95)

George Smith the philanthropist was born at Tunstall in the Potteries in 1831. His father was a brickmaker, and at the age of nine the boy was working up to thirteen hours a day, carrying heavy loads of clay and bricks on his head. He somehow still found time to educate himself and soon rose to manage a large brick and tile works. He discovered important clay deposits at Coalville in Leicestershire, but unfortunately allowed others to profit from his find. Nevertheless, he did move there to become manager of a large concern. But he had never forgotten the hardships of his own childhood and he became a vigorous campaigner for the rights of the brickworkers, particularly the children. His efforts received mixed rewards. In 1871 parliament passed an act allowing inspection of brickworks to check on the working conditions of children and women. Smith received a purse of sovereigns and the plaudits of other philanthropists. The brickmakers were less enthusiastic: Smith was sacked.

For the rest of his life, George Smith was to work for children's welfare. In 1873 he began looking at the life of the boat children, and in 1875 he published his famous book *Our Canal Population*. Largely due to his efforts, parliament passed acts in 1878 and 1884 in an attempt to regulate the conditions on board boats and to ensure some education for the children. But by the time the second act was passed, Smith was already looking elsewhere, this time to gypsy children. Throughout this period he himself was often desperately poor and it was only in 1885 when he received a royal bounty in recognition of his work that he could live in anything approaching comfort. He was not to enjoy it for long: he died in 1895.

decorated. Lace plates with perforations threaded with ribbon were much favoured. The stove had to be kept blacked and all the brass was polished daily. And the ropework from the fender at the front to the horse's tail at the stern of the butty had to be kept white, not by blancoing but by scrubbing. The cabins were true homes and families were very particular who was invited in, and for an outsider to be invited aboard was a rare privilege. Even boat owners had to wait for an invitation from their employees. That everything was so immaculate is a minor miracle. It was thanks to the boatwomen who somehow fitted it in with every other chore. One old boatman recalled the days when the family worked a pair of boats. Mother took the first boat, the easier of the pair to steer. The first job was to make a mug of cocoa which was put on the tow-path at a bridge hole and picked up by the second boat. Other meals and the endless cups of strong tea were dealt with in the same way, Mother hopping up and down between stove and tiller. She managed also to knit sweaters while standing at the tiller, kept the boat clean and when she had a chance took her tub and washboard out on to the tow-path for the family wash-day. Tring summit was a favourite laundry spot on the Grand Union because of its clear water. Few boatmen would disagree with the statement that the women had the harder role, but nor did they question that this should be so. As one said: 'If you told the wife to jump, she jumped – even when she knew she was going to finish up in the reeds.'

This was the life the children were raised to, standing on a stool at the tiller until they were tall enough to reach it. There was little time for schooling. The essential thing was to get a mark in your attendance book. The education officer counted up the marks and, if satisfied, stamped the book. The requirements were scarcely onerous – one mark a week was considered sufficient. The mark, however, only indicated that the child had gone to school. A boy might go to school at nine in the morning and half an hour later his father would be at the door, announcing that the boat was leaving – and there are boat people alive today who received just such an education. Even when they went to school, there was no guarantee that they would learn anything. Never staying anywhere for long, never part of a settled classroom routine, and inevitably way behind their contemporaries who attended school regularly, the boat children were liable to be dumped at the back of the room with a picture book to keep them quiet. A partial solution came when special schools were set up in the 1920s at places such as Brentford where boats often lay up for loading and unloading and waiting between cargoes.

A committee of churchmen established the canal boatman's institute, with its floating school. *The Times* reported on the work in 1930:

> Considering the difficulties, the attainments of the children are reasonably good . . . but it is impossible that they should be equal to those of children of the same age in regular attendance at schools. The chief difficulty is reading; once that is mastered, it becomes possible to arrange for individual work and private study to be done on the boat.

Sadly, in many cases, that first essential step was never taken. Many boat people remained virtually illiterate and resented it. They felt, probably justifiably, that it made it easier for the educated to take advantage of them. One is amazed by the heroic efforts that went into the laborious process of self-help. One old lady told how she had picked up her 'letters' by studying the markings on passing railway trucks. She had taught herself to read, but still found it difficult. That did not prevent her from having a fierce pride in her accomplishments. She would slowly pick out a word, letter by letter, until she had it puzzled out, a process which had some curious results. Her answers were not always accurate by generally agreed standards, but to her they were gospel – for example, if the name over a tunnel said 'Harecastle' and she read it as 'Hardcastle', then Hardcastle it remained and nothing would convince her that she was wrong. And one gets a glimpse of the attempts made at phonetic spelling from this note to a canal company from a boatman's wife, when she explained that he was ill but she could cope in his absence: 'Thay tacken im a way on or count of is stumuck no ned to worey arbout yor

A Boatwoman Remembers

And if I had my choice again and I could go back over those years – I have had a very hard life and a bad one but I would do it all again exactly the same as I had it with the horses, the boats the loading – I have loaded and emptied 25 tons of corned beef, I have emptied 31 tons of spelter, I have done 25 tons of timbers – to me work was nothing, I couldn't care less, I don't even today.

But I liked it and I liked my horse and I liked the boat as it was. When they brought the noisy motors out I didn't like that at all. They frightened me because I don't think it was so peaceful and there was no beauty. I mean you look along the boat as it was going and you see that horse just walking along that road and the hedges and trees and everthing going by. No one could ask for better than that.

What I would like to see now – before I leave this world – I would like to see all those horses come back and the place come back as it was as I knew it.

(Nell Cartwright, 1977)

A special school was established on a converted boat at Brentford for the boat children. Their education had to be snatched during the brief periods when the boats were tied up at the depot (British Waterways Board)

Traditional Dress

By the end of the nineteenth century, the boatman and the boatwoman were as distinctive in their dress as the narrow boat was in its decoration. In the older style of dress, which boatmen now talk of as being of their father's generation, the men wore cord trousers, or occasionally blue velour with drop fronts, like a sailor's. They had 36in (91cm) bottoms with nine rows of stitches, and were gathered below the knee by 'yorks' – bands fastened by brass buckles. No self-respecting boatman would use string. Braces were embroidered and were usually joined by a belt – not so much used to hold up the trousers as to provide a handy lodging place for the windlass – always tucked at the back of the belt, out of the way. 'Up-country' boatmen, those from north of Birmingham, favoured clogs, while the southerners preferred boots. The shirt was generally collarless, with a scarf at the neck and a flat cap topped the outfit, although the trilby later came into favour. Even as late as the 1930s, a boatman might still wear his 'full rig', a carefully assembled outfit. One boatman had his shoes – slightly high-heeled – specially made. His trousers were white cord and above them he wore a double-breasted waistcoat. His shirt was hand-made by a boatwoman and his stockings were hand-knitted. The fancy and colourful belt of webbing and leather came from a saddlemaker, while a cousin provided the braces which were decorated with brass hearts and diamonds. He cut a grand figure.

The boatwomen were even more distinctive. At the end of the last century, they wore ankle-length skirts, often topped by ornate blouses and a shawl over the blouse. A long apron was also frequently worn. In this respect they were little different from other working women of the day, but what really set them apart

continued on page 149

Boats.' (They [have] taken him away on account of his stomach. No need to worry about your boats.)

The life of the boat children was neither so bleak as George Smith painted it, nor so rosy as some romantic commentators suggested. It was also not without its dangers. A moving boat has its obvious hazards and to that had to be added the other perils that inevitably go with small children and moving machinery. Hands and limbs could all too easily be crushed between boat and lock side, and even a good swimmer could drown in the swirling waters of a lock. There were tragedies, yet a surprisingly large number of children seemed to have charmed lives, falling in the water time and time again and emerging unscathed.

There were times when certain precautions were taken. When Noel and Rene James reflected on their own and their children's lives, they remembered that although the extra money for loading coal was always welcomed, the baby had to be fastened by reins to the side of the boat and at the end of the day the baby was as black as the coal. On the move, the children were mostly left to their own devices and they seemed to be constantly getting tangled in tow lines and tripping over things. Rene said she once fell in three times in one day and that was how she learned to swim: 'You knew when you went in, you had to get out.' Noel had been sent once on an errand to the blacksmith's, and he returned riding his bicycle along the coping stones and fell in the river. His mother did not bother to stop the boat, but leaned over as the boat passed him and hauled him out by the hair. But tunnels were a different matter. The children were sent down to the butty cabin and told to stay there. 'Let's come out mam, let's come out mam – and mam kicked us back in.'

The principal memories of most boat people looking back on their own childhoods is of a life of hard work – one that was not resented and often remembered with real pleasure, but none the less hard for all that. Danny Jinks was born in the back cabin of a narrow boat in 1899. There were no midwives for the boatwomen, just help from each other. After a few days' rest, a new mother would return to work. However, not everyone was as stalwart as one boatwoman who was starting to work up a flight of locks. She was still jumping down from the lockside into the boat at the bottom lock, but had had the baby by the time they reached the top. By the time Danny Jinks was ten he was helping his uncle to leg through the narrow, low hole of the old Harecastle tunnel. Busy times were the worst. If boats were using the locks at the north end, the flow of water would suck the boat into the tunnel. It was all leggers could do, straining every muscle, to keep the boat from going backwards. As soon as the flow had abated, they could carry on again with their slow, dark progress. And this at ten years old.

When things went wrong in the boating community they tended to turn first to their own resources: often there were few other resources to which they could turn. Throughout the first century of boating there was little interest shown by the rest of Britain in the floating community that moved among them. Denunciations of drunkenness and violence were heard from the pulpit, but the church did nothing to provide any alternative to the pub. Charitable individuals occasionally looked to the canals. Henry Ward, an Oxford coal merchant, established a floating chapel at Hythe Bridge, Oxford, for the use of the boat people, and weekday classes were held for the children. When the chapel sank in the 1860s a permanent one was built, but such concern was rare. A change took place in 1851 when the Seamen's Society joined with the Inland Navigation Society to form the Seamen and Boatmen's Friend Society. This missionary group became very strong by the end of the century, setting up centres throughout the country. Their prime aim may have been to bring Christianity to a notoriously irreligious group, but they had the sense and compassion to realise that preaching alone was not enough. The pub provided drink, but it also provided a place where people could meet friends, chat, hear the news and gossip and relax a little after the hard work of the day. The society set out to provide rest rooms as alternatives to the bar. They were remarkably successful. This is not to say that the boatman became overnight a sober, God-fearing, evangelical Christian, but the simple fact of having an alternative where, to take just one example, an illiterate boatman could have a letter written meant that he spent much less time in the pub. And there was an intangible benefit, for the boat people found in the society missionaries a group from outside their own world who treated them with respect. Over the years, other groups set about helping the boating community. The Salvation Army ran a pair of boats in the Midlands. There was inevitably a certain cynicism in the attitude to such organisations: one boatman reckoned it was worth attending a couple of 'Sally Army' rallies if it meant new clothes for his children. There was, however, a genuine respect for Mr Chapman of the Boatman's Institute. But no one did more to win and hold the affection of the many boaters who travelled the Grand Union Canal than did Sister Mary Ward of Stoke Bruerne. She had the advantage of knowing the families, for her father spun ropes for the boat people and very good ropes they were considered to be, too. Susan Woolfitt in her account of boating during World War II described her surgery:

> Everything seemed to be white, the chairs were draped in it, and the muslin curtains were tied up with bandages . . . The boat people trust her implicitly. I have often heard them say: 'I'll ask the nurse when we get to Stoke. She'll know, she'll tell me what to do.' One old boatman said, quite simply, 'She saved my life.'

Other groups of workers found mutual help by setting up friendly societies, which later developed into trade unions. The scattered, constantly shifting boat population never had sufficient time together to form organisations, and established unions found it equally difficult to bring the canals under their influence. It was said that the closed shop was as important as anything in getting boatmen into the union. The dockers at places like Limehouse would not load or unload boats unless the skipper had a union card, but in time the canal people, men and women, found that the union brought them real advantages. The trial of strength of the 1923 strike showed that the boaters did have power, and over the next few years there were tangible advances. It was not just a question of wages, although the union did manage to keep rates up in

continued from page 148

were the bonnets. These had stiff brims above which rose an elaborate confection of tucks and gathers, and a long 'curtain' hung down the back to protect the neck from the sun. Originally the bonnets were white or patterned, but at the death of Queen Victoria, the boatwomen joined the rest of the nation and went into mourning black. They never really came out of it and boatwomen could still be seen in this black mourning until as late as the 1930s.

the miserable years of the Depression, but equally important were other benefits and the recognition of the special nature of canal work. So payment was made for waiting time and for those periods when, perhaps due to a canal stoppage, the boats could not get through. And there was a formal recognition of the work done by the boatwomen. The greatest triumph, however, came in 1943 with the negotiation of a minimum wage for the boaties. However reluctantly some may have joined the TGWU in the first place, many a boat family lived to be grateful for the union's efforts.

One of the problems facing boaties in their relationship with the rest of the world lay with the lack of recognition of the skills involved in their work, and this lack of recognition has never quite died away. How often have we heard pleasure boaters boast of their skills at handling boats or working locks and, to be honest, how many times have we patted ourselves on the back for a job well done? But it is a delusion to believe that we have anything like the skill of the working boatmen, and it is even more illusory to believe that we travel the canal in anything like the same way. It is not just a matter of hard labour and long hours, but of a whole different way of working. So let us take a look at the working life, first of the horse-boat crew and then of the motor boat.

To run a horse boat you need a horse, and it was not only the Number Ones who had to provide their own animals. Some companies made the boatmen buy their own horses on a simple hire-purchase scheme, and it was by no means unknown for a horse to die before the debt was repaid, leaving the unfortunate boatman with double payments when he bought a replacement. There were a number of places where boatmen bought horses and mules, and much trading took place with gypsy horse dealers. Horses were also acquired from less likely sources. Caggy Stevens bought a horse that had been pensioned off from a milk float, but the most famous of all was an FMC horse known as 'Bonnie' which had worked in the circus and could always be relied on for a display of tricks outside the pub door. Having bought a horse, the boatman might have to break it in and would certainly have to train it up to the special requirements of canal travel.

There were many stories over the years of mistreatment of horses, and

One of the most famous characters on the canals was Sister Mary Ward who looked after generations of boating families. Here she is seen in her Stoke Bruerne clinic in the 1950s (British Waterways Board)

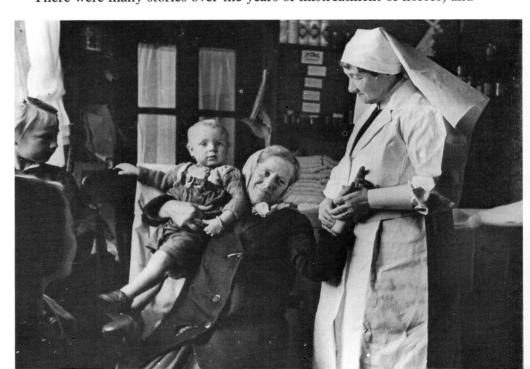

there is no doubt that it did take place. The animals were expected to work extremely long hours and they were seldom beasts of the best quality in the first place. But for many boatmen, the horse was an important investment and needed proper attention. The family might grow hungry in hard times, but never the horse. Boatmen even went so far in really icy weather as to rub their own hands in the water bucket so that the water was not too cold for the animal to drink.

At the start of the day, the horse was harnessed up. The actual harness is not dissimilar to that of the cart-horse, except that instead of the shaft on either side of the animal there was a single tow-rope dragging behind. So traces, laced with beads to prevent chafing of the horse's flanks, led back from the collar to a spreader, a bar with the tow-rope attached in the centre. Now the horse was ready for work, and when the word came to start, it leaned into its collar to take the strain, but once under way it could virtually be left to its own devices, with the occasional addition of a pair of boots tied to the tow-rope to convince it there really was a human being close at hand. When another horse boat was met, the vessel on the outside had to drop the tow-rope to let the other horse step over and snatch it up again quickly to keep the boat under way. The same thing had to be done to allow the inside boat to float across the line.

Steady progress was simple, but locks required good management of horse and boat. The horse was stopped at the lockside, and as the boat floated in under its own momentum, the boatman had to whip a line around a bollard to bring it to a halt before it crashed into the lock gate at the far end. Tunnels presented different problems. Where there was no tow-path, the horse was led over the top, and the horse boat was either legged through or, in later days, taken through by tug. It was also not uncommon for a motor boat to give a tow. Often the traffic through the tunnel was surprisingly heavy. Just taking one random week, for August 1928, there were 169 boats hauled by tug through Blisworth tunnel. The tugs ran a regular service starting at 5am and the last left at 6.30pm. Time for the trip varied from half an hour for an empty tug to an hour for a tow of six narrow boats. But even where there was a tow-path, the horses were often frightened and it was a common practice to tow on a very short line so that the headlamp on the boat lit the horse's way.

Travel by motor boat was at once simpler and more complex. It was simpler because of the greater flexibility of use: the motor went straight through a tunnel and it could charge up to a lock at full tilt and then be halted by reversing the engine. It was more complex because the motor itself demanded the skills of a good mechanic to keep it running well. Boatmen were notoriously proud of their abilities, and secretive about their way of working. Alex Purcell always said that he was ready to repair anyone's engine, but no one could come near the engine-room while he was doing so. Even official company fitters needed permission to go into the engine-room. And the engines themselves were by no means straightforward. On the early Bolinders, the day started with warming up the hot bulb and there were some boatmen who believed – quite erroneously – that the engine worked best when the fuel overflowed to send flames shooting up the chimney. The later Nationals were a little easier, but it was still hard work to crank up the starter and engage the engine. The main differences, however, came from the complications of the working pair – the motor and the dumb butty – as each required different handling techniques. Even what might seem to be the most obvious work, a straightforward tow had its complexities. Boats were run on different lengths of line, depending on whether they were working long pounds or heavily locked sections, and there were even different lengths of line for uphill and downhill working. On a canal such as the Grand Union with wide locks able to take two boats side by side, the aim was, as always, to move as quickly and as efficiently as possible, ideally using a three-person team.

The first person in the team was the lock wheeler who went ahead to set the locks; with the horse boat someone always had to be ahead with the horse anyway. The motor boat would then approach the open lock, go straight in and stop by reversing the engine. The butty was then cast off to nose into the gap beside the motor. If the lock wheeler had not moved ahead, a line could be thrown ashore and the butty stopped. More commonly, a heavy rope or strap was kept near the stern and used in conjunction with a bollard. Coming into a full lock, heading downhill, the most elegant solution was to pass a line around the hand-rail on the gate and back to the stern cleat so that the butty not only stopped but pulled the gate closed at the same time. To go out as efficiently as possible, both boats passed lines with slip knots up to the front gates, so that the reversing of the engine and the natural falling back of the butty pulled the gates open. As the boats moved forward, so the lines slipped free. No time was taken to close gates after boats for the good reason that it was never done. Closing gates took up time, and the steerers preferred the 50–50 chance of a lock being ready set to the certainty of it never being ready at all. Some time, however, had to be used in adjusting and handling the tow-line, although that could be minimised by the use of running blocks. In effect, the line was passed from the butty's towing mast through a series of blocks on the top planks to the stern. This gave the butty steerer direct control of the line, but it needed skilful handling to prevent the coiled rope from becoming tangled or whipping out and injuring the steerer.

Just as there was a quick way to take a pair down the locks, so there were short cuts in locking up. And where boats were travelling empty, they could be breasted up, fastened side by side and handled as a single unit. Loaded boats were too heavy to be worked in this way. Narrow locks presented different problems and were harder work. When the butty was cast off, it simply floated up to nose against the lock gates and then had to be manhandled into position. But for every manoeuvre, the boatman had his own methods of easing the journey and cutting the time.

Moving the boats was only a part of the boater's life: work did not stop when the boat stopped. For the horse boater, there was the animal to feed, groom and bed down for the night. For the women, there were the household chores of washing, cooking and the perpetual polishing. At the end of a trip there was cargo to load or unload, and often there was the long and tedious job of cleaning out the hold. If foodstuffs were being picked up, then the hold had to be scrubbed until it was spotless and there were some cargoes which were always dreaded. Wheat was one of the worst: the dust and the chaff got into everything, and if every last scrap was not cleared out after a trip, the family would soon know it for wheat, when it starts to rot, produces an abominable smell.

If all this sounds like a line of unremitting hard work, then it was. Holidays were virtually unknown until the 1940s, and where today we go away for a break, the boat families mostly enjoyed the luxury of not going anywhere at all for a change. But for most of the two centuries of the working boats, endless hard toil was the fate of most of the population. Unlike the other workers of the Industrial Revolution whose lives were spent in the often dark and deafening world of mill and factory, where the bell tolling in its tower sounded the start and finish of the working day, the boaters had the open air, the constantly changing scenery and, to a very large extent, freedom to control their own affairs. Attitudes change, and in an increasingly organised mechanical and impersonal world, there seems to be an aura of romance surrounding the boats and the people to whom they were home. Perhaps our sympathy and interest has come a little late. So here is a last thought from an old working boatman, who remembered the time when 'respectable citizens' spat on him from bridges – until he took to leaving his shotgun in view on the cabin top: 'Those days then, which is not very long ago, we was bums; now, what are we now, we're marvellous, we're part of the history.'

Painted Boats

Nobody seems quite certain when or how the traditional roses and castles of narrow-boat decoration appeared. Robertson's *Life on the Upper Thames* of 1875 shows a decorated cabin side, but earlier pictures all show boats plain and adorned with nothing but the owner's name and the name of the craft. The most popular theory is that decoration increased as more and more boating families left the land to live permanently on the water. It is all very well working on 'Smith's Canal Carriers' boat 'The Swan', but just as the owners of No 2 Acacia Avenue like to think their house is quite different from No 4 so the family on The Swan wanted to distinguish their boat as their home and different from Smith's other boat 'The Kingfisher'. We all decorate our homes because we find decoration gives personality and a sense of ownership. But at the same time, few of us venture anything very startlingly different from what our neighbours are doing: we follow the accepted fashions and conventions of our age. The boat people were no different, and they developed their own unique style of decoration.

It has been argued that the roses and castles of canal-boat painting have a gypsy origin, either because the boat people were themselves of gypsy families or because they copied designs from gypsy waggons and caravans. Certainly the castles would look rather more at home in Ruritania than beside an English canal, but it is also a design admirably suited to small panels. Only a few brush strokes are needed to convey a romantic, turreted castle, usually portrayed near water, and roses were also produced by a few deft strokes. Altogether, there were three dominant styles of decoration: the castles in their romantic scenery, painted on doors and cabin panels; the flowers – by no means limited to roses – appeared in many different parts of the boat, embellishing names, for example, and decorating all kinds of ware from the water bucket to a simple stool; and finally there were geometrical designs, such as lozenges and stars, used on the side of the boat and bold, sweeping patterns on the outside of cabin doors. Within this broad canvas an infinite variety of changes was possible. Different canal companies favoured different patterns, and individual painters each had their own very personal style. An expert can as easily differentiate between a Frank Jones daisy and a Jess Owen daisy as a visitor to an art gallery can tell apart a Constable from a Turner. But the canal narrow boat was not, and was not intended to be, a floating gallery for folk art. It was a cheerful home on the move.

This is a superb example of canal
art at its finest – and Barlow's boats
were always noted for the quality of
the decoration. All the traditional
features can be seen. The rudder is
decorated by a simple roundel and
topped with elaborate rope work.
The octagonal tiller has two
alternating colours. The shadow
lettering for the boat's name and the
owner's name is particularly fine.
At the stern of the boat between the
boat name and the rudder post, one
can just see a small painted anchor,
very much an essential part of the
scheme. At the other end of the
name is an equally traditional
diamond pattern. The cabin is
decorated with roses and castles and
roses appear again on the Buckby
can on the cabin roof (Michael E.
Ware)

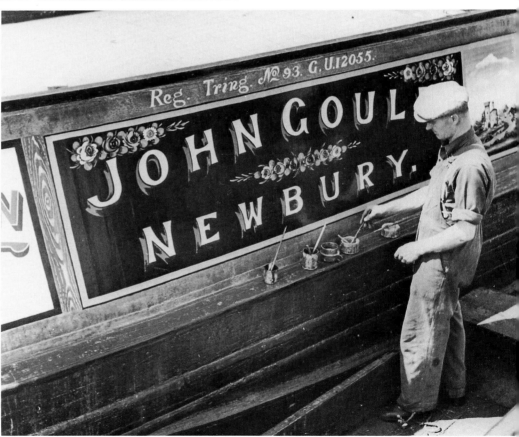

Frank Jones painting John Gould's
motor boat Colin at Leighton
Buzzard. The boat is also shown
with the butty Iris on pp204 (British
Waterways Board)

10 THE YEARS OF DECLINE

Had you been standing on the Glamorganshire Canal wharf at Abercynon on 13 February 1804, you would have been given a glimpse of the future, and had you been financially astute, you might well have sold your canal shares, for coming towards you would have been a rattling, shaking, puffing and smoking monster, dragging a line of wagons along the little tramway that ran down from the ironworks at Merthyr Tydfil. Richard Trevithick's steam locomotive was having its first run and the railway age was being born – well, almost, for you might have heard above the hiss of steam a series of sharp crackling noises as the brittle rails broke under the weight of the new machine. That was enough to deter manufacturers from putting the engine into regular service, and for a few more years the steam locomotive seemed more of an entertaining novelty than a serious threat to the booming canal trade. But the threat was real enough, and now at that same spot a railway can be found running down the valley of the Taff, but scarcely a trace of the canal remains – just a plaque mounted on tramway rails recording that day and marking the site of the wharf.

The first railways could almost have been thought of as aids to water transport, little more than an extension of the tramway system bringing coal from the mines to boats on rivers and canals. The first commercially successful railway did just that, linking Middleton Colliery near Leeds to the Aire and Calder navigation, and it was followed by other railways serving the collieries around the town. Indeed, while Tyne traffic prospered, the Tees traffic to the south was suffering, and in 1810 a resolution was passed in Stockton Town Hall authorising a survey for the line of a canal or railway from Darlington. John Rennie was handed the job, but very little happened and the plan was dropped, only to be revised in the 1820s. The task was now passed to an avid enthusiast for steam railways, a local engineer, George Stephenson, and all thoughts of canal building were dropped. In 1825 the Stockton and Darlington Railway was opened. It may have begun as just another tramway – and indeed in its early days horses worked the line as well as steam locomotives and inclines were a notable feature – but what attracted everyone's attention was that this was a public railway, built from the first with the steam engine in mind. Its success really did open the doors for the railway builders.

As a direct result of the success of the Stockton and Darlington Railway, Stephenson was invited to plan a new line from Liverpool to Manchester. Now here was a real and direct threat to the waterways, promising to take goods which before had been carried on the Mersey and Irwell, the Sankey and the Bridgewater Canal. Just as the river

navigation authorities had fought hard against the Bridgewater Canal bill, now the canal companies fought the railway interest. They got off to a good start, for Stephenson had rushed his first survey in order to get it ready in time for the parliamentary session of 1825. The canal companies had, it turned out, done their homework rather better than Mr Stephenson and their lawyers pulverised the unfortunate engineer. Here is their squirmingly embarrassing demolition job on the proposal to build a bridge across the Irwell with arches a mere 10ft (3m) above the water – barely navigable at low water and totally submerged during floods:

> Did any ignorance ever arrive at such a pitch as this? Was there ever any ignorance exhibited like it? Is Mr Stephenson to be the person upon whose faith this Committee is to pass this bill, involving property to the extent of 400,000 *l* or 500,000 *l*, when he is so ignorant of his profession, as to propose to build a bridge not sufficient to carry off the flood water of the river, or to permit any of the vessels to pass which of necessity must pass under it, and to leave his own Railroad liable to be several feet under water.

But they had only won a temporary reprieve. The line was built and a network of rails spread with extraordinary rapidity, south to Birmingham and on into London. The threat to canal trade was now an all-too-obvious reality.

In the event, the darkest fears of the canal companies seemed not to be realised. Some received compensation from the railways: £10,000 in the case of the Great Western Railway and the Kennet and Avon Canal, and there was even a period of brisk trade carrying the building materials for the new enterprise. Although the canal companies grabbed whatever small compensation they could and were ready to carry for the rapidly developing rivals, they were by no means eager in their co-operation. Brunel's railway was to follow the same line as the Kennet and Avon through the narrow valley that runs down past Limpley Stoke and Claverton to Bath. On his reconnoitre of the line, Brunel commented as follows:

156

The side of the hill is a rotten description oolite laying on clay . . .
Many slips have occurred owing no doubt to the washing of the clay
by the river and considerably assisted by the bad management of
the canal. Blakewell the Canal engineer, a bigoted, obstinate
practical man says the road will make the hill slip, but could not tell
us why.

The canal companies, after having spent a great deal of cash fighting off
the competitor, often found that in the early years the railways' initial
success was in passenger carrying which had never been of more than
minor importance on the canals. True, the railways offered the obvious
advantages of greater loads carried at greater speed, but a good many
industries had been built on canalside sites precisely so that they could
take advantage of direct links, especially to the collieries. Nowhere was
this more true than in that complex maze of waterways that make up
the BCN. The canals in this region were now in fact feeling the full
benefits of their earlier success. The space in and around them was
crammed with industries, large and small, which relied on the boats for
cheap coal and raw materials coming in and finished goods going out.
Even had the railways had their eyes on such a trade – which they surely
must have had – there was precious little space left for the multitude of
branch lines and sidings that would have been needed completely to take
over the canal trade. The place of Birmingham at the heart of the canal
system was at least assured, and as long as the heart beat strongly, there
was every hope that the body as a whole would survive.

The 1790s were the years of the canal mania, when everyone saw a
canal share as a ticket in a lottery in which there were no losers. Quick
profit was the universal cry and the devil take the hindmost. The same
was to happen all over again on the railways in the 1840s, when a vast
number of railways were promoted, huge sums of money were invested,
and numerous railways were even built. A large number of railways,
however, were not built although all the money was spent, and some

Three generations of transport can be seen in this picture. On the right is the rough rutted road, whilst navvies repair the track of the North Midland Railway. Above these are the high embankment and aqueduct of the Cromford Canal (The Science Museum)

A Canal Carrier's Complaints

The following letter was from the carrier, James Thomason, and was sent on 15 May 1885:

Henry Collier Esq

Dear Sir,

Referring to our interview of 21st February, we beg to enclose a statement of our charges against the Lancashire and Yorkshire Railway Company for mismanagement of the Manchester Bury and Bolton Canal during the last seven years, the effect of which has been calculated to prejudice canal transit arrangements in favour of their own competing Railway lines.

The statutory obligations devolving upon the Canal Proprietors have been departed from in almost every particular and we desire to call your attention to some of the more important.

The Canal is required to be efficiently maintained throughout and at all times kept open and fit for navigation. Numerous instances have occurred of the silting up of the Canal bed with mud and stones by subsidence of the neglected banks, and the removal of these dangerous obstructions, when brought under notice, was only attempted after long and harassing delays, our flats meanwhile sustaining damage with its consequent heavy repairs. We need only however mention that the present breakdown, which has stopped the navigation for upwards of twenty-six weeks is the sixth breakdown of the kind since 1878, to prove that the neglect has been habitual and the most culpable character.

During the thirty-five weeks in which the three breakdowns of 1880–81 were in process of repair and traffic completely suspended we frequently urged

continued on page 159

that were built never prospered. Nevertheless, it is interesting to compare the peak year on the canals, 1793, when 19 canal acts were approved, with 1845, when 108 railway acts were passed and, according to Bradshaw, no less than 27 new railways were actually opened. Those who put their money into the ventures wanted the best possible return in the shortest possible time, which meant that they took a particularly dim view of all rivals, and rivals included canals as well as competing railway companies. The process of buying up canals began and few efforts were spared in the battle to win trade for the railways. It was not an edifying spectacle, as a commentator on the scene, Thomas Graham, wrote in a treatise on transport published in 1834:

When the project of a new canal or railway is promulgated, it is universally represented as a public undertaking, of deep importance to the community: and, on this ground, its interference with the rights of individuals and their proprietors, is justified. If objected to by the trustees of a turnpike road, or rival canal or railway, the opposition is stigmatised as the defence of a monopoly. The act of incorporation, however, once obtained, the alleged public enterprise, sinks into a matter of private speculation and monopoly: in the protection of which, the public cease to have any interest.

Public interest should have been the concern of parliament, but instead parliament concerned itself with minor legislation designed not so much to promote the general good of transport in the country as to minimise the damage to the canals. It was not notably successful. Railway companies bought up canals and it was some time before there was much in the way of regulation regarding what they did with them. There were statutory obligations relating to tolls and keeping the canals in good order, but as Arthur Hugh Clough wrote in his modernised version of the ten commandments:

Thou shalt not kill; but needst not strive
Officiously to keep alive.

That could well have been taken as the motto for many canal-owning railway companies. Repairs were carried out, but with no great sense of urgency; stoppages were prolonged in the often well-founded hope that merchants and manufacturers would grow tired of the delays and convert to rail. Wharves and warehouses were allowed to deteriorate, and in general many canals took on the mournful appearance of threadbare poor relations. This was a situation that was also harmful to the more successful, independent canals, which could also be affected by a delay on any canal which formed a link in the complex network.

Against this view it could be argued that railways did provide genuine competition which was bound, in any case, to harm canal trade, and that some canals would have gone bankrupt in time without railway purchase. In some cases being bought out by the railways was the best news shareholders had had since they made their first investment; and there was undoubtedly more than one canal, often beset by engineering

158

THE YEARS OF DECLINE

problems such as chronic water shortage, which might well have closed down in the nineteenth century but for the statutory obligation on a railway company to keep it open. Certainly, in the endless arguments between canal and railway companies that continued to roll and rattle on into the twentieth century, the railways made much of the burden of canal ownership. In evidence before a parliamentary commission, O. R. H. Bury of the Great Northern Railway claimed that his company was losing £30,000 a year on its canals. The railmen argued that what the world wanted was speed, and when the case was put to S. Fay of the Great Central Railway that there were goods where what mattered was a regular cheap supply, he replied bluntly: 'I have not met any.' Yet at that time there were many examples of large concerns who welcomed the delivery of cargo to their own wharves rather than to a distant goods yard.

The arguments were batted backward and forward and from time to time parliament became involved with acts which ensured that railway companies made at least some sort of effort to maintain their canals. Other important legislation appeared, such as the act of 1845 which gave the canal companies much more freedom to carry goods on their own behalf and to vary the tolls for their customers. That at least gave them a chance to compete, although cost-cutting inevitably had its effect throughout the canal community. It bore particularly hard on the boatmen who found themselves working longer hours on longer runs and often for less pay. What was the truth of the story that the railways set out deliberately to damage the canals? A parliamentary committee of 1872 decided that this was indeed the case, and there is certainly good evidence to support the argument. A committe in 1883 found that the tolls on railway-controlled canals were five times those of independents such as the Grand Junction and the Leeds and Liverpool. And it was not just the inevitable fall of cargo carrying on the railway-owned canals that created a problem, for those canals would normally have been feeding goods on into other parts of the system. Damage to a part brought trouble to the whole. Statistics sometimes give an unduly rosy picture. The following figures were produced for the Royal Commission of 1905:

	Independent Canals	Railway-owned Canals
Miles (kilometres)	2,556 (4,113)	1,266 (2,037)
Tons carried	28,168,313	14,191,073
Revenue	£1,502,959	£546,287

The figures look very even, but what is hidden on the railway side is the highly successful BCN. Take that out and you have this comparison: the independents were carrying 11,000 tons per mile and the railway canals a mere 200.

The cause of the canals' decline cannot be laid just at the door of the competing railways. Much of the blame must attach to the canals themselves. The piecemeal way in which they developed, with a bewildering variety of lock sizes, meant that it was impossible to organise efficient long-distance haulage without trans-shipment. It was theoreti-

that the canal should be efficiently repaired throughout its entire length, but notwithstanding the opportunities of these eight months, little or nothing in that direction was done – and during the succeeding eighteen months stoppages occurred almost weekly – the period of suspension of the navigation during that time including Sunday and night stoppages being three-fifths of the whole period.

Our correspondence with Canal proprietors of which copies are before you, admit the neglect, and their numerous promises regarding completion of repairs which on their Railway system would have been faithfully executed have always been greatly delayed in execution and not done so as to endure . . . .

While we have sustained heavy loss and have been serious prejudiced by constant stoppages the Railway Proprietors of the canal by ingenious diplomacy, insisting all the while on maintenance of canal carriage rates by us, have, by covertly championing the merchants cause in a successful raid upon canal carriage rates obtained unwitting approval of reductions from the authorities and so emphasised the prejudice their canal stoppages had already induced that it has resulted in an almost entire withdrawal of our traffic to their Railway.

cally possible to run wide boats on the Grand Junction, but what was the point when at Birmingham they were faced by a barrage of narrow locks? So the boats worked in pairs, with all that that involved in terms of extra manpower and slower journeys. The railways had their own divisions for a while between Stephenson's standard gauge and Brunel's broad gauge, but they achieved eventual standardisation. The canals never achieved standardisation and suffered for it. There was a general feeling that nothing could be done or would be done to the narrow canals, so modernisation was concentrated on the big, broad waterways, with most satisfying results. The 1883 committee may have shown independent canals to be far cheaper than railway canals, but that was nothing compared with the difference between modernised waterways and the rest: the same committee reported that charges on the Aire and Calder were one-tenth those of the Leeds and Liverpool. There were many canalmen who saw the way in which commercial trade would eventually move. J. E. Palmer, a director of the Irish Grand Canal Company, wrote these words in 1910:

> Railway men sometimes allege that the Aire and Calder and the Weaver Navigations are exceptional cases that ought not to be taken as indicating, in a general way, the capabilities of inland water transport. But these waterways are only exceptional really in the sense that there are no other barge canals of equally large capacity in this country. They are not exceptional in showing the economy of improved water transport. They coincide with inland waterways of somewhat similar capacities abroad in showing the economic advantages of waterways of adequate dimensions.

That same argument has been repeated by proponents of water transport ever since, and has always had to contend with the view that canals were of the eighteenth century, had only a minor role to play in the nineteenth century, and have none at all in the twentieth – they were simply out of date. A fast goods train with its long line of loaded wagons seemed so obviously superior to the narrow boat with its plodding horse that the railwaymen could not see that there was any room for argument. The waterways argument was given support by the report of a royal commission set up in 1906. They recommended widening and deepening the main trunk routes of the cross linking the Severn, Thames, Trent and Mersey to take barges with a minimum of 100-ton loads and up to 300 tons on certain favourable sections. The Birmingham maze was to be left untouched as a sort of clearing house for the new system. Recognising that no private investors were likely to come forward, they proposed nationalisation, with the new controlling body as the canal owner, but with other concerns running the boats. Nothing was done.

The canals did survive, however, and some prospered, often, in spite of their frequent public arguments, working very successfully together. Goods from the docks, for example, could be easily and cheaply moved to railway interchange warehouses on the Regent's Canal at Camden Town. Of the 8 million tons of goods carried annually on the BCN at the end of the last century, 7 million finished or started their journey by rail. But both railways and canals were soon to face a new competitor, and Mr Palmer, who had made such a sensible prognosis of the canal problem, came up with a gloriously wrong prediction of twentieth-century traffic: 'The chief use of road motors seems likely to be in acting as feeders for railways and canals, and carrying traffic for short distances, thus superseding horse-drawn traffic.' That may have looked like the sensible view in 1910, but the Great War was to change the picture out of all recognition. The end of the war brought the start of a series of changes which have affected the country ever since: a decline in the old manufacturing industries of the North, accompanied by a rise in new light industries in the South. That in turn meant that the men who came home as heroes to the flag-waving crowds soon found themselves in the considerably less heroic position of unemployment. The canals and railways had both been built to fit the old patterns of industry, so both entered this new period at a distinct disadvantage. But the biggest threat of all was the motor vehicle. In 1920 the Ministry of Munitions sold around twenty thousand war surplus vehicles at knock-down prices. For many men they were the key to open the door that would take them out of the gloom of depression and into a prosperous future. No one was paying much attention to regulations, and there were in any case few rules to follow. Fellows, Morton & Clayton suddenly found their lucrative sugar contract under threat from small operators willing to work a hundred hours a week for little pay, ready to do their own maintenance in their 'spare time' and not in the least averse to carrying 6-ton loads on 5-ton trucks. The road hauliers reduced their rates by a quarter to grab the trade. Competition was intense, with the small men quoting the lowest price that would make them the minimum of profit for a trip. Having got the job of, say, hauling a 6-ton load for 100 miles (161km) they then faced a return journey with an empty truck. So anything that could be picked up at any price was profit to them. With low overheads and no worries about such matters as tolls and road maintenance, this new generation of hauliers could undercut just about anyone, and offer the advantages of door-to-door delivery. They might not be well placed to take the heavy loads of big industry, but they were beautifully set up to carry the lighter loads of the new industrial world.

The canal response was amalgamations, of which the best known was the formation of the Grand Union out of the old Grand Junction, which had already absorbed the Leicestershire and Northamptonshire Union, the Regent's Canal, the Warwick and Birmingham, the Warwick and Napton and the Birmingham and Warwick Junction. The new company now controlled all the main routes from London to Birmingham and the more important branches. Improvement and modernisation went ahead at a good pace, but there was no serious attempt to increase the width of the canal to take barges rather than narrow boats, for although wide boats could use the locks, there would have been endless delays at bridges and other narrow points. Rather more dramatic changes came in the North East with a major lock-building programme to improve the navigation of the Trent to bring big craft all the way to Nottingham. A tug pulling barges could now haul loads of 600 tons on the waterway, giving the city a through route to the Humber and the sea.

The twentieth century brought a fresh competitor to the canals: road transport. This prophetic cover for a 1924 magazine shows a modern motorway, for which tolls are charged. Cars speed past the slow moving narrow boat on the adjoining canal (Michael E. Ware)

Other canals were less fortunate. As trade dropped away, so the dismal roll-call of closures extended. The Grantham went and the Grand Western, the Thames and Severn and the Droitwich, the Bradford and the Aberdare and many lesser canals all said goodbye to the boats. Others survived but trade declined. Maintenance work was neglected and although some canals were nominally still open, they were scarcely in a position to attract trade. Yet more were truncated. The Union Canal from Edinburgh to Falkirk remained open, but the locks that joined it to the Forth and Clyde were filled in: isolated from the rest of the system, no one could have predicted anything but a gloomy future. Among the worst affected by decay were the canals of Wales. The Glamorgan Canal above Abercynon stopped being a waterway for boats and became a water-pipe for Cardiff Corporation. The Neath Canal was nominally open, but there are no records of any commercial movements whatsoever after World War I, while its connecting link, the Tennant, remained open through the 1930s, but paradoxically was closed to commercial craft. So the story continued, of traffic gradually disappearing from South Wales, leading to dereliction which could only end in abandonment. Things were little better elsewhere, and even canals which survived were forced to reduce operations. The Shropshire Union and the Rochdale gave up carrying and simply reverted to the old pattern of toll collection. They were caught in an unbreakable spiral. The canals needed modernisation, but modernisation cost money and money could only come from revenue; but revenue was falling on the unimproved waterways so there was no money. Improvements could not be made so

The post-war years brought nationalisation to the canals, and a drabness to the boats. But although this pair are given the standard British Waterways paintwork, the brass still gleams and the ropework on the butty is as immaculate as ever (Anthony Burton)

trade slipped further and further, with revenues dropping to the danger point where the question was not 'Is there money for improvement?' but 'Can we afford maintenance and repairs?'.

Matters would probably have taken an inevitable course but for the outbreak of war in 1939. The government that had been unwilling to take an interest in the country's waterways in peacetime had no option but to act to keep them open in wartime. There was a ruthless pruning out of some canals, including the Manchester, Bolton and Bury and the Huddersfield Narrow, but resources were put into others which were felt to be necessary for the war effort. Much now came under government control; many were to stay there. On 1 January 1948 the great majority of the canals and river navigations of Britain passed into the control of the British Transport Commission, with canals coming under the Docks & Inland Waterways Executive. The boat people were suitably scathing about the new bosses from the government. One described the Executive as 'a playground for generals' and prophesied the end of the waterways. This was not exactly fair to men like Robert Davidson who had managed the Leeds and Liverpool and George Cadbury of the Severn & Canal Company. There were others who saw, however, that without the sort of investment that could only come through public funding, the entire system would collapse. There was even, for a moment, the glorious prospect of a unified transport policy where road, rail and canal interests would all work together. In the event, as is the British way, events were neither as bad as the pessimists forecast nor as good as the optimists hoped.

Nationalisation brought many changes to the waterways and the new body set about drawing up a list of priorities. It needed to. Some waterways, notably those which could take big, modern motorised barges, were seen as having a definite potential for commercial development, and there was for the first time a recognition of the new and increasingly important form of traffic – pleasure boating. So the system was carved up into three categories. Top priority went to a small group of canals and rivers – the Aire and Calder, the Severn and the Grand Union up to Berkhampstead which could be developed. Next in line came those which were thought still to have commercial life in them, such as the rest of the Grand Union and the Leeds and Liverpool. There was then a third category of canals which, on the whole, the authorities would have been glad to get rid of to anyone who wanted them.

The last thing the new canal owners had in mind was running a large fleet of narrow boats, but they soon found themselves acquiring the biggest fleet on the cut. All the canal company fleets went with the canal, and major private operators also dropped out. Fellows, Morton & Clayton decided that nationalised waterways were not for them, and certainly saw in the new body a ready purchaser for an increasingly unprofitable business. The new fleet obviously needed a new image. There seemed to be two conflicting thoughts at work here. The old traditional decoration of roses and castles and the quaint names all smacked of nostalgia and were considered out of keeping with an ambitious new enterprise. On the other hand, they felt that the boats should be bright and cheerful, that they should stand out and be

Canals Owned by Railway Companies at the Beginning of the Twentieth Century

Great Western Railway
Kennet and Avon
Stratford-on-Avon
Stourbridge Extension
River Tone Navigation
Bridgewater and Taunton
Grand Western
Stover
Brecon and Abergavenny
Monmouthshire
Swansea
Somerset Coal Canal

London, Midland and Scottish
Ulverston
Manchester, Bolton and Bury
Huddersfield Broad
Huddersfield Narrow
Lancaster
St Helen's or Sankey Canal
Shropshire Tub Boat
Trent and Mersey
Ashby
Cromford
Shropshire Union – including the Chester, Llangollen Montgomeryshire, Middlewich branch and Shrewsbury

The LMS also controlled the Birmingham Canal Company.

London & North Eastern Railway
River Derwent (Yorkshire)
Pocklington Canal
River Ure Navigation
Ashton
Peak Forest
Macclesfield
Chesterfield
Grantham
Nottingham
Fossdyke

The LNER also owned the navigation previously controlled by the Norwich and Lowestoft Navigation Company

Southern
Gravesend and Rochester

instantly recognisable. So away went the decoration, the names were replaced by plain numbers and in came a new colour scheme of garish blue and yellow. The *Daily Mirror* sent a reporter along to see this process of refurbishment and obtained a suitable quote from a boatman.

'British Waterways 279,' he snarled. 'Blue paint and yellow paint,' he growled.

He spat once more and said bitterly: 'It's all a lot of bloody red tape.'

There were many who agreed wholeheartedly with those sentiments and it was not long before traditional decoration began to return to the boats. There was a general feeling in any case that the new owners did not understand canal life. One boatman found an official peering into his back cabin, and hauled him out by the scruff of the neck.

'Do you know who I am?' demanded outraged officialdom.

'No, and I don't . . . care,' replied the boatman.

'How would you like me to go to your house, march in the front door and go upstairs and start poking round your bedroom?'

Other changes were more important and had a more lasting effect, especially changes in the political complexion of the government. Enthusiasm for central planning was not a part of the Conservative philosophy, and in 1953 the Transport Act resulted in the break-up of the Transport Commission. Road haulage mostly went back to private ownership, and railways and canals went their separate ways. There followed even more fragmentation as docks were split off from waterways. None of this might have seemed to have much effect on the working lives of the boat people, but it did. The young and fit found that they could make a reasonable living by working hard for long hours and taking a fairly ruthless attitude towards their fellow boatmen. Many old families left the cut, and many who had been away to the war never returned. And those who stayed were not sure how they felt about the steadily increasing number of pleasure boats with which they were now sharing the waterway. Some just regarded them philosophically as part of an inevitably changing scene. The young tearaway boatman in a hurry regarded them as at best, confounded nuisances, although 'confounded' was not perhaps the adjective that would have been used.

One boatman – named Fred for the purpose of this story – told of an encounter with a pleasure boat on the Grand Union. Fred was still in his teens but already captain of a boat and heading for London. On the way he met a boat coming up and received the good news that the locks in the next flight were all set and with him. He reached the first and it was set against him, so someone must have got in front of him. Another working boatman passed on the news that there was a pleasure boat just in front; all he had to do was pass that and he was on his way. Sure enough, the pleasure boat appeared. Fred shouted to him to move over. There was no response from pleasure-boater, who went by himself into the double lock, slammed the gates and began drawing the paddles. That

was too much for Fred. He wound up the Bolinder and, with flames shooting from the chimney, he rammed the lock gates flat out and burst through into the lock. He leapt out and wound the paddles full open, so that narrow boat and 20ft (6m) cruiser were left to crash about together in the lock. When the gates were opened there was apparently very little argument about who would leave first and claim the right of way! Such incidents were comparatively rare. Most of us who started pleasure boating in those days as rank novices were much too nervous of the great iron narrow boats to do anything other than stay meekly by the bank to let the monsters through. Cowardice, I seem to recall, was a more potent motive than respect for a working boat carrying a man with a hard living to earn.

In the end, it was not so much the plans of men in offices nor even the inexorable working of economic forces that wrote the effective end to narrow-boat trading, but the weather. The winter of 1962–3 was desperately harsh. Canals froze up in December and boats were locked into the ice until March. Customers who turned to the roads to get their goods through simply never returned. It coincided with yet another change – the establishment of the British Waterways Board. The end would have come anyway, for the narrow boats were losing money and they simply could not be adapted to the new world of containerisation. But it was a traumatic time for the boating families. BWB allowed them to live in the butties while they made new arrangements for their lives, and there were maintenance jobs on the canals for some. No one could doubt that a new canal age had now begun. It was formalised in 1968, when the divisions that had been talked about for so long were made into legal realities. There were to be commercial waterways, cruising waterways and remainder waterways. 'Commercial' meant waterways that could take large, economical vessels. Cruiseways were for pleasure boating and were at least assured of survival. Remainder waterways were, in effect, being marked by a large sign 'Not Wanted'. But whether a waterway was designated for cruising or was earmarked for eventual abandonment, one thing was clear: no one saw any place in the new plans for the trading narrow boats. They were to be allowed quietly to slide off into history.

None of that, of course, meant the end of the canals: the holiday trade boomed, continued in part at least by those old narrow boats, either cut down as cruisers or converted to hotel boats. A restoration movement was begun and went from strength to strength, while commercial traffic still runs on parts at least of the system. But the great days were over. The decline that set in with the coming of the railways and which was speeded on its way by the motor lorries finally reached its inevitable conclusion with the boatman's oldest enemy – the ice.

Invoice for work done on the Coventry Canal (British Waterways Board)

11 THE CANALS AT WAR

It is difficult to imagine anything further removed from images of war than a pleasure boat chugging along an old canal somewhere in the depths of the British countryside. But the effects of war, even a war fought on foreign soil in the days before the aeroplane made such a distinction a good deal less important, are invariably felt throughout the country. The canals were far from immune.

The American War of Independence had its effect in drying up capital for canal building, and the same was largely true when war broke out with France in 1793. The furious rate of expansion of the canal-mania years began to slacken off, but effects were to be far greater than just a general tightening of the purse strings. America is a long way from Britain, and even the fastest sailing ship would have taken weeks rather than days to cross the Atlantic, so no American muskets were likely to be fired in the British Isles. The war with France, however, was a different matter. It was popularly believed that it would be easily settled: the British lion would make short work of the pack of yelping dogs that were said to constitute the French army. In the event, revolutionary fervour, able generalship and modern techniques overwhelmed the decidedly incompetent, badly led and less well-equipped forces of Britain and her allies. It seemed for a while as if the unthinkable might actually be about to happen: that the French would invade Britain. If it had come to a French landing, then it would have been essential to get troops to the area as quickly as possible. And here the canals were seen as having an important role to play.

One of the facts of war was that for all Britain's proud boast of ruling the waves, the navy could not guarantee full protection of the sea routes of the coastal trade. This threatened the vital coal supplies from the North East and made the movement of troops by sea too risky a business. There were earnest discussions about the possibilities of building new canals to take over parts of the coastal trade. Some, such as a proposed route from the metal mines of Devon and Cornwall up through Somerset to the Bristol Channel, were scarcely sensible and, given the nature of the terrain, scarcely practicable. One new canal, however, was built: the Royal Military Canal from Seabrook around Romney Marsh to the River Rother near Rye. It was a military canal in every sense, with the conventional roles of promoter and engineer being taken by the Quartermaster General and Colonel Browne. The canal had two functions: first to act as a defensive barrier against an invading army, and second to speed troop movements in the south-east of England. As it was never required for either function, the canal rapidly fell into disuse and now it is a peaceful backwater mainly used by rowing boats. Other

PEGASUS

WOT TH'—

The Grand Union Canal Bill, 1943—now awaiting the Royal assent—makes history by empowering the Company to take part in the operation of all forms of transport—by land, sea and air. The canal horse thus "takes wings."

A cartoon from the Birmingham Mail *commenting on the Grand Union Canal Bill of 1943 empowering the company to use transport by land, sea and air* (British Waterways Board)

canals were, however, called into service. In 1798 the canals along the route from London to Liverpool were given notice that there was to be a major troop movement involving fifteen boats which were to be given absolute priority. Ordnance stores were also sent by canal and they, too, were given priority rating. The most remarkable survivor from this time is the military depot at Weedon, which was built at the end of a short arm off the Grand Junction Canal. It was heavily fortified and there was even a suggestion that the king could be rushed there by water should the dreaded Frenchmen cross the Channel. There is a certain charming incongruity in the notion of King George and his cabinet being hustled away to a horse-drawn narrow boat. Being legged through Blisworth tunnel was hardly a high-speed escape. Very little has changed at Weedon over the years, so that this little branch can claim the distinction of being the only canal which can be closed off by a military portcullis.

There were times when the threat seemed real, and there was a rush of patriotism on the canals as there was in the country. Pickford's offered to make their fleet of boats available to the government, and canal staff pledged to fight to the death to preserve the waterways. The fact that invasion never came does not make the anxieties of the time any the less real. In the event, the main effect of war was the more mundane one of raising prices and costs. This included a very high cost of fodder for the horses and it was the expense of foodstuffs that provided the impetus for early experiments with steam locomotives. The railway war which followed the French wars had, in the event, a far greater effect on life on the canals.

The wars of the nineteenth century took place at a distance far enough removed from Britain for the impact at home to be minimised. The two world wars of the twentieth century left no part of the community untouched. The effect on the canals was immediate. Those which were owned by railway companies came at once under government control. There was no problem with legislation, for the takeover had been authorised as early as 1871 with the Regulation of the Force Act which allowed for a railway takeover in time of war. The actual management of the railways and their canals was left to the Railway Executive Committee, which was made up of the managers of the leading companies. The government was able to control traffic and in return the companies received more than generous compensation. The independent canals continued in their own way and, with the government understandably sending goods where possible on the system which they had under their own control, they began to suffer. Events were not helped by the steady flow of young men to the carnage that was the battlefields of Europe. And it was not just men who were sent to the front; horses were also requisitioned. At home, many men left for the better paid work of the munitions factories. It was some time before the government realised the seriousness of the situation. Lord Curzon was later to say that 'The Allies floated to victory on a wave of oil'. It was quite true that Britain's huge merchant fleet played a vital role in ensuring that essential supplies reached the country's ports, but goods still needed to be moved inland as well. And the canals had a role to play which it was increasingly difficult for them to play well. Somewhat belatedly, the government

168

acted and in 1917 they set up a Canal Control Committee. The damage, however, had already been done: it is far more difficult to recoup trade lost to a competitor than it is to get new trade. The canals were carrying over 30 million tons of cargo a year at the start of the war: at the end it was 10 million less. It was a catastrophe for which compensation only offered a temporary palliative.

Some canals did benefit. The Basingstoke was in a fairly wretched condition at the start of the war, but it ran conveniently close to Aldershot Barracks, so the Royal Engineers took it over and used it to bring supplies down from Woolwich. Authority, however slow it might have been to recognise the importance of the British canals, did at least recognise that, in Europe, there was a very modern, efficient waterways system which could take a vast amount of cargo for the military, provided that the military knew how to use it. So soldiers were sent to the British canals to receive instruction in the art of canal-boat handling. Given the large numbers of boatmen who had enlisted in the army, the exercise smacks more than a little of administrative incompetence. This official acknowledgement of the role of well-run, modern waterways in a country's transport system does not seem to have set anyone thinking about what might be done to Britain's increasingly outmoded system once the war was over. There were even less likely uses found for the canals. The Red Cross ran a converted narrow boat as a trip boat for convalescent soldiers, which puts it well in the ranks of pioneering holiday craft on the Kennet and Avon.

The outbreak of World War II found the pattern of the first being repeated, thereby bearing out George Bernard Shaw's dictum: 'If history repeats itself, and the unexpected always happens, how incapable must Man be of learning from experience!' The Ministry of Transport at once took over the railways and their associated canals, leaving the independents more or less to their own devices. They then discovered, just as they had in World War I, that this was not a sensible way of running the nation's transport and they set up an investigation to see what should be done. The enquirers discovered just as they had before, that some form of overall control was necessary. The appointment of Brigadier

Troop Movements by Canal

The first division of the troops that are to proceed by the Paddington canal for Liverpool, and thence by transports for Dublin, will leave Paddington to-day, and will be followed by others to-morrow and Sunday. By this mode of conveyance the men will be only seven days in reaching Liverpool, and with comparatively little fatigue, as it would take them above fourteen days to march that distance. – Relays of fresh horses for the canal boats have been ordered to be in readiness at all the stages.

(*The Times*, 19 December 1806)

During World War I soldiers were sent for training in boat handling on the Basingstoke Canal, so that they would be able to make use of the extensive waterway system of France and Belgium (Imperial War Museum/ Michael E. Ware Collection)

Not creatures from outer space, but the Fire and Air Raid Squad at Goole Docks on the Aire and Calder in World War II (British Waterways Board)

General Sir Osborne Mance was not universally applauded among the boating community who had a not unreasonable distrust of outsiders, in particular of military outsiders. It was not, however, all bad news for the boat people who, for the first time ever, were given a whole week's holiday. As the importance of their work was finally recognised, boating was made a reserved occupation and boatmen were required to stay on the canals – but not before many of them had left. The lack of boaters became a serious problem.

When the first men went to war, the women simply carried on as best they could, wives taking over their husbands' roles to add to the burdens of an already hard life. That alone was not enough, and carriers were encouraged by the authorities to start bringing in recruits to train for the boats. Many were brought in to the scheme, but by far the best known were the women who were to make up all-female crews. These new recruits were given special badges which indicated that they worked for Inland Waterways on essential war work. The initials gave one of these women, Susan Woolfitt, the title for the book of her experiences, *Idle Women*. The title was ironic, for idle they most certainly were not. Perhaps their importance to the war effort on the canals has been exaggerated. There were, after all, never very many of them and at the best they represented only a tiny fraction of the boating population – no more than fifteen pairs were worked by women on the cut at any one time. There were, and are, however, good reasons why their efforts are still remembered. First, they earned the respect they eventually received. These young women, mostly from impeccable middle-class backgrounds, totally unused to hard manual work, whose boating experience was usually limited to a cruiser on the Broads or a dinghy in Brixham harbour, turned themselves into first-rate boaters. Second, they told the world about what they did. The traditional canal-boating families could seldom read a book, let alone write one, but these

170

THE CANALS AT WAR

articulate educated young ladies could both read and, as they proved, write. Emma Smith's *Maidens' Trip*, Susan Woolfitt's *Idle Women* and Eily Gayford's *The Amateur Boatwomen* all appeared after the war and Margaret Cornish put her experiences into fiction and followed up with her own account of those years entitled *Troubled Waters* in 1987. If they earned the respect of the boating community, they also showed their own respect for it. The books represent perhaps the closest thing we have to an insider's view of the working life of the canals, not just as seen in the special circumstances of war but as part of a long continuing tradition. The books are far more than accounts of the adventures of a small group of women in what was to them a strange and bizarre world; they are social documents of real value. If they do nothing else, the books give a vivid picture of the working practices of the professional boater.

The women's training scheme began in 1942 when the GUCCC and later Samuel Barlow agreed to give the idea their support. The first necessity was training, and the first to be trained were the trainers themselves. There were two of them, Kit Gayford and Daphne French, and the office work was organised by the redoubtable Miss Mimms. It is difficult now to appreciate just how different the world that these young women entered was to anything they had known before. The canal community was still essentially a closed one, having its own tradition and its own way of life. Fashion was probably not the subject uppermost in their minds in the war years, but it must nevertheless have come as a shock to find some boatwomen still wearing long black skirts and costumes that would not have looked out of place in Victorian England. But that was as nothing compared to the shock of the working life and the boats themselves. It is one thing to be brought up in a back cabin, but quite another to be presented with a first sight of one, together with the startling information that this was to be your home, and you were going to have to share it. Margaret Ridout, who wrote as Margaret Cornish, remembered one girl who sat patiently in the cabin waiting to be shown the main living quarters.

As 'intruders', the women had to be careful. They had a certain glamour – one pair were known as 'the Dresden chinas' – and it was all too easy to breed jealousy among the boatwomen. Generally, they wore trousers and severely practical clothing, and were very careful not to appear too friendly with the men folk. They learned the canal etiquette: never to go on board someone else's boat unless they were asked, and because they knew what it meant, an invitation to a cabin was an accolade as valuable as a medal won at the front. Not that all this information came at once. There was a brief training period, a period of learning on the job, six weeks of working from 8am to 5pm, and then they were out and carrying and working every hour of daylight that was available.

All the women agreed that they had to earn respect, and they could only do that by standing up for themselves: no one was going to do them any favours. Susan Woolfitt remembers getting the locks ready at Hillmorton when a pair of jossers came round the bend and, in spite of the trainees' shouts, headed straight for the open lock. The women were having none of this and promptly set off for the lock, with the result

The Culinary Delights of the Wigan to Liverpool Packet Boat

The cook generally begins her operations by ten o'clock in the morning, frying bacon, eggs, beef steaks, potatoes, and mutton chops; roasting meat, warming meat pies, &c., and seldom finishes before 3 or 4 o'clock in the afternoon; for most people who go in the tail end of the packet seem to think that eating and drinking is the most delightful amusement of travelling. The generality of those who sail in the upper end seem to have very different ideas. They appear as if ashamed of such a piece of vulgarity as the indulging a propensity to eat and just as one begins to think that they have learnt to exist without eating, perhaps they bring forth a dainty bit of chicken, ham, or game; a pot of veal, or shrimps, or a little tart that will scarce be two mouthfuls, just to convince the rest of the company that they do eat sometimes. The perfumes of tobacco, spirits, and hot meat, which are often very plentiful in a conveyance of this kind, form a very cheap substitute for some people; who, so far from requiring more food for the day than what they took at breakfast, frequently bestow a part of that meal upon the fishes with the greatest liberality, the various smells of the cabin being quite enough for them.

(Miss Weeton, *Journal of a Governess, 1807–11*)

171

Two pairs of boats passing on the Grand Union; worked by women trainees. By the end of the war, boat families accepted that the newcomers were as good at their job as anyone else on the canal. The photograph also shows the system of running blocks carrying the line from the motor to the butty in the foreground (Kit Gayford)

that the two motor boats arrived simultaneously and jammed together in the mouth. There followed the usual pleasantries in which views were expressed on, as Susan Woolfitt put it, 'the doubtful domestic habits of one another's forebears', and when the shouting was over, the women reluctantly gave way. Although they had lost the first encounter, they certainly had not conceded the campaign. They worked as hard and as fast as they were able, constantly on the heels of the other pair so that they could stand around with an air of resigned patience at a lock to imply that waiting for the other boats to get on with things was all very well but they, 'the so-and-so trainees', would have been well on their way by now. By the time they had reached the last lock, the children from the jossers were being ordered to close the gates for the ladies. That was a minor victory – but a greater triumph lay ahead. Rounding a corner, they found the professionals stuck on the mud – a rare experience for a professional boater at any time, a uniquely humiliating one in the circumstances. The women pulled them clear. Susan Woolfitt summed up the experience in these words:

From that day on, that particular pair of Jossers were always firm allies of ours. In case anyone should think that we lowered ourselves by such an unseemly brawl, I would like to say that it was nothing but a trial of strength. They were out to do us down and they knew

172

it. If we had taken it lying down they would, rightly I think, have despised us for ever. They got no more than they deserved and they respected us for it ever after. They are a queer crowd, the boat people, and they can't be treated quite the same way as other people. Their whole life is a fight for existence and the things they understand best are: strength, skill, giving a helping hand, and at the same time pulling the fastest of fast ones on a fellow who is not as quick as they are. Once you have got their trust, they will place implicit faith in you, but it takes a bit of getting. If they decide to dislike you then heaven help you, for they won't – ever.

All the other women had similar tales to tell. They were regarded at first as interlopers and, to earn the respect of the boating families, they had to work hard and to be hard. They succeeded. Alan Brooks, who was born on the boats, remembered them as far better than the men who came off the land. By the end of the war, he said, he never even tried to pass them on a run, knowing that they would work through a lock as quickly as anyone. He awarded them his finest tribute: 'You couldn't tell them from ordinary boat people.'

There were some things, however, which the women never learned to accept, and foremost among these was the unnecessary squalor to which the boating families were occasionally subjected. This was seen at its worst on the Bottom Road from Coventry through Tamworth approaching Birmingham from the north-east. On this route the butty had to be bow-hauled on the short pounds, which was bad enough, but the conditions made it seem far worse. Margaret Cornish wrote:

These locks must have been – and probably still are – some of the dirtiest on the Cut. The locksides were greasy with a thick, viscous, greenish-grey slime, and the tow-path was coated with coal-encrusted cinders. Inevitably, the towing line from the masthead became contaminated with the combination of oil and cinders so that hands became chafed and roughened, clothes were indescribably filthy and tempers fermented with every delay or misjudgement.

Susan Woolfitt saw the same conditions endured by boat families and even pregnant women helping with the bow-hauling and she imagined the effects of all that filth and grease on a family boat with no room and precious few facilities for cleaning: 'I felt that we had progressed not at all since the scandal of child labour during the Industrial Revolution.' But her greatest wrath was reserved for officialdom who sent them on the Bottom Road when it could easily have been avoided. One of the great virtues of all the books by the former trainees is that they form a great corrective to the over-romanticised view of canal life, which it is all too easy to hold.

It was an odd interlude in the wartime story, but it has left us with a picture of the times which we might otherwise never have seen. There is not a great deal said, however, about the dangers of the work. Boats were trading into areas such as London docks and Coventry, which were

The Women Volunteers

It must have been an astonishing imposition for the canal people when war brought them dainty young girls to help them mind their business, clean young eager creatures with voices so pitched as to be almost impossible to understand . . . For years, for generations, they had worked out their hard lives undisturbed, almost unnoticed. Then suddenly – the war; and with it descended on them these fifteen or so flighty young savages, crying out for windlasses, decked up in all manner of extraordinary clothes that were meant to indicate the marriage of hard work with romance. For the most part the boaters took it stoically.

(Emma Smith, *Maidens' Trip*, 1948)

favourite targets for bombers. Surprisingly, few boats were sunk or even very severely damaged, although some of the trainees were lucky to escape from a rocket attack that hit City basin in London. There were air-raid shelters in Birmingham for the boaters, which was perhaps as well, for in November 1940 a raid resulted in a direct hit on New Warwick Wharf in which four narrow boats were sunk. The boaters, working hard and far from immune from danger, received less than generous treatment from the government. Except for the occasions when they went out on tidal waters, boaters never received the extra rations which were given to merchant seamen. Indeed, far from receiving the extra rations thought to be necessary for those doing hard physical work for the war effort, they often found themselves getting a good deal less. Being constantly on the move, they had to have emergency ration cards and in those times of scarcity, shopkeepers tended, not unnaturally, to keep back what little they had to supply their regular customers. Fortunately, there was the occasional 'damaged crate' that could be relied on for a tin of corned beef.

Central organisation was supposed to ensure that boats were used to the best possible effect. Runs which had traditionally been one way, such as the regular supply of chocolate crumb for Cadbury's, were re-scheduled so that back cargoes could be carried on the return trip. The old rules still applied, with fly boats getting precedence over other craft, with the perhaps surprising result that a boat loaded with coal for a

Bomb damage to Banbury Locks in 1942. Fortunately the lock-keeper was living in a house in the town (British Waterways Board)

Tunnel tug tickets (British Waterways Board)

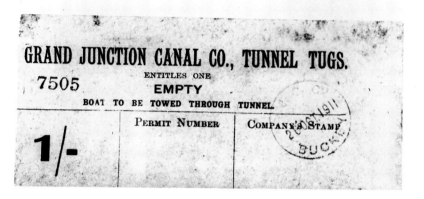

factory had to give way to another on the Guinness run. Whether this was merely a continuation of tradition or an acceptance of the importance of beer in raising morale seems uncertain. But, in spite of efforts to rationalise cargoes and make maximum use of the canals, there was still a steady decline in carrying. There were many reasons. Old problems did not go away just because there was a war on. Weather still played its part. Boats were iced up in winter. Margaret Ridout recalled being stuck for a week on the Grand Union. She and her partner hitch-hiked into Leamington Spa where they had tea in the Pump Room while a string trio played. There could hardly have been a greater contrast with their working lives. Far more serious was the water shortage following a series of dry summers. Although the importance of canals was recognised, they did not enjoy a very high priority in transport planning. The numbers of canal workers steadily shrank, and cargoes continued to decline, from around 13 million tons in 1938 to little more than 10 million at the end of the war. With this went a small but nonetheless important closure programme, which resulted in the loss of some 200 miles (322km) of canal.

The end of the war did not mark a return to the old days of privately owned canals, for the first post-war election brought in Attlee's Labour government and the nationalisation programme. A measure of state control had brought a greater rationality to the canal scene in wartime, but it was already clear to many people that the movement of trade figures was inexorably pointing in one direction – downhill. Tonnage on the canals at the end of World War II was less than half of what it had been at the end of World War I. But whatever the future might hold for the canals, those who stayed behind to work them through the war and those who came from the land to help them, could feel just as proud of their war effort as those who went into the services to fight.

12 PASSENGERS AND TOURISTS

When I took my first canal holiday in 1961, it seemed to be an adventure, something different, out of the ordinary. My wife and I made our way up to Middlewich, where BWB had their hire boats, to take over one of their tiny two-berth cruisers known as Water Babies. We were blissfully ignorant of canals and canal boats and a 70ft (21m) narrow boat looked to us just about as manageable as an ocean-going liner. A day being blown about in a high wind, which sent our little fibreglass craft skittering over the water, taught me a thing or two about not judging by appearances. But at first, as we set out for distant Llangollen, we felt very grand. We also felt like pioneers. The previous year we had canoed down the Thames, but we knew that there was a long history of passenger and pleasure boating on the river. My only previous experience of canals had been as a boy when I had seen the occasional working boat. Pleasure boating on the old trading routes was, I felt, something decidedly new and exciting. I could not have been more wrong, for passenger travel, as I was later to discover, is just about as old as the canals themselves.

As early as 1766, the Duke of Bridgewater's records show that he was carrying some passengers on the canal, in sufficient numbers for him to decide that it was worthwhile establishing a regular service in specially built craft. At first they were called passage boats, but later they took the more common name, borrowed from the seafaring world, and were known as packets. The name stuck and came to be applied to any canal boat running a regular passenger service to a fixed timetable. The duke's vessels were grand affairs. His first service was begun with two craft, one capable of carrying 80 passengers, the other 120, and each of them boasted a 'coffee house' which not only dispensed coffee but also more potent beverages. There was first-, second- and third-class accommodation. Like the fly boats running to a set timetable, the packets had priority over other craft and the Bridgewater boats carried a curved, shining blade in the bows to slice through the tow-rope of any lesser craft so impudent as to get in the way.

Sir George Head wrote a wonderfully vivid account of a journey on a Bridgewater packet in the summer of 1835. His general remarks on the delights of canal travel are just as valid today as when they were written. Happily, the second half of his comments no longer applies.

This mode of travelling, to an easy-going individual, provided it be not repeated too often, is far from disagreeable; – there he sits without troubling himself with the world's concerns, basking in the sunshine, and gliding through a continuous panorama of cows, cottages, and green fields, the latter gaily sparkling in the season with buttercups and daisies . . . It is true, there is one drawback to the comfort of the traveller, – namely, that within a dozen miles of Manchester the water of the canal is as black as the Styx, and absolutely pestiferous, from the gas and refuse of the many factories with which it is impregnated.

The smells of Manchester were by no means the only disadvantage to this form of travel: fellow passengers were not always on their best behaviour. Although there was accommodation in the cabins, there were also benches set on the flat roof. Sir George was enjoying his buttercups and daisies when the peaceful scene was distrubed:

A woman contrived to pitch herself head-foremost off the top of the platform where she was sitting, down upon the deck. She fell with such violence that I really thought she must have been killed. As it was, she was not hurt, and as I picked her up, she sent forth a sigh, which smelt so strongly of rum that I was happy to consign her collapsed form into other hands.

Sir George was no better off in the cabin and, apart from the fact that few people these days travel with their servants, who has not met the couple with the raucous child whose noise seems to delight the parents as much as it infuriates their fellow passengers?

I think I never saw a couple more rich in their own conceits, or more inclined to be satisfied with themselves and the things about them – and these were all on a small scale. He was a slight, weasel-shaped man, like a stunted stay-maker; – the wife, little; – the child, by appearance, an abortion; – and the maid-servant, little, – fresh from the country – with clattering thick-soled shoes, and hair tied

Pleasure boating on the Regent's Canal at the beginning of the nineteenth century. It would be difficult to find such rural delights on the canal today (Bodleian Library/JJ Collection Canals)

back, evidently, on her promotion, in a little knot like a shaving-brush, the length of one's thumb. The man and wife smirked and smiled on each other, and both gloated with eyes of affection on the dear baby. The lady, anxious to show to the rest of the passengers that she kept a maid-servant, ever and anon was calling her from one part of the vessel to another to give her some trifling order. The little maid, nevertheless, seemed truly happy, and the more the child cried, the more she jiggled it, and the more her active eyes travelled round and round, looking first at one person and then on another, while they sparkled with delight as she inhaled the pure fresh air.

Even that, it seems, was better than the company he met with on a Mersey and Irwell packet, where not only were the passengers a little on the rough side, but, worse still as far as the aristocratic traveller was concerned, they would not keep to their place and wandered in to the first-class cabin smoking and drinking beer while the women picked winkles from their shells with a pin.

One might think that, with the rules and regulations governing right of way for the packets, they would be skimming through the water, dragged by a team of galloping horses such as one sees pulling stage coaches on a thousand Christmas cards. Reality seems to have fallen some way short of this pleasing fantasy.

> The boat was towed at the rate of about five miles an hour by a couple of clumsy cart-horses, driven beyond their natural pace, and working under all possible disadvantages, for half the strength of one horse was continually exerted to prevent itself from being dragged into the canal by the other . . . In the present case, the two small boys who rode each on one of these unfortunate horses, exhibited an utter insensibility to that lively state of muscle which is the result of a well-tutored mouth. They whipped and kicked as if sitting across a tree; while the horses tugged and reeled, exhibiting a perfect specimen of ill-applied force, one literally pulling continually one way, and the other another. In the meantime, the riders, in worsted stockings, with thick country-made shoes, were healthy and active, jumping on and off, according to their fancy, without stopping the boat or creating any delay . . . Each boy was about twelve years old, yet these little fellows rode every day the whole distance, – one day up, the next down, – two-and-thirty miles, hot or cold, wet or dry, winter or summer.

In spite of all this, the trip was a success, not only in the opinion of Sir George Head but in the view of the thousands of other passengers who took the packet boats. The system soon spread to other canals. The best-known service was undoubtedly that of the Lancaster packets, which worked with an eye to the tourist trade. The Lake District was just becoming fashionable and passengers could leave industrial Lancashire and travel in comfort to Kendal. These were the days, too, when the name Wigan Pier was more than just a music-hall joke. By the time George Orwell heard of it, the pier was no more than the staithes where coal was tipped into waiting boats, but in the eighteenth century there was a passenger pier. At the very modest cost of a halfpenny for every 2 miles (3.2km) – or 10 miles (16km) a penny in today's coinage – you could take the boat to Liverpool. Or, if you felt like a little bracing sea air, you could get off at Halsall to pick up the coach down to Southport. In some cases, the canal itself was the appeal – and horse-drawn tourist boats still run on the canal at Llangollen. There the attraction is the scenery culminating in the lovely Horseshoe Falls. But one tends to forget that at the beginning of the canal age what seems to us to be commonplace was then the wonder of the times. The Rev Stebbing Shaw visited Harecastle tunnel on the Trent and Mersey, although his memory was a little wobbly on the dates, as it was not, in fact, open until 1777:

I visited this tunnel about the year 1770, soon after it was finished, when pleasure boats were then kept for the purpose of exhibiting this great wonder; the impression it made on my mind is still very fresh. The procession was solemn; some enlivened this scene with a band of musick, but we had none; as we entered far, the light of candles was necessary, and about half-way, the view back upon the mouth, was like the glimmering of a star, very beautiful.

It is interesting to contemplate what the band of music would have sounded like in the middle of a tunnel nearly 2 miles (3.2km) long and only 9ft (3m) wide. But all too soon there were other marvels for travellers to enjoy, as Sir George Head discovered when he turned from the boat pulled by a pair of cart-horses to the still new world of the steam railway. He visited the Leeds and Selby Railway which had opened in 1834, so was less than a year old at the time of his journey. He recorded, with admirable precision, that he travelled 19 miles 7 furlongs (30km) in 1 hour 4 minutes.

The sensation created by our transit, at this early stage of affairs, was particularly striking. Had the double-tailed comet passed that way, the country-people would hardly have been more interested by the spectacle; the men at work in the fields and quarries stood like statues, their pickaxes in their hands, in attitudes of fixed attention, and immovable as if turned by the wand of a magician into blocks of stone; and women in troops, in their best gowns and bonnets, fled from the villages, and congregated at the corner of every intersecting lane.

Faced by the glamorous competitor, dashing along at nearly four times the speed of the Bridgewater packet, the canal companies could see their trade vanishing unless prompt action was taken. One obvious answer was speed. Packet boats were proving particularly successful on the Scottish canals, and Scotland had a considerable reputation for engineering innovation and a scientific approach to design. It was very soon realised that putting more and faster horses on the tow-line did not necessarily result in a faster boat. It was William Houston who identified the problem and set about finding a solution for it. With a wide vessel

The Company Boat

For real luxury travel there was nothing to beat a trip in a company boat, normally used by directors and senior engineers viewing the canal. In 1829 the engineer Francis Giles went on a trip down the Basingstoke Canal in the most enviable style.

Our boat was a fine long one, extremely neat and clean, and was drawn by two horses; towards the stern there was a covered cabin large enough to contain twenty people, and it was of sufficient height to allow a man's walking in it up right. It was furnished with chairs and a long table, and there were books to read and a fire to warm ourselves by – but at this season of the year a fire not being necessary, still we had one for our cooking. At the head of the boat there was an awning made of water-proof material under which were safely stowed large joints of cold boiled mutton, pickled salmon, venison pastry, cheese, bread and potatoes, and for our drink we had to put up with hock, burgundy, port, ale, perry and cyder. In the space between the cabin and this awning which was open to the air we had two splendid rows of divans, one on each side of the boat, made of square bundles of hay, arranged side by side.

in a narrow canal there is a limit to how much water can be forced back between the sides of the boat and the bank so that a bow wave builds up. Applying more power simply results in a bigger bow wave and no noticeable increase in speed. The answer was a narrower vessel, and Houston tried several shapes, including an alarmingly narrow and presumably unstable vessel, 60ft (18m) long and only 4½ft (1.5m) wide, like an overgrown entrant for the Oxford and Cambridge boat race. He soon discovered that, by using suitably fine lines for the hull, he could increase the beam and still have a vessel able to reach speeds of up to 12 miles (19km) per hour. These became variously known as Scotch or swift boats and were widely used not only in Scotland but on English canals as far apart as the Lancaster and the Kennet and Avon. One of these vessels was sent down to the Lancaster in 1839. She had an iron hull, was 70ft (21.5m) long by 6ft (2m) beam and could carry 90 passengers. There was a cabin with first-class seating at the front, second class at the back and a bar in between. Once the packet business was finally given up, she continued in use as an inspection boat *Waterwitch II* and survived right through to the 1930s.

The obvious alternative to the fast Scotch boat and galloping horses was the steamer. Again, Scotland was the scene of experimentation culminating in the highly successful running of the *Charlotte Dundas* on the Forth and Clyde Canal. It came a little too soon, however, to rouse any great enthusiasm, as the railways had yet to appear over the technological horizon. When they did, the Forth and Clyde was again

The old Lancaster Canal packetboat Waterwitch II, *photographed in 1952. She was built in 1839 and continued on as an inspection boat, but was finally broken up. The diagram* (right) *shows the arrangement of the accommodation (Lancaster City Museum and British Waterways Board)*

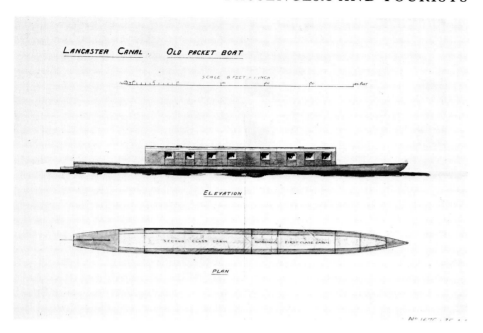

LANCASTER CANAL . OLD PACKET BOAT

SCALE 8 FEET = 1 INCH

ELEVATION

PLAN

to be the scene of a series of experiments designed to test hull shapes and different types of drive. The engineer Thomas Grahame looked for ideas across the Atlantic to the stern-wheelers of the Mississippi, seeing the obvious advantages of having the paddle wheel behind the vessel in the restricted waters of a canal. His account of the trials with the stern-wheeler *Cyclops* in 1830 was quoted by another advocate of steam power, William Fairbairn, in his *Remarks on Canal Navigation*, 1831:

> The boat, except as regards shape, is replete with errors. She is too heavy; viz. she bears about with her a quantity of iron, sufficient to build nearly two boats of the same size, and of equal strength. Her engine, which ought to have been high pressure, is low pressure, and, though a sweet-going machine, is much too heavy. Her paddle, which from its position must necessarily labour under the disadvantage of a deficient supply of water, is so placed as to enjoy this disadvantage to its greatest possible extent . . . I could state a number of other faults but will not trouble you with them. The party most opposed to stern paddles could not have desired a trial, where every possible disadvantage was more decidedly experienced. With all these disadvantages, and taking them to be irremediable, I am decidedly of opinion, that, in all cases where the breadth of a boat is limited, or where the paddles are subjected to risk of damage from narrow banks, &c. stern paddle-boats will be introduced, as best adapted for boats intended to carry large cargoes of goods, at a moderate pace.

Cyclops may have been seen as a prototype for a cargo vessel, but the passenger steamer soon found a regular home on the wide canals of Scotland. They afforded as much local excitement as the arrival of the railway, and some saw the steamers as a new source of revenue, as this notice posted on the Crinan Canal indicates:

Children and Others are hereby Prohibited from Running along the Canal Banks after the Passenger Steamer; and Passengers are requested not to encourage them by throwing Money on to the bank.

Children are further warned not to throw Flowers into the Boat.

The packet boats were supplemented by market boats, an extension of a system already in use for centuries on the river. These were cargo vessels which ran to a rough-and-ready schedule and had some space available for passengers. In the special craft there was generally a cargo hold in the bows and behind a well that was covered by an awning for the passengers. Some vessels, however, made no special provision and the passengers perched wherever they could find a space. There were also special arrangements for special passengers. Pickford's had a contract with the Admiralty for carrying troops, and there was what appears to have been quite a regular business carrying Poor Law families. These unfortunate people were paupers who were either being sent back to their original home parishes so that they could get relief there, for the law made it clear that it was only there that any relief would be available, or were being shipped off by the Poor Law authorities to the manufacturing districts where work was available. 'Get on a barge' appears to have been the nineteenth-century equivalent of 'Get on your bike'. Most of the working class, when they moved of their own accord, travelled by foot, but the fly boats did offer a relatively cheap and quick way of covering long distances.

There were regular arrangements for canal passenger travel of all kinds and varieties, and there were irregular arrangements as well. The canals had their hitchhikers just as our roads do, and a surreptitious shilling to a boat's captain was often all that was needed to ensure a cheap journey. The companies frowned on such affairs and even issued stern warnings against the practice – and the frequency with which the warnings appeared is itself good evidence that it was widespread. All this seems a long way from our modern notion of canal travel. Most passengers, rich or poor, used the canal because it was a convenient and sensible way of getting from A to B. Interesting sights or lovely scenery were welcome bonuses, but not a reason for travelling. There were short excursions to see specific, spectacular sights in the early days, but these ran only for as long as it took for the novelty to wear off. By the middle of the nineteenth century, narrow boats and barges were being hired for the day for such events as Sunday school excursions, but it was not until the latter part of the century that we find people writing accounts of travelling the canals simply because travelling the canals seemed like an entertaining thing to do.

An article in Harper's *New Monthly Magazine* in 1885 described a trip on the Regent's Canal. The canal is called the 'unknown river' that runs through the heart of London. But clearly it was finding some popularity:

Small pleasure-boats are allowed to ply on parts of the canal, and have given life to the scene. A long barge is anchored in front of a green field, and its owner informs us by a sign that he has 'boats to let for school and picnic parties'.

GIPSY QUEEN AT SHIRVA.

Reading the descriptions of the canal scene, one wonders who would want to take up the offer:

> Meantime we have been slowly passing, on the right, the great dreary goods station and the yards of the Great Western Railway. Then we come to Paddington work-house, a long dreary brick structure, set in a vast dreary field; and next beyond it, at the side of the Harrow Road, stands the Lock Hospital for destitute fallen women.
>
> Passing under Harrow Road bridge, we burst into a silent sea of shabby gentility, drearier in its assumption than all that has gone before. A pretentious terrace stretches away on either hand, faced with a make-believe massive balustrade, cracked and broken; the heavy houses fronting upon it are stuccoed shams, seamed and shabby; its few disconsolate trees seem tired of trying to keep up appearances, and the faded grass is completely discouraged and is going back again.

The anonymous authors travelled part of the way by narrow boat, with a skipper whose views of the canal were even less enticing:

The Gypsy Queen *operated as a pleasure steamer on the Forth and Clyde Canal in the last century, and this picture shows what a very pleasant waterway this can be* (Strathkelvin District Libraries)

183

It's never clean, an' it's allers low water, and there's nothin' but naked men a bathin' and thieves wot robs your barge and takes all they can git out of 'er, and blackguard boys wot calls yer names and spits on yer, and throws stones at yer.

The appeal for the writers clearly did not lie in contemplating the peace and calm of the waterways, but in a fascination with the working life of the canal, with the sense of visiting another world about which ordinary Londoners knew next to nothing. It was a world where men were legging boats unseen in a dark, deep hole far beneath the pavements, a world where cargoes from all around the world were carried in a rich mixture of craft. It was a world very different from that of everyday life, as this brief description of a journey through Mile End indicates:

The smoky air gives weird effects: the long low sheds of the Great Eastern goods station seem to stretch to the horizon. There are vast spaces stretching out on either hand, dusky distances far ahead. Amid all its strangeness there comes towards us a barge, dead black from stem to stern, no horse pulling it, no rower visible. The ghostly vision passes, and is resolved into a steam monkey boat, well laden, its tarpaulin stretched taut, its screw merrily whirling, its little engine gasping.

Many of today's canal travellers would be equally excited at finding a steamer coming towards them through the haze. But somehow the reader of this account cannot help feeling that the authors took the

One of the earliest accounts of travelling the canals for pleasure in a narrow boat is Two Girls on a Barge, *written in 1891. Here they are, with friends, at Watford Staircase on the Leicester Arm of the Grand Union* (Bodleian Library)

journey to get copy for the article as much as for the pleasures of the trip itself. The next account is very different.

Two Girls on a Barge, written in 1891 by V. Cecil Cotes, is exactly what its name suggests, an account of a journey by two highly respectable young ladies who decided to take a canal holiday. They managed to persuade a canal company to hire them a narrow boat complete with its captain and his wife, referred to somewhat coyly throughout as 'Mr Bargee and Mrs Bargee'. They then proceeded to have the hold partitioned off into cabins and to turn those cabins into passable imitations of the artier type of Victorian drawing-room.

> There was still much to do before we could begin to take Barge life in earnest. There were the curtains to hang, Liberty curtains that had taken a whole day to choose, and 'dhurries' to be draped over the fresh-scented pine of the little cabins; and Liberty again in innumerable hangings to be arranged all round the bulwarks gracefully.

The boat finally ready, the girls set off on what was obviously 'a great adventure'. They travelled up the Grand Union and loved it all. They were on the hunt for new and different experiences, something out of the ordinary, as different as possible from the polite life of London society. They found just that at Blisworth tunnel:

> We were in a black, domed passage, and it was deathly still; in all that string of barges no one spoke or moved. The gloom of the place encircled us. An indefinable Presence moved with us in the blackness. The nearness of the damp stones impressed itself upon the eyes and played fantastic tricks with the imagination. Every sense became distorted, unnaturally acute; the silence was appalling. The story the Bargee had told us of the great White Spectre, boding evil to the boatmen whenever it appears, came back to me with a meaning and a terror that yesterday had seemed impossible. 'Ye just slips yer foot, or over balances, and the black water swallows ye.'
>
> A vision of a barge, like the one I was on, engrossed all my attention. It was covered up, as ours was, with tarpaulin, to keep the cargo dry; but two boards, small, mean boards – 'wings' the bargee had called them – had been placed far out over the cruel water on either side of it. They were narrow, unprotected, slippery boards, and on one of them a little, clinging, frightened boy was lying on his back 'legging' the boat along, with nothing to prevent his slipping off the plank but a hand twisted under him and grasping it. It was the first time he had done it, and he was 'well-nigh skeered'. 'For his father had seen it,' the Bargee said, 'only the day afore, and so then *he* slipped and the black waters swallowed he.'

The book is pervaded by this sense of total absorption in a world that could seem as exotic as anything that one might expect to find in a trip up the Amazon. The canal holiday was chosen as 'something different' – which is why I chose to go on my first canal holiday over half a century later. No one ever expressed this view better than E. Temple Thurston in his classic work *The Flower of Gloster*, which was published in 1911:

> 'I'll go,' said I one day, 'where there are no guides and scarce a map is printed. Who knows his way about the canals of England?'
> 'They begin at Regent's Park,' said a man.
> 'And then?' I asked him.
> 'There's one passes near Slough on the Great Western. I've seen it from the train.'
> 'If that's all that's known about them,' said I, 'I'll get a barge myself and go on till I stop.'

And so he did. He bought *The Flower of Gloster* and hired Harry from Eynsham and a horse to take him on his voyage of discovery, a leisurely voyage with time to look around and relax in the peaceful countryside.

The nearer one comes to one's own lifetime, the more recognisable attitudes seem to be. We all know the 'lock bashers', the boaters whose sole ambition is to cover as many locks and miles as possible in one day. I met just such a gentleman in print, P. Bouthron, whose book *My Holidays on Inland Waterways* was published in 1915. Here he describes a day's travel, starting on the Stratford Canal:

> Leaving Hockley Heath at nine sharp, we at once encountered 19 locks in 2¾ miles, doing this in 1 hour and 35 minutes. This finished the Stratford-on-Avon Canal. We were then shunted, on to the Warwick and Birmingham Canal, on which we did some eight miles with 24 locks to Budbrooke junction. This canal is well kept up, and has some fine bits of wooded scenery as one gets along. In the afternoon we made a passing call at the ancient town of Warwick, which is well worth a visit. In doing a trip such as this one feels inclined to land at many places en route to view the cathedrals and explore the town thoroughly but we found to adopt this would entail a serious loss of time, our route being pretty well mapped out for each day's programme.
>
> It was at this fine old town that we entered the Warwick and Napton Canal (14 miles with 25 locks), which took us down to the junction of the Oxford Canal, passing the well known town of Leamington (Warwick) on the way. This canal we found also in good condition. A lot of traffic passes through here in transit between Birmingham and London.
>
> We were really rather pleased with our run on that day, as altogether we had done 25 miles over part of the three canal companies' properties, and the very large number of 66 locks – an excellent piece of work we considered – constituting, as far as we know, a record for a single day's lock work.

It is perhaps worth mentioning that the self-congratulatory tone was a little misleading since the author and his friends had nothing much to

This elegant steam launch, Alexandra, *with its company of gentlemen was touring the Leeds and Liverpool in the 1890s. Here it can be seen at Bank Newton* (Rolt Archive)

do but to sit back and let the hired help work the sixty-six locks.

Rather more to my taste is C. J. Aubertin, whose book title *A Caravan Afloat* (1916) is a good description of his boat, a sort of floating box, 33ft (10m) long which was poled or bow-hauled. Originally, it was fitted with a paddle-wheel, worked by a cog and chain like a bicycle. Even the proud owner described it as 'a place of torture'. Not that all his travel was done this way: like other early tourists he, too, journeyed with a working boatman, and found a way of life very different from that of the land.

A strange life this barge work! Here to-day and gone to-morrow. A barge passed us. 'How d'ye do, Jim?' 'How d'ye do Harry?' 'Where for?'

'Macclesfield with bricks. What's your game?'

'Pleasure trip.' No time for more. 'That was my brother. Haven't seen him a many year.'

He found a working life full of quirks and oddities which delighted him. Here, by way of example, is what he found on the Suffolk Stour:

On this river the boats always travel in pairs. The bow end of the fore boat has a deck large enough to provide standing room for a horse. Whenever the tow-path crosses the river a small jetty is built out into the stream corresponding to another on the further bank – not opposite but a few yards up or down stream. When a crossing

187

is to be made, the horse ceases to pull and goes to the pier head. The boat is steered close alongside and the horse leaps on board, some litter having been considerately placed on the deck to afford him foothold. The boat is then steered sharply over to the opposite pier, where the horse leaps out ready to begin work again.

Reading accounts such as this fills me with envy, for by the time I came to the canals, much of the richness of the working life was already fading into memory. Perhaps the last writer to catch the spirit of the working days was L. T. C. Rolt. In *Narrow Boat* he described a journey through England immediately before World War II. Even then, he could still write of a world largely unknown to his fellow citizens, but infinitely worth knowing. He saw, however, that the days of the working boats were numbered and that 'the bright boats will rot at the wharves, to live on only in old men's memories'. That his other sad prediction that the last of the canals would soon be 'a weedy stagnant ditch' did not come true was due in no small measure to the efforts of Tom Rolt himself and others who fought to keep them open. The canals now are busier with holidaymakers than even the most optimistic of the early tourists could ever have dreamed possible. They are a joy to thousands, but they will never again be what they were in the days of Rolt and Temple Thurston, or of two young Victorian ladies who decided to leave the city one day for the strange, peaceful world of the waterways.

Narrow boats could easily be adapted as pleasure boats for special events such as school and club outings. This is Mabel *at Market Harborough in the 1950s* (Anthony Burton)

A Trent and Mersey Canal milepost (Anthony Burton)

Pontcysyllte

Pontcysyllte is the most dramatic, and the most popular, structure on British canals. It is an unforgettable sight: nineteen stone arches carry the iron trough 121ft (37m) above the River Dee, and the span from one side of the valley to the other is 1,007ft (307m). It is seen at its most impressive by those who cross it by boat, for although the trough is 12ft (3.7m) wide, the tow-path is cantilevered over the water reducing the available width for boats to just over 7ft (2m). The result is that the steerer invariably finds the boat running right against the side of the trough and, which makes it a unique and even slightly alarming process, the iron plates are usually out of sight below the level of the gunwales. The result is that one seems to be flying rather than boating: the same effect obtains on other iron-trough aqueducts, such as Edstone on the Stratford Canal or Wolverton on the Grand Union, but no others have such a dizzying drop.

Originally, the chief engineer William Jessop had put forward two proposals for the crossing of the Dee valley. One was for a conventional aqueduct, roughly the same dimensions as Pontcysyllte; the other, and cheaper, version was to lower the canal by 24ft (7.3m) via three locks. A pump, powered by water from the Dee would be used to supply the water for the locks in a straightforward pump-back system. When Jessop's assistant, Thomas Telford, returned from his work on the Shropshire Canal, where the River Tern had been crossed by a successful, if somewhat crude, iron-trough aqueduct, he was an enthusiastic advocate for the use of iron for the Dee crossing. Jessop was very familiar with ironworks being himself a partner in the Butterley Ironworks in Derbyshire, so needed little convincing. The balance was tilted back in favour of the long valley crossing, which removed the need to build locks. The aqueduct has to be seen as part of the whole design of the canal for this mountainous region. Further to the south, the canal had to be carried over the River Ceiriog at Chirk, but beyond that the only sensible solution for the hill that now lay across the line was a tunnel. Tunnelling was always difficult and expensive, and the deeper and longer a tunnel was the more difficult and costly it became to build. Keeping the canal at a high level reduced tunnelling problems to a minimum. It was in order to maintain that level that the engineering works at Pontcysyllte were needed, and the great aqueduct was only the culmination of the whole scheme. After Chirk tunnel came the shorter Whitehouses tunnel, but then a huge embankment had to be constructed to bring the waterway to the point where it could fly off across the Dee. The embankment was, at the time, almost as great an achievement as the aqueduct itself.

The building of the aqueduct was seen by contemporaries as a major event: engineering on a scale previously unknown. Jessop worried about the effects on the stonemasons and builders working at such giddy heights, and few of us would envy the job. The stone piers were constructed of solid masonry up to a height of 70ft (21m), above which they are hollow and braced by cross walls. The iron work above was designed in consultation with William Hazeldine of the nearby Plas Kynaston Ironworks, where the various parts were to be cast. It is no straightforward box, but a complex jigsaw of pieces, angled so that they could act against each other to withstand water pressure. The pattern is more complex than strictly necessary, but who can blame the pioneers for making safety doubly sure on such an ambitious project? It was officially opened in 1805 and declared a wonder and a marvel: nothing has happened in the intervening years to change that judgement.

13 CANALS FOR PLEASURE

When considering using canals for pleasure, most people think first and foremost about boating. British Waterways commissioned an opinion poll from NOP in 1986 which showed that an estimated 140,000 people took canal holidays in hire-boats, which seems a great many people. On the other hand, against that figure, there were 770,000 anglers and nearly five million people who use the canals for what was described as 'other informal' purposes. So how does one justify devoting the whole of this chapter to what now appears to be a minority use? Well, first, the average boater will see more canal than the others who use it. Even a week's cruising can cover the best part of 100 miles (161km) of travel. Most anglers seem, at least to the admittedly prejudiced eye of the passing boater, never to move at all, not even to pull in a fish. In fact, in more than twenty years of boating, I have only once seen anyone catch anything at all, and that was an eel which the angler was too squeamish to touch. The truth, of course, is that anglers enjoy the peace of canals as much as the rest of us – and would often prefer that it was a good deal more peaceful than it is – but their prime concern is not scenery but those slippery, elusive, silver creatures darting about in the murky waters. The canal is viewed by their expert eyes not in terms of what might delight the human eye but as what might appeal to a fishy instinct. That corner by the gasworks may be less than salubrious to the rest of humanity, but if the angler sees it as just the spot for carp or roach, then he will set down his rod, his umbrella, his tins of bait and all the complex paraphernalia needed to lure the beast on to the hook. There are anglers, I am sure, who delight in the canalside scene, are learned in canal history and lore, and I know from talking to them that there are many who appreciate the boats. Irritating though they may be as interruptions, boats are valuable in keeping channels open and unsilted. But the angler's first love is line and rod, and he does not really care whether the pond he is fishing is a natural lake or an engineer's answer to a canal water shortage. Nor is he especially interested in whether the canal on which his float bobs was constructed on the principles of contour or cut and fill. These seem to be more than adequate reasons for not attempting to deal with fishing in this chapter.

So much for angling, but what of the five million casual users? Many of these are people who simply find themselves living near a canal and use it as a place to stroll by, or they wander down to canalside pubs and watch the passing boats. There are a few who make a point of walking tow-paths, and there are many derelict canals which are only accessible to those prepared to use their feet. It can, indeed, be a most rewarding activity, and we shall be returning to the subject later on. The dedicated

If any one structure can be said to exemplify the technical brilliance and innovation that marked the work of the greatest canal engineers, this is it: Pontcysyllte, the aqueduct that carries the Llangollen Canal across the River Dee. (Anthony Burton)

tow-path walker will usually tell you that the pleasures are, in any case, much the same as those enjoyed by the boater, without the noise of an engine or the smell of diesel. These pleasures come from enjoyment of the scenery, both in the widest view and in the more particular sense of appreciating the narrow world, which is at once both artificial and natural in that what man has begun on the canals, nature has continued to shape. The walkers will, I hope, excuse the concentration on boating since they and boaters have so much in common. Boating also has an added element: the pleasure of boating itself, which perhaps should come with a slight correction to read the pleasure of boating well.

This is not going to be a manual on boating. Those with their own boats presumably have some notion of what they are doing. There are incompetent boat owners in plenty, but sadly their incompetence is often joined to, and even explained by, a disinclination to listen to advice. Beginners setting out on hire-boats will find practical advice at the boatyard a better start than reading theory, although to them I would just like to point out that they should beware of falling into a common trap. A boat with a steering wheel at the front may look reassuringly like the family car, but it is in no way similar in practice. The boat designed along traditional lines with a tiller at the stern is the end product of two hundred years of canal-boat building practice. There really is no need to be frightened of it; just remind yourself that in the working days 70ft (21m) boats were managed quite competently by small children standing on stools to reach the tiller. Happily, however, the training run given to hirers does not use the technique reported by one Thames waterman. He started his steering career standing on a box and on his first day out banged against the side of a bridge. Next thing he knew his ears were ringing, he was seeing stars and his father was standing over him saying, 'You get one of those every time you hit anything.' He learned, he said, very quickly.

This will not, then, be a training manual. But there is one question that I am asked more than any other: 'Which canal should I start on?' Occasionally, the question is addressed in a slightly different form: 'Which is your favourite canal?' The answer to the first question is complex, but comes down to finding out what the questioner is hoping to find. The answer to the second is far simpler: 'I haven't got one.' And the reason why there is no real answer to either question is the same in both cases: the splendid complexity and variety of the British canals. What is full of pleasure and interest to one may well be a miserable interlude to another. So what follows will be a series of impressions of what I find especially pleasing about canal travel, what it is that has brought me back year after year since my first tentative excursion to Llangollen.

It all begins with the pace. There is no way you can hurry on the canal. Some will try to: you hear a frantic revving of the engine, which results not in extra speed but in the stern dipping ever lower in the water above a gurgling mass like chocolate blancmange in a mixer. The canals have a comfortable, natural pace, where the engine runs smoothly, there is no wash to harm the banks and the boat does not attempt to shake itself to pieces. And that comfortable pace will get you to your destination in

as good a time as any hectic thrashing around. It is the pace of a not
particularly energetic walker, a human pace which allows ample
opportunity to see what the world around has to offer of interest. For
me, to stand at the tiller of a canal boat is one of life's real pleasures. It
is not just a matter of the scenery passing by in leisurely parade, for the
boat itself always demands attention. There is as much delight in
knowing that you have shifted the tiller by just the right amount at just
the right moment to move the boat easily round a difficult, sharp bend
as there is in the sight of a rainbow standing proud above a field bright
with corn. It would not be the same at a greater speed; it would inevitably feel mechanical, while the gentle drift of the canal boat is still not
so very different from what it would have been when the only motive
power was the ambling horse on the tow-path. It feels natural, which is
probably why I seldom worry very much about the weather. Obviously,
like everyone else, I prefer sun to rain, warmth to freezing cold, and day
after day of gloom and downpour can make anyone depressed. But it is
part of the sense one has of canal travel being a very close, intimate
affair, at one with the natural world, that one has to accept the worst
the weather can do as the price for that sense of closeness. So, on bad
days as well as good, I am still reluctant to be prized away from the tiller.
Even the very worst days have their compensation: like the man hitting
his head with a hammer, it is wonderful when you stop.

Things never seem quite so bad in retrospect as they may have seemed
at the time, and, just as memories of childhood holidays are of
successions of golden days, so one remembers days on the canal when
the sun turned the water into a necklace of brilliant diamonds. Rain, in
our selective memories, not to mention sleet, hail and snow, become at
worst passing irritations. So I turned to words set down when experience

was all too fresh in the mind, and this is what I wrote about the climb up the twenty-one locks of the Wigan flight:

As we started up the locks, the rain started down: not even down, really, more horizontal, blown flat by a cold wind. Working a flight of locks in the rain is not much fun, and when the locks are right pigs that don't want to be worked in the first place it is least fun of all. And that's what we got at Wigan. Half the paddle gear was out of order. The jack cloughs, big wooden levers that slide covers across the faces of the sluices, seldom worked. Many of the rest had to be heaved and bullied and cajoled into working. And just to make it that much more difficult, all the gear was locked and chained to preserve it from vandalism. We were constantly fumbling with keys and locks, fastening and unfastening the chains with numb fingers. It was sheer misery. We must have looked like a collection of little clouds coming up the hill. The cold rain combined with hot sweaty bodies to give each of us our own, personal aureole of steam. Three and a half hours that flight took us, and what did we see on the way? Precious little, apart from a factory that described itself as a waste manufacturer. I'd always suspected they existed. As we reached the top, the lock-keeper came out and asked if we meant to go on. No, we said, that was not our intention. Right, he said, you can tie up right where you are, so we simply fastened the boat up to the top gate and called it a day.

Trees lean their branches over the beautiful Brecon and Abergavenny Canal at Mamhilad (Derek Pratt)

Is there really any compensation for such misery undertaken in the name of pleasure? There always is. There is the pleasure of getting out of wet clothes into dry, and exchanging the damp and cold of the great outdoors for the snug warmth of a friendly pub where, if there is any justice in the world, you can find good ale and decent food. Fortified and restored, the day's horrors become a good story, full of incidents rather than just a curse.

It is just as well that one has learned to accept the weather, since there is nothing whatsoever that can be done to change it. And the true pleasures, the pleasures that lie with the world of the canals themselves are always there regardless of what the elements contrive. It is not always easy to identify exactly where that enjoyment lies in a particular sense, but the most obvious must be the beauty of the scenery. I said that there is no answer to the question 'Where do I start?', but I have found that most people setting out on their first holiday put the answer to that question on the top of the list. Which canals, then, offer the most spectacular scenery?

The Brecon and Abergavenny is a name that always comes very high on the list, if only because it is a canal that runs through much of its length within the boundaries of a national park, the Brecon Beacons. It is a route dominated by hills. Once clear of the outskirts of Pontypool at its southern end, it follows as twisting a path as any canal in the country, and with good reason, for it occupies a narrow ledge on the hillside and has to follow every fold and indentation. It has, perhaps, its grandest section on the approach to Llanfoist, where the waterway is dominated by the steep wooded hillside of the Blorange. All the time the canal is following a high-level route with superb views down over the Usk valley. In all this journey through the hills of Wales, there is just one short flight of locks, and inevitably, as the canal reaches ever higher up the valley, it meets the river itself. The crossing on the Brynich aqueduct is altogether delightful and forms a fitting prelude to the run up to Brecon. I was caught out here. The map showed a winding hole some way from the town, but at the end it said, 'Brecon Basin'. The words proved a delusion. Basin there undoubtedly was, but it is no more, just a dead end, which meant that I had to start the return journey by travelling for ½ mile (0.8km) in reverse.

There is scarcely a sour note on the whole of the Brecon Canal, and if any waterway deserves the epithet 'unspoiled', this must surely be it. It is the sort of canal that people come to who do not want to be reminded of the fact that the whole system was built in the first instance to serve the needs of the Industrial Revolution, not to provide pretty routes for holidaymakers. But industry was most certainly here, and for me, much of the appeal of the canal derives from the almost hidden, secretive remains of the past. Take Llanfoist, for example, as superb an example of a little canal wharf set in a truly lovely position as you could hope to find. But everywhere there is evidence that there is more here than can be taken in at first glance. For a start, why is there such an extensive wharf with manager's house and large warehouse at such an out-of-the-way spot? Why, instead of the familiar hump-backed bridge, is there a flat-topped bridge across the canal, and, even more mysteriously, why is there a tunnel under the canal at the same point? If you stop to investigate, clues soon begin to appear. The warehouse is the place to start. There is a wharf, but also a boat hole where vessels could be brought in for loading. On the land side, the roadway runs round the back of the warehouse, higher up the hill so that goods could be unloaded at first-floor level. That trackway then seems to connect with another leading straight up the hillside, with a branch crossing the flat-topped bridge. On my last visit a little truck was sitting on iron rails and a few pigs of iron were laid out alongside. The final piece of the jigsaw is now in place. This was a canal-tramway interchange. The flat-topped bridge carried rails and the tunnel was for pedestrians who did not wish to be run over by trucks hurtling down the incline. The wagons brought iron to the wharf, then loaded it into the upper storey of the warehouse from where it could be lowered into boats that floated in underneath. Those who have a strong sense of curiosity about such places can follow the incline up the hill and find numerous stone sleeper blocks in place. Those prepared to walk far enough can eventually trace a route right back to the start where they will find themselves confronted by the blast furnaces of the eighteenth-century ironworks at Blaenafon, as majestic in ruined old age as the crumbling walls of a medieval castle. So, having started out recommending a canal entirely on the basis of great scenic beauty, I have now ended by praising it for its wealth of historic material. Some will go in search of the one, others will be on the look out for the other, but those who take equal delight in both will get most from the journey. This, happily, is true of the great majority of canals.

If one stops for a moment with canals in hilly country, the same rich mixture seems inevitably to occur. The upper end of the Peak Forest canal between Whaley Bridge and Marple, for example, follows a high-level route above the Goyt valley, not dissimilar to that taken by the Brecon and Abergavenny and similarly lock free – though not, alas, free from swing-bridges which all too often show a marked reluctance to budge at all, let alone swing. It, too, has its tramways and, in Marple, a fine old warehouse built to serve cotton mills rather than blast furnaces. This canal has also to come to terms with the river valley and does so in the grandest of manners. A lovely flight of locks with side ponds and little stone bridges starts the journey down the valley side. It is full of appealing details, including a horse tunnel under the main road. It all ends with the river crossing on the breath-taking aqueduct. After that, the canal heads off towards the centre of Manchester – at which point some holiday boaters immediately lose interest. That, to many, is the workaday world they have tried to leave behind and the very last thing they want to encounter on holiday. This was just as true of the early canal travellers. This quotation comes from *The Flower of Gloster* and the author is just setting out with his boatman from Oxford:

'Is it like this all the way?' I cried.

He left his horse. She stopped at once to nibble by the hedge.

'Is the canal like this all the way?' I asked him as he came back along the path.

196

The towering arches of Marple aqueduct carry the Peak Forest Canal over the River Goyt. The holes in the arches are not decorative devices, but serve to lighten the load without weakening the structure (Derek Pratt)

'Oh no, sur,' said he: 'look you, there's fine country soon as you come past Thrupp.'

'And where shall we stop for the night?'

'Well, that's as it likes you, sur. We reach Shipton Church 'bout seven this evening. There be a good flow of water under, and we shall make Shipton Church 'bout seven.'

'Right away, then,' said I. 'Go along as fast as you can till we get away from these damned red brick villas.'

Now this has never been my view. I enjoy the urban canal as much as the rural, and, having started on the Peak Forest, let us stay with it on into the Ashton, the Rochdale, the Bridgewater, the Trent and Mersey and finally come back to Marple on the Macclesfield Canal to complete a popular cruising circuit, the Cheshire Ring. I am not, as a rule, much in favour of rings, when I have only a fixed amount of time available. Once well set on your way, you feel bound to hurry on to complete the task, ignoring all temptations to stray, however enticing they may be. But the Cheshire Ring contains such an extraordinary mixture of scenery, such a contrast between town and country, that it serves beautifully to illustrate the contention that variety is certainly the spice of canal life.

As one leaves the Goyt valley behind, so a steady spattering of isolated cotton mills punctuates progress, like a trailer for coming attractions. At Dukinfield, the Peak Forest runs into the short Ashton and now the mills and warehouses begin to crowd in on the waterway, closing off the view. Admirers of Lowry and enthusiastic industrial archaeologists will find it fascinating, even attractive, while others may see only the ugliness of a crowded industrial world – but you cannot ignore it. Like it or hate it, you have to admit that it is mightily impressive. But we are still only on the B feature; the main attraction comes with the Rochdale Canal. Once the junction was marked by massive warehouses, now long gone, and the twentieth-century world of offices has taken over from the old cotton kingdom, but in doing so it has produced the most bizarre entrance to any canal that I know. After going down just one lock, the canal apparently disappears into an office block. Only when you get nearer do you discover that the entire tower block stands on concrete stilts, and somewhere in the dark of the foundations is not just the canal but a canal lock. After that, almost anything might be expected to prove an anti-climax, but not here. Emerging out into the light, you find yourself faced by a man-made canyon as the canal slices through the heart of the old commercial centre of Manchester, surrounded by imposing buildings erected in the days when cotton ruled the city. It can be an exciting trip, too, for unsuspecting lock-wheelers. There is no room here for by-weirs, so that the opening of a lock sends a wave like a miniature Severn bore rushing down the canal. It is likely to overflow on to the tow-path, so Wellington boots are no bad thing on the Rochdale.

After the Rochdale with its flurry of locks there is time to relax on the lock-free Bridgewater Canal, bringing you away from the city and back to the country. On this pioneering waterway there are 23 miles (37km) without interruption all the way to Preston Brook and the junction with that other early waterway, the Trent and Mersey. It is, and seems to be, a different world, as one exchanges the broadness of the one for the

One of the most remarkable locks on the whole canal system can be found here where the Rochdale Canal passes underneath an office block in the heart of Manchester (Anthony Burton)

narrowness of the other. The contrast seems all the more marked because of the rather tentative nature of the works on the old Grand Trunk Canal. Tunnels are low, narrow and crooked; the course of the canal is winding and at times can seem almost arbitrary. Everything about it declares that it was built at the beginning of the canal age, and, just when you are getting used to the fact, you reach Anderton and the extraordinary lift that carrries boats between the canal and the River Weaver down below. The Trent and Mersey turns out to be a canal full of contrasts: in places it is as idyllically rural as one could find, but elsewhere passes through a weird, unnatural landscape of old salt works where the underground workings have literally undermined the land, causing it to sink and crumble.

The Trent and Mersey offers several landscapes, while the Macclesfield is predominantly a back-to-the-hills canal. If the Anderton lift can seem like a modern, mechanised folly, then this canal starts out under the shadow of a genuine folly. The hill Mow Cop is topped by a romantic ruin, but there is no point in trying to guess what was there before the collapse, for there was nothing. The ruin was built as a ruin, as artificial as a film set with no function other than to sit on top of the hill and look splendid. The canal is unmistakably of the North, its dark stone bridges echoing the stone that forms a hard edge to the nearby hills. It is not a country-side that lends itself easily to canal building and the engineers had to force a way through in deep cuttings and stride over valleys on high embankments. A walker in the hills tends to have one type of view, which can be excellent but which cannot match the variety that comes from diving into the heart of the land only to come out again on to the grandeur of a high bank with immense views taking over from the closed world of the cutting.

The Cheshire Ring has something for everyone: scenery of every conceivable type from flat plain to tall hill. It has the canal that began it all and in the Macclesfield one that only just crept in at the very end of the canal age. It has a town where you occupy an almost private, secretive world of your own, and the widest of wide spaces. It would be fair to say that anyone who travelled the Ring and failed to find anything at all to enthuse over is someone who will never really take to canals.

Inevitably, one thinks of the northern canals in terms of hill country. The Leeds and Liverpool takes a great swing round to the north to avoid the worst of the Pennines, but it is still the hills that provide the dominant mood. Greenberfield locks, for example, seem to belong absolutely to their particular place; everything tells the same story from the strong swell of the hillside above the water to the drystone walls that mark the canal's progress through the land. Further south, the mood can be very different, altogether gentler, but that is not to say that there is no drama to be found. The Staffs and Worcester on its way up from the Severn passes through an area of red sandstone, so that in places the canal is quite literally overhung by cliffs of most startlingly vivid colours. Those making the journey with no set plans and time to spare – quite the best way to travel – can dawdle up this most lovely route of quiet pleasures and then take one from a variety of choices. Two junctions, sounding confusingly similar but offering very different prospects –

Aldersley and Autherley – appear within ½ mile (0.8km) of each other. You can ignore them both and continue serenely on your way, enjoying the slow progress through a peaceful countryside that seems to be the principal feature of the Brindley canal; or you can turn north on to the Shropshire Union for the most extreme example of the late canal, with its deepest of deep cuttings and highest of high banks; or you can turn south and climb the long flight of locks up to Wolverhampton and the heartland of the English canal system, the BCN.

I remember a day in what was alleged to be spring when I had come up the Worcester and Birmingham in driving rain that turned to hail thrown like bullets on a fierce wind. At Farmer's Bridge, where three canals meet, the wind was so strong that I was una   to steer the boat round to the moorings, even with the engine goi.g rd and the tiller pushed right over. We finished up with the family bv -hauling round the turn as I heaved at the tiller, while the water strea ied down my neck; and the only things that stood out from the surrounding gloom were the lighted windows of unlovely tower blocks. 'What on earth are we doing here?' my wife shouted above the row of the engine and the howl of the wind. For the life of me, I could not think of a sensible answer.

People will tell you there is ugliness here and I would not disagree, although I would point out that there can be a surprising beauty. I have seen the deep cutting sides of the Birmingham Canal blaze out with gorse and flowers, and I have chugged through smiling to myself in the knowledge that there was probably no brighter spot that day in the whole of the Midlands. The fact that it was here in so unexpected a setting made it all the more enjoyable. But such experiences are more the exception than the rule, and I can only agree that much of what is seen from these canals is a reminder of a harsh world of industry where men and women worked in appalling conditions, where filth and dirt and smoke and grime were accepted as the norms of existence. But even Temple Thurston recognised that there was something special here:

> In fact, whether you believe in it or not, those belching furnaces and that poisoned land must make you marvel as you pass it by. The black sweeping hills with scrubby bushes leafless and dead; the men and women, white-faced and dirty with the everlasting falling of the sooty air; the thousand factories and the countless furnaces; the utter lifelessness in all this seething mass of life, however much he might shudder at it, a man must stop and realise its greatness.

Like it or not, it was for this that the canals were built and for anyone who says that they would like to see industrial canals in their historical context, then Birmingham is the place to be. But there is more to it than that. The BCN is like a world within a world, a well-kept secret. You know that all around you life is going on at the sort of pace one expects from Britain's second city, but it seldom reaches quite down to the canal. And if you turn off the main route, you can feel like an explorer in a foreign land – with many of the difficulties explorers face, including being regularly stopped by unforeseen obstacles. I once collected an astonishing object, an indescribable mass of wire and cloth, on one of the less-used byways and it had to be cleared from the prop by an oxyacetylene burner. There is, too, a special magic in the names of Birmingham: some blunt enough to tell you all you need to know – Gas Street, Rough Hills, or Bug Hole; others offering promises of romance, country freshness or just plain oddity. Even if the reality does not match imagination, they still act as a lure. When were farmers last seen at Farmer's Bridge and what culinary delights were once to be found at Pudding Green? Is Watery Lane as delightful as it sounds, and what lies behind such curious names as Oozells Street, Spon Lane and Wednesbury Oak? There always seems to be something lurking in the Birmingham area waiting to be discovered, and if I cannot quite explain clearly why I keep returning, I can at least recall the fact that I do, and that I am far from alone in finding endless interest in this complex web of canals.

Wansford bridge on the peaceful River Nene (Jenny Burton)

The word 'complex' seems to keep recurring when one talks about canals, and it often seems that it is in that complexity that much of their charm lies, in the knowledge that each new canal will offer a very different experience from the last, and that whatever you are looking for in the canal world is probably to be found somewhere. Those with the taste for getting away from it all, combined with a sense of history, might turn to the lovely Caldon or the little-used Chesterfield. The idle might enjoy the lock-free Ashby or Lancaster, while those who really want to avoid crowds can take a trip down one of the loveliest of all our rivers, the Nene, to connect into the system of waterways that spreads out through the Fens. I started by talking about the joys of travelling through the hills of Wales and nothing could make a greater contrast. This is a world of whispering reed-beds, where the scenery of the land can seem far less impressive than the ever-changing pageant of the wide skies, repeated in mirror image as a shifting pattern of light and dark on the water. Which is best? There is no answer, for there is no comparison, just as one cannot compare travelling the wide, commercial waterways of the North East and their still busy traffic with a quiet meander up a narrow canal of the Midlands.

There are canals to be enjoyed which the narrow boat does not reach. The ship canals of Scotland are one example, such as the short but exhilarating Crinan which in 9 miles (14km) climbs up the hill from the sea by seven locks and swoops down to the sea again by eight more. The Caledonian is altogether grander, with its long sections of natural loch which, in stormy weather, can seem as choppy as the North Sea. It is the only canal to offer at least the possibility of a sighting of its own resident monster, still regularly hunted in Loch Ness. But there is, too, a far larger group of canals that are inaccessible by conventional boat – the derelict and abandoned waterways. Some are undergoing restoration, but even before that is complete they can still be enjoyed by those prepared to exchange their boats for boots and engine power for leg power.

Having boated the Rochdale Canal on its dive down through Manchester, I decided in the summer of 1987 to see all the remainder right down to its junction with the Calder and Hebble at Sowerby

Bridge. A distance of 33 miles (53km) is rather more than I can face in a day's stroll, but it is on occasions like this that one is grateful for the fact that railway engineers often followed the line laid down by their predecessors on the canals. The old Lancashire and Yorkshire Railway was built alongside the canal and, as it is still in use, it makes it easy for the walker to get a train back to the start at the end of a day's walk. I found it a most enjoyable experience. The scenery is true Pennine, with the mixture that I love of crag-topped hills, drystone walls and the tight, clenched-up mill towns down in the valley bottom. It was certainly no hardship to walk and it did occur to me that with 92 locks in its 33 miles (53km) travellers by boat would probably finish up walking just about as far as I did.

This was tow-path walking at its simplest, but there are canals which have been so long abandoned that they have almost disappeared from the landscape. Searching for them can combine healthy exercise, decent country walking and the attractions of the treasure hunt. The south-west of England is a particularly fine hunting ground. In the past, I have gone to search out the handsome aqueduct that carried the Rolle Canal across the Torridge. I have tried to trace the Stover and the Tavistock and on occasions when the canal search was leading to nothing very inspiring, I have found surprises and delights. It was while trying to find the site of a lock on the canal from Liskeard to Looe that I heard the unmistakable sound of a large theatre organ wafting across the fields. I abandoned the lock hunt and went in search of the source of the music. I found it in Paul Corin's Mechanical Music Centre with everything from player pianos to the mighty Wurlitzer that had drawn me to them. Perhaps there is only the most tenuous link between theatre organs and canals, but if I had not gone looking for the one I should never have found the other. It is really an important part of the appeal of canals, surely, whether walked or boated, that they take you away from the ordinary, everyday world and introduce you to the extraordinary.

Canals for me are a source of inexhaustible pleasure. There are still those which I have not fully explored and there are many abandoned canals I have yet to trace. There are canals which are now derelict but which will one day be restored and on which boats will again float. And even when there is nothing new to be done, there will still be old friends to revisit. The canal I knew at one particular time and at one particular season will be very different at another time and another season. The charm of the canals may defy definition, but it never goes away.

The Old Clyde puffer ViC 32 *is still a coal-fired steamer but these days earns her keep by carrying passengers instead of cargo. Here she can be seen edging slowly up the Crinan Canal* (Anthony Burton)

14 RESTORATION

Even if L. T. C. Rolt's *Narrow Boat* was not the excellent book that it is, it would deserve a special place of reverence on every canal enthusiast's shelf, for it was the trigger that set off the canal restoration movement in Britain. After its publication, many people wrote to the author, including Charles Hadfield, who was to become the doyen of canal historians, and a literary agent. The latter wanted to form a society of like-minded canal enthusiasts, 'a sort of cross between the Light Railway Transport League and the Friends of Canterbury Cathedral'. The agent was Robert Aickman, who was to become chairman of this unlikely hybrid. The first meeting was held in London in May 1946 with Aickman, Rolt who was appointed secretary, Hadfield as vice-chairman, and a friend of Hadfield's, Frank Eyre as treasurer. During that evening a stranger appeared, Captain R. L. H. Smith, who enquired politely if this was the meeting of the Inland Waterways Association. The new movement had been given its name.

The founding fathers were to have serious disagreements, partly over policy and partly as a result of a clash of personalities. What was the new society to do? At first Rolt and Aickman were agreed that the first priority should be to keep the canals open for working narrow boats, with the notion that some might also be used for pleasure boating tacked on almost as an afterthought. Rolt's own views were expressed with his customary clarity and obvious depth of feeling in the autobiographical *Landscape With Canals*, 1977:

> What chiefly appealed to me about the canal system was its indigenous working life. On the narrow canals this meant the working narrow boats and their crews which were so essential a part of them. These working boaters, so many of whom I knew and admired, unconsciously supplied that subtle traditional patina of constant use – the worn and dusty towpath, the polish that generations of 'uphill or downhill straps' had given to the bollards of cast-iron or grainy oak at the locks; it was an essential part of that blend of utility and beauty which used to compound the particular magic of canals. This was something which some members in the I.W.A. could never fully appreciate. They could value canals aesthetically as an important contribution to landscape beauty, but they could not assess to how great an extent utility was responsible for this.

Charles Hadfield shared Rolt's enthusiasm for the working life of the narrow canal, but felt that their days were finished and nothing could

be done to stem the inevitable decline of a transport system which was soon to celebrate its two hundredth birthday. He was, in any case, about to join the Civil Service and felt that he would not be the ideal person to stand at the head of an organisation that was very likely to be arguing vigorously against government decisions. There was also a problem in working in harmony with the extrovert, flamboyant personality of Robert Aickman.

Tom Rolt was an active, indeed vital, figure in those early years, but he began to have doubts about the way in which the organisation was moving. Aickman's view was simple and, with hindsight, probably correct: all canals should be saved. Rolt wanted the emphasis to be placed on, and all the limited resources to be set to, those canals which still carried working boats. It seems, looked at from this distance in time, to be no more than a shift in emphasis, the sort of disagreement that could easily be resolved. Once again, however, personalities were to play a crucial part. When Rolt resigned as secretary, partly because of policy disagreements and also because the voluntary work was taking an impossibly large portion of his life when he had a living to earn, the acrimony bubbled to the surface like marsh gas in a swamp. Rolt and his wife were advised not to bring themselves or their equally famous boat *Cressy* to the first IWA boat rally, although the rally had been Rolt's idea. The whole sorry business ended when Rolt was expelled from the association. It was done by the most formal of formal letters, with no mention of his role in the formation of the IWA. The memories of the bitter feud between the 'Roltites' and the 'Aickmanites' lived on for very many years, and arguments about the rights and wrongs of the issue still occasionally rumble on. It is worth reviving these accounts of old wars, however, for they demonstrate a truth which is applicable far beyond the bounds of canal societies. It is in the nature of protest movements – for that is what the IWA was in its early days – to be started by passionate idealists. It is also in the nature of passionate idealists that they can seldom work together for more than a limited time, so that there is always a threat of splits and schisms. If, however, the cause is good enough, there is every chance that the organisation will outlast the quarrels of its begetters. The IWA proved to have that strength.

It is perhaps difficult now to appreciate the size of the task facing the infant IWA. Who would now consider closing the canal to Llangollen? But we live at a time when pleasure boating is almost the only form of boating seen on the British canals. It is not just fun for a few, but an important, thriving business for many. For Tom Rolt, taking *Cressy* to Pontcysyllte was more than just an adventure, it was the achievement of a long-held ambition and an affirmation of the importance and unique character of the canal. This was important, for it was threatened with closure, and the early years of the association had necessarily to be more concerned with keeping what was there already, rather than worrying about restoring what had gone. In the early campaigning years, vigorous action was needed just to maintain the status quo, and achieving recognition that a waterway existed and could be used for something other than dumping old prams was a priority. Campaign cruising began on the Stratford Canal in May 1947, when navigation was obstructed at King's Norton. The authorities said that, given twenty-four hours' notice, they would shift the obstruction for a boat to pass. This involved jacking up a steel bridge at Lifford Lane and Rolt took *Cressy* along after due warning had been given. The bridge was duly raised and *Cressy* scraped underneath to the clicking of camera shutters. A point had been made, publicity had been obtained for the new organisation, and it was not long before a lift bridge was in place. This trip was followed by many others, together with boat rallies at spots specially selected to highlight the importance of some threatened part of the system. Threats, however, were becoming more real and more menacing.

In the early years, the IWA was a campaigning organisation, writing leaflets and pamphlets, sending letters to the press and drawing in such famous men as Peter Scott and A. P. Herbert to help advance the cause. But in spite of all this hard work, some waterways were visibly being allowed to crumble and decay. The most important of them, simply because of its size, was the Kennet and Avon. Newbury Council declared that, as far as they were concerned, the canal could fall into disuse – not a view shared by one local citizen, John Gould. He decided that it was worth fighting for and he also decided that the most practical way of keeping the canal open was to use it. He bought a pair of narrow boats, *Colin* and *Iris*, and in 1949 brought a load of paving stones from Birmingham to Newbury. He was also one of the prime movers in setting up meetings to discuss the future of the canal. As a result, a local branch of the IWA was formed which was to be open to anyone who had an interest in the Kennet and Avon. Meanwhile, control of the canal passed to the new British Transport Commission, a body initially enthusiastic about road transport, fairly keen on railways but with very little enthusiasm at all for canals. In fact, it would not be unfair to say that the BTC regarded canals as tedious left-overs from a bygone age and the activities of men such as John Gould as a confounded nuisance. A series of stoppages of unspecified duration were suddenly announced: commercial carrying was over. The infant IWA branch was also running into choppy water, as the waves from the Rolt/Aickman dispute spread along the canals. They tended to side with Rolt and by 1951 the IWA branch was no more and the Kennet and Avon Association was born, later to be changed again into the Kennet and Avon Trust. The story of the Kennet and Avon is one of fluctuating fortunes, as opinions at the top of the canal hierarchy went through many a change of direction. While the enthusiasts eagerly fought the battle for a navigable canal, the old BTC fought just as hard for closure. The BTC had one great advantage: they were the body who looked after maintenance. All they needed to do was neglect that maintenance and time would close the canal for them.

The 1950s, however, saw the beginnings of a new canal trade – hireboats for holidaymakers. Canal Pleasurecraft began operating out of Stourport, New Way Holidays offered the first hotel boat and thousands had a glimpse of the canal world when the trip boat *Jason* began its travels up and down the Regent's Canal. It was clear that some new thinking was needed about how canals were to develop, and the job was handed to a committee headed by Leslie Bowes. As they began their deliberations, the BTC applied to parliament for permission to close the Kennet and Avon. The issue was hard fought, with the Kennet and Avon Association organising a petition which collected twenty thousand signatures and was taken to London from Bristol by canoe. The outcome was a mixture: neither closure nor reopening was foreseen for the immediate future, but everything was to be halted, frozen at an instant: no restoration, but no more deterioration to be permitted. The Bowes Committee report in 1958 summed up the current state of thinking. The gloomy part came first: 'We have found no justification for restoring the section from Reading to Bath.' But it was suggested that it was 'a case for redevelopment' which should give 'due weight to amenity and recreational values'. There followed an interim period when the status quo was more or less maintained by groups of volunteers acting as unofficial lengthmen. On 1 January 1963, control of the canal passed to the British Waterways Board, and to meet their new masters the enthusiasts also changed hats. From a campaigning association, with a little muscle work on the canal, the movement changed its name and character. The Kennet and Avon Trust was formed and a new way forward appeared when, it was fervently hoped, co-operation could take over from the old form of confrontation. BWB was to divide the £40,000 spent each year, half to go on maintenance and half on restoration, while the trust would raise funds and provide volunteers to help with the work. In time, the work element dropped away and the fund-raising became of paramount importance. So the branch of the IWA became an association and the association became a trust and in 1987, when the trust celebrated its silver jubilee, the chairman's report was bandying figures about that would have seemed unbelievable at the start:

At last year's AGM I told you that, based upon the costs given to us by the Director of Engineering BWB, we needed to raise £625,000 by the end of 1989. A reassessment of certain costs and a prudent decision that we should include a fairly substantial sum for 'contingencies', led to this being revised upwards to £¾ million.

You will understand, I am sure, what pleasure I have in telling you that we are now assured of this sum. What a happy chance we should achieve this at our Silver Jubilee!

And to add to that, there was the news that completion was set for the end of 1989. The canal that looked doomed in the 1940s was to see boats making the trip from Bristol to Reading in the 1990s.

The Kennet and Avon is by far the longest running continuous saga on the canal, and will, as they say on the hoardings, 'run and run', for the trust will have a continuing interest even when restoration is complete. Along the way, the whole range of restoration problems and solutions have appeared. Official hostility has been replaced by co-operation; volunteers have come, and gone again; restoration by amateurs has given way to fund-raising for the professionals, and so it goes on. And all the time, the canal world has been changing. Other schemes have been started: some completed, a few abandoned, and different approaches to problems of restoration have been tried. The Kennet and Avon group parted company with the IWA in 1951, but by then the IWA had a great many projects to worry about. It is not possible in one chapter to cover over forty years of restoration work, so to give an idea of the tremendous range of activities of the IWA and other independent bodies, we shall look at just a few schemes – which, if it does nothing else, will at least prove that there is more than one way to restore a canal.

The first on the list is the Lower Avon. In the years after the war, the river from Evesham to Tewkesbury had become unnavigable, and the old company had long since run out of funds to pay for its regular upkeep. In 1950 the Midlands IWA took a bold and decisive step: they bought the waterway for what now looks like the remarkably good bargain price of £1,500. The Lower Avon Navigation Trust was then established to raise funds to pay for its restoration, and early on they received help from an unexpected quarter. The Royal Engineers offered to help rebuild Chadbury Lock. This not only saved the trust a considerable amount of money in the short term, but it gave a welcome boost to finance in general, as people now came to believe that a bunch of well-meaning amateurs actually could restore the aged navigation to life. It was eventually to be completed in 1962, and the next stage of restoring the Upper Avon could be started. But long before that, the success of the scheme caused eyes to be turned to other parts of the system. What if, the dreamers dreamed, we could restore the Avon to Stratford and then restore the Stratford Canal? Boats could complete a wonderful waterways circuit – up the Avon to the Stratford, on down the Worcester and Birmingham to the Severn and along the Severn back to the start. We could have an Avon Ring! Work had begun on the Avon and it was time to look at the Stratford.

The Surrey and Hampshire Canal Society's venerable steam dredger is no museum piece, but a useful working machine on the Basingstoke Canal (David Robinson)

Rolt's cruise had shown the value of getting a boat on to the canal. It highlighted the problems, and even persuaded the authority to do something about one of them. But the canal as a whole was a wretched affair then: undredged, weedy, silted pounds were linked by dilapidated locks with bulging walls and sagging gates. The chances of getting a narrow boat through were precisely nil, but early in 1957 a canoeist made the journey which had rather more in common with Humphrey Bogart's trip on *The African Queen* than with a conventional canal cruise. But what a valuable effort it proved to be, for in 1959 Warwickshire County Council applied to parliament for permission to abandon the Southern Stratford on the grounds that they were legally allowed to do so because there had been no traffic on the canal in the previous three years. They were wrong, and along came one lone canoeist with a handful of toll receipts to prove it. The canal was not closed and instead the National Trust stepped in to lease it from BWB for restoration and eventually to buy it. Another stage in the journey of the ring was now begun. The National Trust was, and is, a body with a considerable reputation and a large following. There were obvious advantages in having that prestige tied directly to a major restoration plan. Money was raised and volunteers came forward, some rather more voluntarily than others, since a good part of the work went to prisoners from Winson Green and men from the army and RAF.

The work of the Avon Ring will always be associated with one man, David Hutchings. He is one of those individuals who, once fairly set on a target, is as stoppable as a runaway express train. He got help, however, from wherever he could, and was always clear about his objectives: to get a waterway open for boats. Everything else was of merely secondary importance. In June 1964, Evesham Town Lock was formally reopened, to be followed by an even grander event the following month when the Queen Mother came to Stratford to declare the canal officially reopened. Canals, for once, made the front page. They also ceased to be merely mucky ditches crawling round the backs of grubby towns. They were respectable; they had the 'royal stamp of approval'.

If canal restoration had been a cricket match, one could say that the gentlemen had been first to take the field. The players were about to have their innings. Volunteers were at work up and down the country in the 1960s on a whole variety of schemes. It was becoming obvious that some of them actually enjoyed the work for its own sake. A new movement was about to develop from the unlikely base of the London and Home Counties branch of the IWA. The name 'Home Counties' seems to carry overtones of gentility, but that would not be the word that comes first to mind when describing the branch secretary who started a new magazine *Navvies Notebook* in 1966. He was to become as prominent a figure in the restoration movement as David Hutchings. Graham Palmer soon moved from magazine production into organising an army of volunteers who shared his enthusiasm for the canals but, just as importantly, also shared his enthusiasm for getting stuck in. They became the Waterways Recovery Group, and one had the feeling that if they ever managed to produce an official motto it might have been 'The muckier, the better'.

For those who have never been on a working party, it is difficult to describe how filthy it can be. I recall a day on the 'Deep-cut Dig' in 1977 when, as one of about six hundred volunteers working on the Basingstoke Canal, I was helping to clear a lock. This involved shovelling black slime, piling it into a wheelbarrow and then wheeling it away over planks to dump it. As the day wore on, the planks became less and less distinguishable from the surrounding sea of silt and the inevitable happened. I trundled the barrow right off the planks, at which point, to my horror, it began to sink out of sight. By the time I had got my barrow back, I was no more distinguishable from the mud than the planks were. It was generally reckoned by the assembled amateur navvies to have been one of their better days.

The Waterways Recovery Group won their spurs when they tackled what was thought by BWB to be both a useless and impossible task: the restoration of the Ashton and Peak Forest Canals. This was to be part of another ring project to match the Avon Ring, the Cheshire Ring. Once again, the restorers were faced by scenes of dereliction and neglect. As early as 1959 BWB were putting up notices saying that the Peak Forest was not recommended for boating – a challenge which the IWA met in 1961 by organising a cruise on the Ashton and Peak Forest. This would have been difficult enough at any time, but was made more difficult by the mysterious burning down of one set of lock gates the night before the procession of boats was due. The point, however, had already been made – that the canals were navigable. A more daunting challenge than vandalised locks was thrown down by the elements when the severe winters of 1962 and 1963 caused widespread damage, notably to the lovely Marple aqueduct. The Peak Forest Canal Society and the IWA campaigned hard, but it is much easier to make people understand the value of a lovely rural canal such as the Stratford than it is to explain the value of an urban waterway running through an old industrial area such as Ashton-under-Lyne. Eventually, the time came when everyone agreed that the volunteers should at least be given a chance. Graham Palmer organised 'Operation Ashton', which sounded a touch military, but then the whole project was run like a military campaign. Some six hundred workers descended on Manchester one weekend in 1968 and everyone had a job to do. To the amazement of almost everyone except Graham Palmer, everyone did their jobs. An astonishing collection of rubbish was removed and burnt, and 2,000 tons were carried away to a dump. Operation Ashton had been set a target and that target was triumphantly reached. The big work party was a success; the canal could be restored and the amateur navvies could play a vital role. After the Ashton weekend no one doubted that the Cheshire Ring would become a reality – and what a splendid reality it is. And, after Ashton, it was equally clear that the Waterways Recovery Group was going to be a major force in the whole restoration movement. Camps are still being held at sites all over Britain, where, for a very modest sum, one can enjoy a week's holiday digging out muck and sleeping in church halls – a pleasant alternative, perhaps, to the Costa del Sol.

The success of the early schemes brought varied rewards. It was not just that a few derelict canals had been reopened: local authorities, too,

Making new lock gates for the Huddersfield Narrow Canal at the Colne Valley workshops (Huddersfield Canal Society)

Getting into the muck: members of the Waterways Recovery Group clearing out a lock at Woking (Clive Durley, Waterways Recovery Group)

were gradually coming to realise that their canals need not be unpleasant eyesores, but might actually be valuable amenities. Canals were becoming fashionable. Those who had seen the houses at Marple, when the owners tried to shield off the view of rubbish and mud by fences and hedges, could now come back and see the hedges removed and lawns stretching down to clear waters, busy with passing boats and water fowl. Estate agents – handy barometers for testing the economic weather forecast – began to put 'Canalside property' at the head of a description, where before they had studiously avoided mentioning anything so offensive as a waterway. Slowly but surely, the long years of campaigning were beginning to pay off.

Restoration increasingly became a tripartite affair, between BWB, local authorities and volunteers. By the late 1970s a new factor appeared on the scene which was to become increasingly important in the 1980s – mass unemployment on a scale that matched the years of the Great Depression. Government funds were used to back various youth employment and job creation schemes under the Manpower Services Commission. Suddenly there was money to spend on canals, and full-time workers could be brought in to do the job. Canals which might once have been thought impossible to restore saw work beginning and going ahead at a phenomenal rate. Many of us had looked at the two great trans-Pennine routes, the Rochdale and the Huddersfield Narrow, and declared them superb, but had doubted whether they could be saved in part, let alone restored throughout. Energetic enthusiasts, however, were not deterred, and almost before anyone knew it, the locks were being refurbished and the old filthy ditches became clear waterways. One now has the feeling that perhaps nothing is impossible. Canals which seemed doomed forever echo to the sucking squelch of the dredger. Will the Thames and Severn Canal ever be fully reopened? Perhaps not, but many people are prepared to have a good go at making it work – and anyone who has ever strolled the old tow-path down the Golden Valley, as lovely in reality as the name suggests, can only wish them well. But what about canals that have all but disappeared from view, so that it requires detective work even to find out where they were in the first place? The Wilts and Berks has got lost in Swindon, is now just about visible as part of a roadway in Abingdon and is not very much clearer along many other parts of its way. But that has not stopped the dreamers having visions of a grand reopening. And if that seems far-fetched, well, so did the idea of a navigable Avon Ring or a Cheshire Ring not so very long ago.

The restoration movement is probably more buoyant now than it has ever been. British Waterways were even able to announce in 1988 that a new Canal Act had just received royal assent to allow the Montgomery Canal to be restored to the standards of a cruising waterway. But in the euphoria surrounding fresh restorations and new beginnings, there are still a few sour notes to be heard. While funds and efforts can go into restoration, what about the old canals that never became derelict but which are increasingly showing their age? They, too, often need restoring, while the two-centuries-old structures – bridges, aqueducts, tunnels and the rest – not only need looking after, but require the sort of sensitive treatment that can be seen in the best of the restoration schemes, such as Aldermaston Lock on the Kennet or the restored locks of the Huddersfield Narrow. And then there are the other conservationists, who, seeing the ugly ducklings they had ignored for years emerging as beautiful swans, suddenly declare that they are valuable wildlife habitats, far too beautiful and serenely peaceful to be ruined by noisy boats and oafish boaters. The restoration story is a success story. One only has to cruise canals such as the Caldon, or the Brecon and Abergavenny, or to look at what is happening on the Wey and Arun or the Droitwich to see that. One thing now seems certain: the amateur and the professional restorers will have no shortage of work to do or problems to overcome in the foreseeable future.

Sapperton Tunnel

Sapperton tunnel on the Thames and Severn Canal is not the longest canal tunnel in Britain – Standedge on the Huddersfield Canal claims that title – but it can surely claim to be one of the most majestic. When work began on the canal in 1781 it was described by contemporaries as 'the most historic exploit of the century', for this was not to be a narrow canal, but one capable of taking river barges up to 11ft (3.4m) beam. The tunnel was thus on a scale never before attempted: a wide bore well over 2 miles (3.2km) long. It had to be driven through difficult ground, passing through fuller's earth and limestone, in an area beset with springs. The work was as difficult as any to be found anywhere, and the techniques were crude, relying on muscle power and blasting by black powder. Inevitably there were casualties, but the achievement was great. This wide bore 3,817yd (3,490m) long tunnel was completed in five years, and it was said to be so straight and true that it was possible to see right through from one end to the other. This can be compared with the first Harecastle tunnel of 1766, a narrow bore, nearly half a mile shorter and notably crooked: that took eleven years to complete.

The owners of the canal, Gloucestershire County Council, were given official permission to abandon much of the canal, including the tunnel, in 1927. Rock falls closed it off and gradually it and the rest of the canal fell into dereliction. In 1972, the Stroudwater Canal Society was formed and three years later it expanded to become the Stroudwater Thames and Severn Canal Trust. Restoration was under way. In the autumn of 1988, the first official party of visitors was taken to see part of least of the tunnel – following good royal precedent. In 1788, George III was taken on a similar excursion into the tunnel by Earl Bathurst, and the eastern end of the tunnel became known as 'King's Reach'. The Coates entrance is suitably regal, a splendid portico complete with pillars, parapet and niches. Once inside two things strike one, the total clarity of the water and the neat stonework of the arch. The tunnel has no tow-path, yet there are no marks of wear on walls or roof to suggest that boats were legged through – and as one gets deeper into the tunnel it soon becomes obvious that legging would have been impossible. It seems likely that the barges were pushed through using shafts with a broad base so that they did not stick in the clay floor.

As the little boat penetrates deeper under the Cotswold hills, so the character of the tunnel changes. In places it is brick lined, and it is obvious from the size, shape and colour of the bricks that this was part of the original work. The most spectacular sections, however, are those where the bare rock is exposed. The walls are fissured and stratified presenting a decidedly uneven surface – hence the absence of legging. All along the walls one can still see what appear to be semicircular grooves cut in the rock. These are the remains of blasting. The rock would have been drilled by hand, packed with powder and when that exploded, the rock split away leaving just half the original drill hole still visible. There is no shortage of things to see: distances are marked off in the good old-fashioned measurement of chains. In places walls have been built against the rock at water level. This is because the oolite was very prone to leaking and the walls kept the water in the canal. Not that there seems to be a shortage of water, for springs can be seen pouring merrily in from the sides. Contractor's shafts can still be seen rising up out of the darkness; no glimmer of light at the end for they are all capped. There is also evidence of the last attempt to keep the tunnel open. When Gloucestershire County Council took control in 1901, they put in hand a lot of repair work, and the concrete in the sides and the pipes through which springs are ducted date from this period.

This first trip stopped just short of the rock fall, but everyone who was fortunate enough to be invited came away not just excited by what they had seen, but with new admiration for the engineers and workmen who burrowed deep under the ground two centuries ago.

15 CANALS IN THE FUTURE

'The canals will never be what they were in the past' – a statement usually made with an accompanying sad shake of the head and mournful look. And the statement is quite true. It was equally true in the 1940s when the canals were nationalised; it was true in the 1920s when trucks began to take more and more trade away to the roads; and at the beginning of this century when the motor boat appeared alongside the horse-drawn boat. It was true when the first locomotive hauled the first waggon on iron rails; and the statement was probably first heard when a second generation of engineers turned away from the theories of James Brindley to adopt new and bolder building techniques. Change is an inevitable part of any great enterprise. The narrow canals that were the main arteries of trade for the Industrial Revolution are now, to many, no more than watery equivalents of country lanes, suitable for holidays and nothing else. There is no point in trying to turn back the pages of the history book, hoping to bring back to life those charming illustrations of horses on the tow-path, narrow boats bright with roses and castles, and a busy, thriving commercial trade. The trick will not work; the past cannot be relived. But that is not to say that there is no role for water transport in Britain. It is, in a way, unfortunate that the very name 'canal' conjures up such a romantic image, for it seems so clearly a thing of the past that it is hard to conceive of any future in the commercial, cargo-carrying sense. But when the engineers came to conduct their famous experiments in the eighteenth century, which showed that a horse pulling a boat on a canal could shift twenty-five times the load of a horse hauling a waggon on a well-made road, they were producing results that are still valid today. We may not use horses, but we still think in terms of horse power for our engines. What was true of the 1hp horse is just as true of the 1hp engine – or the ten horse power or the hundred. Moving goods by water requires less power than moving goods by land.

Is there a future for commercial carrying on Britain's waterways? Only the incurably romantic can look forward to a time in which cargo carrying will again play an important part in the world of narrow canals – which is not to say that there is not a commercial future for these waterways, but that it will not be based on carrying goods. British Waterways are not the sole proprietors of the canal system, but their role is so central that it is simplest to look at the whole story in terms of the BWB system. The 1968 Transport Act divided their empire, like Caesar's Gaul, into three parts, whose names adequately describe their function: 542 miles (541km) as commercial waterways, 1,100 miles (1,770km) as cruising waterways and the 600 miles (965km), known for want of any better word – and lack at the time of any idea what to do with them – as the remainder. In terms of the carrying trade, it is the smallest section that was and is the most important. However, in terms of the total quantity of goods carried in Britain, it was not very important.

In 1982 BWB produced a booklet *Transport: The Water Way* in which they set out their stall at what seemed a particularly propitious moment. After years of pleading and arguing their case with the government, they had finally achieved one of their prime objectives – the improvement and modernisation of the Sheffield and South Yorkshire. The report does not, however, make at first glance very cheerful reading. The waterways took less than ½ per cent of the nation's goods, compared with 10 per cent for their old rivals, the railways, and all the rest went by road. But there is more than one way of looking at figures. What about efficiency? What about looking at the amount carried compared to length? The figures show the waterways carrying 9,458 tons per 0.6 mile (9,612 tonnes per kilometre), 9,393 tons (9,546 tonnes) by rail and only 4,636 tons (4,711 tonnes) by road. And as the roads are so desperately overcrowded already while the waterways could take ten times as much

The 1950s saw an attempt to improve the commercial waterways of Britain. This photograph was taken on the Lee Navigation shortly after the new lock was completed (Anthony Burton)

traffic without any undue strain, is there not a message to be read here? So, before looking at the question of whether there will be more traffic on the commercial waterways, let us look at the question that should be asked before any decision is taken: is there a case for taking more cargo by water?

There are three basic arguments in favour of using the waterways, the three Es: environment, efficiency and Europe. The environmental argument is the most immediately appealing. Every motorist stuck behind a heavy truck grinding slowly and painfully up a steep hill knows it; every villager seeing the fabric of their old buildings being destroyed by juggernauts asks why the trucks are there. Even on the new roads, the motorways, specially built for modern demands, the everlasting cones are reminders that the sheer weight of traffic on Britain's roads is getting close to a limit. The only answer seems to be to build more motorways, more bypasses, and to widen and straighten. And that means taking more land and spreading the noise, the rumble and the fumes of traffic ever further afield. Now waterways are not going to take more than a fraction of that traffic; even if it doubles it will still be less than 1 per cent of the whole. But there are areas where a significant improvement could be made. Look, for example, at the waterways in the London area: the Lee Navigation to Enfield and the Grand Union to Brentford. Here is a real potential for moving traffic out of hopelessly clogged city streets and on to the water. You have only to stand on a bridge over the Seine in Paris to see what could be achieved – and if that does nothing else, it shows how much more pleasant it is to watch boats go by than it is to watch HGVs.

The environmental argument is, at first glance, unanswerable: boats are on the whole quieter, and cause less air pollution and less damage to buildings than road vehicles. But, as with so many environmental arguments, there will always be the opposite case to be put by the practical businessman. 'All very well,' he says, 'you chaps going on about the quality of life and so on, but I have to live in the real world.' The real world, in this context, invariably refers to something downright unpleasant which we all have to put up with for our own good. It is rather like the Victorian nanny dosing the children with castor oil: the nastier it tasted the more virtue it was assumed to have. One of the main preoccupations of the businessman is cost, and here at least the water-ways argument is sound. Advancing forward a little from the engineers of the first canal age to more modern times, numerous tests have been carried out to estimate how much energy was needed to move goods by different means. An American survey of 1973 was particularly thorough and gave specific figures in terms of kilojoules per tonne/kilometre or, in plain language, how much effort you had to put in to move a set load over a set distance. The results for railways and waterways were almost the same, but each used a quarter of the energy of road vehicles and about one-sixtieth that of planes. An important consideration is the conservation of fuel, and the more fuel you save the more money you save as well. In terms of fuel costs, waterways fare better than roads. But fuel is not the only cost: wages also must be taken into account. The truck driver thundering up the motorway can cover hundreds of miles

for a day's pay, while the boatman has scarcely left base. But the boatman's load will be many times that of the driver, so for his one day's pay he is carrying the equivalent of many trucks full of cargo. What he loses in distance, he makes up for in quantity. Not all cargoes are suitable for waterways, but where they are, costs are very much in favour of the boat.

'Very good,' says the hard-nosed businessman, 'but my trucks go door to door. They don't have to be loaded and unloaded and my goods don't have to be transferred from one system to another.' This is very true, but the argument looks less convincing when one brings in E3 – Europe. Britain is part of Europe, yet separate; part of the economic community but physically still an island. Whether we like it or not, a good part of our trade with the rest of the EEC must go by water. Europe has a vast integrated system of modern waterways, so that it is possible for seagoing vessels and large barges to penetrate deep into the heart of the continent. It is not only theoretically but also practically possible to move cargo between Europe and Britain without any trans-shipment at all being needed. Where that can be done you have a transport system that on every criterion is a sensible one – a system that is cheap, efficient and does less harm to the environment than the alternatives. So why are more goods not being carried in this way nowadays and are we likely to see more goods being carried by water in the future?

The first question to ask now is 'Can it be done?' It certainly can be, and the evidence is there to be seen in other countries, especially those of Europe. Huge amounts of capital have gone into improving the waterway system, building bigger and better canals and navigations with

Waterways vs The Rest

The arguments in favour of waterways have always rested on their greater efficiency. Eighteenth-century engineers produced these results, for the load that could be hauled by a single horse:

	Tons
Average pack-horse load	1/8
Stage wagon, soft road	5/8
Stage wagon, macadam road	2
Barge on river	30
Barge on canal	50
Wagon on iron rails	8

Two centuries later, American engineers did their experiments, which were enumerated in the IWA book compiled by Mark Baldwin, *British Freight Waterways*, 1980.

Mode	Specific Energy Consumption Kilojoules/tonne-km	Index
Pipeline	325	0.66
Rail	484	0.99
Waterway	491	1.00
Road	2,023	4.12
Air	30,353	61.80

ever-better facilities, including some spectacular modern boat lifts. Alongside this has come the development of new inland ports and new vessels to take advantage of the system. But where Europe has leapt forwards, Britain has tentatively edged along, and it sometimes seems that for every pace taken in the right direction there has been another back to the start. Improvement has been horrifically slow. It took years of argument for modernisation of the Sheffield and South Yorkshire to take effect. In 1973, a proposal was put forward for the canal which was to cost £3.5 million, a sum which an enthusiastic motorway builder could use up before breakfast. It was turned down, then argued over and eventually when the logic of the arguments won through, the cost had inevitably soared. And why was improvement necessary? In the 1970s one could see the ludicrous spectacle of three modern barges pulled by a tug on the waterway, arriving at a lock which was still manually operated and only big enough to take one barge at a time. So one barge could go through with the tug while the rest had to be man-handled. This sort of situation could only lead to a downward spiral. It is so absurdly outdated that no one wants to use the system; the authorities can then argue that there is no point in modernising a canal that no one wants to use. One also has to ask how much traffic was lost to the canal forever while the government dithered over what was to be done.

Modernisation is at least a step forward, but what about new ideas? The most ambitious proposal ever put forward was by J. F. Pownall in 1942 for what he called a Grand Contour Canal. The idea was for a wide canal running at the 310ft (94m) level right through Britain – the only locks would join it via side arms to cities and rivers all the way from Newcastle to London. In the proposer's own words:

> The natural canal line creates the remarkable possibility, never before known, of having a canal ... through the length of the country and serve the great indus... ...as without any variation from the one level.

What happened to the proposal? While ... ...ching this book at the Waterways Museum at Stoke Bruerne, Powna... ...apers were delivered. They were ready to join other documents that had passed into history and were now destined for the archives. Was the scheme practical? Perhaps not, but we can never be sure because it was never properly considered. It seems all too likely that any other schemes for extending the waterways would suffer a similar dismal fate so that one is left with doing what can be done with what exists already. The trouble has always been a lack of funds and the fragmentary nature, not just of the transport system as a whole, but even of the waterways themselves. The saddest example of what can go wrong when people think only in terms of conflicting interests and not in terms of co-operation is to be seen in the story of BACAT.

One of the keys to successful waterways operations not just in Britain, but in Europe and America as well, is push-tow. It is, in a way, a development from the old working pair, where one boat, the motor, towed another, the butty. It was taken a stage further with the Tom Puddings, where one tug hauled a whole train of small compartment boats. The next step was to design barges which could be pushed as well as pulled – a system which developed on the wide rivers of the USA, particularly the Mississippi, to the point where one push-tug was in charge of a raft of barges, like a small moving island. On the Mississippi it is possible to see a single push-tow consisting of forty 984-ton (1,000-tonne) barges. British vessels are of somewhat more modest dimensions, the norm being a group of three barges each holding about 138 tons (140 tonnes). Not much perhaps, but better than a narrow boat and better by far than even the biggest juggernaut on the roads. The point that was obvious to many people was that such barges could travel equally well on the canals of Holland, Belgium, France or Germany. All that was needed was a method of getting them across the Channel. If you could do that you could load a barge in Rotherham and then unload it in the heart of Europe. This was the job for which BACAT (Barge Aboard Catamaran) was designed. The barges were the standard BWB push-tows and the mother ship had space between the twin hulls for three barges to be locked into place, and a further ten could be lifted by a special elevator and secured on the deck. Mother ship and barges were then ready for a cross-Channel voyage.

There was trouble from the start, although not with BACAT itself, which worked well. But the new system bypassed old ports such as Hull and Goole which were under the control not of BWB but of the British Transport Docks Board who also controlled navigation on the Humber estuary. BWB were charged high tolls for using the Humber, which was bad enough. Worse was to follow. Dockers seeing their facilities bypassed decided unofficially to block the BACAT system. The whole scheme collapsed. The end benefited no one. The trade that had been carried by BACAT never came back to the Humber dockers anyway and BWB's bold experiment which would have linked North East England with Europe came to nothi   n that sort of story it is hard to take an optimistic view of the   o that you can add countless other tales of woe that are cor   eard from the waterway users. Loudest of all the cries is, as it   een for years, that of unfair competition. One can imagine the   ry from the road-haulage companies if they

BACAT 1 (Barge Aboard Catamaran) being loaded in London. Two barges are being pushed by a tug to lie between the twin hulls of the mother ship. The failure of this enterprising scheme is one of the sadder stories of post-war waterways development (British Waterways Board)

The Functional Tradition

Throughout the history of English – or for that matter of any other – architecture, there is a continous thread running parallel with the historical styles but owing little or nothing to them. It might be called a timeless tradition of fuctionalism if the term had not become confused by being used to define a far more sophisticated phase of contemporary architecture. For its constituent elements are geometry unadorned, and it owes its effects to the forthright, spare and logical use of materials. To this extent it has affinities with the architectural effects sought by the architects of to-day, which no doubt explains why, looking back over the centuries, our own eyes are especially apt at picking out structures that owe their charm and quality to this tradition of functionalism, whether seen in a gothic fortress, the roof of a Wiltshire tithe-barn, a groined sea-wall, a lighthouse, a Thames-side warehouse, or one of those grand, breath-taking viaducts by which the early nineteenth century engineers carried their railways across river valleys. But the best place of all to study the functional tradition is the English canal system, perhaps because canals were mostly built at a time when the new engineering techniques aroused enough enthusiasm for pure structure to be acceptable without self-conscious adornment, and perhaps also because they perfectly combine an architectural programme with a strict engineering discipline. The architectural qualities come from a close partnership with the natural landscape and from the drama of simple geometry, with its robust and endless interplay of basic elements: steps, arches, ramps, bulging bastions and subtly concave

continued on page 219

were told that to pay for the roads they used they would have to pay tolls for every ton carried and every mile travelled. Yet that is what commercial craft using the waterways must do.

The technology for an efficient waterways system exists. Bigger locks can be built, improved cargo-handling facilities installed. There is already a great variety of vessels able to travel far inland with good-sized cargoes – there are tankers and coasters, push-tows and motorised barges. There are already systems, similar to BACAT, where barges can be taken across the sea on mother ships. Europe boasts such vessels as the BACAT-liner, able to take twelve barges each of 787 tons (800 tonnes) which float in through the bow doors, while 500 containers can be stowed on deck. It is possible, but will it happen? Several factors count against it. The government seems irremediably wedded to the notion that canals are outdated anachronisms. The British Waterways Board summed up their view of the situation in *Transport: The Water Way*:

> The need to maintain a competitive edge has been blunted as a result of lack of adequate finance to maintain a competitive route standard, uncertainty over the extent to which the mileage of the Commercial Waterways would be maintained, and frustration created by changes in Government and Government policy. Most important of all has been the lack of any comprehensive transport policy. The financial regimes under which the road, rail and water transport systems operate are widely different, and in practice confer considerable benefits to road and rail which are denied to the waterways.

A further difficulty has arisen with the decline – in some cases the total disappearance – of traditional heavy industry in the 1980s. Sadly, these were just the areas which the waterways were best positioned to serve. And yet, the old arguments still hold good. Water transport is cheap, efficient and environmentally desirable, and there are signs at last that co-operation is being seen as an essential part of any future improvement. BWB has worked with local authorities on a variety of schemes such as the promotion of Sharpness Docks and with venture companies, such as the Humberside Sea and Land Services Limited, to build a new wharf at Keadby. Other plans are also going forward. So perhaps the obituary notices for the commercial canals can be put back in the drawer after all. Who knows, the unbelievable might even happen one day and the waterways might be – not given an advantage, that would be too much to hope for – but put on a fair competitive footing with other forms of transport. In fact a modest start has been made. The Transport Act of 1981 gave companies the opportunity to apply for Freight Facilities Grants if they had been previously sending goods by road, and could show that changing to the water would be a benefit to the environment and local communities. The grants could account for as much as 60 per cent of the capital cost of changing from road to waterway.

The cruising waterways present a very different picture. Once it is accepted, as it surely must be, that the only cargo likely to be carried in the foreseeable future is holidaymakers, then the questions that are asked about the commercial waterways become irrelevant. Holidaymakers have no interest in such matters as efficiency of movement. People largely come on the canals to 'get away from it all' – all being interpreted as the world of work and business, of dashing around from home to work and back again, and all the stresses that are a part of everyday living. Look at any canal brochure, and what you are being offered usually turns out to be an amalgam of leisurely travel, lovely scenery, peace and a sense of history. Schemes for 'improving' these canals, in an engineering sense, are meaningless. Traffic on the Southern Oxford could be greatly speeded up if it was given the same treatment that the northern part received in the last century. But just ask any holidaymaker which they find the more enjoyable to travel – the straight new canal or the wandering old one. A totally different set of priorities come, or should come, into play.

The canals obviously cannot simply be neglected. The results of lack of maintenance are decay of structures, silting up of channels and sometimes dramatic and catastrophic collapses. A modest amount of money spent on maintenance can save large amounts of cash being needed after catastrophes. One of the great problems of recent years has been the lack of funds for essential works. But there is more to it than that. What do you do when a bridge begins to crumble, when banks erode and paddle gear wears out? Do you bring in new technology in place of the old, or do you repair where possible and if replacement is necessary, do you keep as close as possible to what was there before? This may sound like a matter of the smallest imaginable importance, but it is not. The visual effect of a canal depends very little on the great, grand statements – no one is, in any case, likely to recommend the demolition of Pontcysyllte and its replacement by something more up to date. They are, however, very liable to miss the importance of small details – the use of the right type of brick, the nature of piling at the banks and the visual impact of locks. The latter are like a signature to a canal, an identifying mark. They are made up of a collection of small things which might seem singly insignificant but which, taken together, convey personality. Tradition was born out of a combination of practicality and simplicity, and age and use have added their own distinctive patina. There will always be those who cannot see why it matters that Grand Union paddle gear is different from that of the Leeds and Liverpool, but once a move towards standardisation gains momentum, it is difficult to stop. It is as well to remember that cruising waterways are something more than linear boating parks – they are survivors from one of the greatest historical changes the world has known. You can rebuild a Greek temple in concrete, but is it any longer a Greek temple? You can modernise the canals in a grossly insensitive manner, but what do you have at the end of the day? It is very easy to do as heavy-handed Victorian church restorers did – restore to the point where the original is no longer recognisable and its true nature is irretrievably lost.

There are things that can be done that have a value far beyond that

continued from page 218

parapet walls, all contrasted with the massive solidity of platforms and masonry retaining walls.

(Eric de Maré, *The Canals of England, 1950*)

City centre sites are always tempting for developers. The old warehouses in Coventry basin have been sympathetically converted into offices and workshops. Further development will be following on and it remains to be seen whether or not the atmosphere of the canal will be preserved (Anthony Burton)

which their modest cost might suggest – simple things like adopting an appropriate colour scheme or using the right materials. BWB's *Waterway Environment Handbook* shows with admirable clarity what can be achieved and how to achieve it. Other matters, however, are necessarily expensive. Funding is a perpetual problem and BWB have much valuable real estate. It is tempting to say, 'Sell it off and spend the money on restoration and renovation'. But when it is sold, where is the next bag full of cash to come from, and who is to say what is built on the land? A more sensible approach is to collaborate in the development process. The first steps are already being taken, sometimes in collaboration with local authorities, sometimes with private companies and sometimes with everyone combined. Schemes may be no more than bringing order to dereliction and chaos so as to make the whole canal environment more attractive, not just for those who might travel that way by boat but for the wider community who live and work near the canal. As with the houses at Marple, the canal can be transformed from eyesore to attractive feature, and the gain in value can apply just as much to businesses as to homes. If that message is understood in the commercial world – and when one finds that a major scheme such as Birmingham's new convention centre is to incorporate the canal as an important feature, then it seems to be – this is good news for everyone. New plans include ever-more ambitious schemes, such as whole new canal villages. They will not be like the eighteenth-century villages – although it would be easy to fall into the trap of what might be called 'Disneyfication' – a world of phoney cobbles and pastiche. Will the new be as good as the old? Sometimes it can certainly be quite startlingly bold as with the new pub at Gas Street Basin, which is proving extremely popular. In other places, such as Coventry Basin, restoration has enabled the new to blend seamlessly with the old. The point to bear in mind is that a new canal world is being developed which is primarily about leisure activities, but which can affect the whole life of the community. But even the grandest schemes occupy only a small part of the canal system. For most of its length it remains what it has always been, a network of waterways built to carry boats.

Canal travel for pleasure looks certain to continue, but if future generations are to enjoy the richness of association with the working world of the waterways which is so much a part of their appeal, then it is essential that conservation is given at least as great a role as any other factor. There will be changes, there will have to be changes, and one can only hope and pray that those who are responsible look long and hard at the system over which they are temporary guardians. In the course of this book I have tried to explain those elements in the canal scene which make it so attractive for myself and many others. They cannot be easily summarised, but some seem to spring at once to mind – a basic, robust honesty where appearance and use go together, and a sense of place, of materials being used that seem to fit naturally into their particular environment.

There are those who would simply stop all development and say, 'This is the historic canal scene and this is how it should stay for ever more'. That is quite unrealistic, but one can insist that when the inevitable changes do come, those responsible for design and planning will take full account of the old when providing the new. A system with no change eventually becomes a dead, sterile system. The canals have survived for two centuries and have managed to keep their essential nature intact. Perhaps in another two centuries they will still be here. Perhaps some of that great and odd collection of seemingly unwanted and unloved 'remainders' will thrive again. They will exist in a world we can no more imagine than James Brindley could conceive of living with television, Concorde and the microchip. But, with luck and care, the canals will still bring delight and will still survive as monuments to an age when Britain was the birthplace of a whole new world. The great days of the canals are not over yet.

FURTHER READING

The following list of books is a personal selection from a growing literature on canals. It is not intended to be comprehensive, and is chosen primarily to provide exactly what the heading suggests – further reading for those who want more information on particular aspects of the subjects treated in this book. Wherever possible, the list has been restricted to books currently in print: older works that have been reprinted are indicated by (R) at the end of the entry.

Hadfield, Charles, *British Canals* (1984) (7th edition)
Rolt, L. T. C., *Navigable Waterways* (1969)

Chapter 1
Allsopp, Niall, *Images of the Kennet and Avon* (1987)
Clew, Kenneth R., *The Kennet and Avon Canal* (1973), (2nd ed)

Chapter 2
Willan, T. S., *River Navigations in England, 1600–1750* (1936), (R)

Chapter 3
Burton, Anthony, *The Canal Builders* (1981), (2nd ed)

Chapter 4
Boucher, C. T. G., *James Brindley, Engineer* (1968)
Hadfield, Charles and Skempton, A. W., *William Jessop, Engineer* (1979)
Malet, Hugh, *The Canal Duke* (1977)
Rolt, L. T. C., *Thomas Telford* (1958)

Chapter 5
Burton, Anthony and Pratt, Derek, *Canal* (1976)
De Maré, Eric, *The Canals of England* (1950), (R)
Harris, Robert, *Canals and their Architecture* (1980), (2nd ed)

Chapter 6
Hanson, Harry, *Canal People* (1978)
Ware, Michael E., *Narrow Boats At Work* (1980)
—, —, *A Canalside Camera, 1845–1930* (1975)

Chapter 7
Faulkner, Alan H., *Barlows* (1986)
—, —, *Claytons of Oldbury* (1978)
—, —, *Fellows, Morton & Clayton* (1975)
—, —, *Severn and Canal and Cadbury's* (1981)

Turnbull, Gerald L., *Traffic and Transport* (1979)
Wilson, Robert J., *The Number Ones* (1972)
—, —, *Too Many Boats* (1980)

Chapter 8
Chaplin, Tom, *The Narrow Boat Book* (1978)
Ellis, Tony, *The Sailing Barges of Maritime England* (1982)
Lewery, A. J., *Narrow Boat Painting* (1974)
Paget-Tomlinson, E., *Britain's Canal and River Craft* (1979)

Chapter 9
Hanson, Harry, *The Canal Boatmen, 1760–1914* (1975)
Smith, George, *Our Canal Population* (1875) (R)

Chapter 10
Russell, Ronald, *Lost Canals and Waterways of Britain* (1982)
Ware, Michael E., *Britain's Lost Waterways* (2 vols) (1979)

Chapter 11
Cornish, Margaret, *Troubled Waters* (1987)
Smith, Emma, *Maidens' Trip* (1948) (R)
Woolfitt, Susan, *Idle Women* (1947) (R)

Chapter 12
Rolt, L. T. C., *Narrow Boat* (1944) (R)
Vine, P. A. L., *Pleasure Boating in the Victorian Era* (1983)

Chapter 13
Burton, Anthony, *Back Door Britain* (1977)
McKnight, Hugh, *The Shell Book of Inland Waterways* (1981), (2nd ed)

Chapter 14
Ransom, P. J. G., *Waterways Restored* (1974)
Squires, Roger W., *Canals Revived* (1979)
—, —, *The New Navvies* (1983)

Chapter 15
Baldwin, Mark, *British Freight Waterways Today and Tomorrow* (1980)

INDEX

Page numbers in *italic* denote illustrations

Abercynon, 84, 155, 162
Abingdon, 210, *26*, *35*
Accrington, *136*
Aickman, Robert, 203, 204, 206
Alrewas, 86
Anderton lift, 78, 83, 89–90, 199, *89*
Aqueducts: Almond, 82, 93; Avoncliff, 12, 13, 14, 15; Barton, 40, 41, 42–3, 78, 82, *41*, *67;* Brynich, 90–3, 195, *62;* Chirk, 82, 93; Dove, 82; Dundas, 15, 77, 82, 93, *62;* Edstone, 93, 189; Engine Arm, 86, *62;* Hazelhurst, 82; Longdon upon Tern, 82, 93, *93;* Lune, 77, 82, 93, *62;* Marple, 77, 82, 93, *209, 197;* North Circular, 93; Pontcysyllte, 42–3, 71, 75, 76, 82, 87, 90, 93, 189, 205, 219, *51, 71;* Sow, 90
Arkwright, Richard, 70
Ashton under Lyne, 47, 209
Atkins, Charlie, 137
Aubertin, C. J., 187–8

Baird, Hugh, 93
BACAT, 216–18, *217*
Baldwin, Mark, 216
Banbury, 106
Barlow, Samuel, 126, 135, 171, *154*
Bartholomew, William, 98
Bath, 11, 13, 15, 17–19, 85, 94, 156, 206, *18*
Bathampton, 17
Bathurst, Earl, 211
Bedworth, 135
Bennett, Arnold, 139
Bentley, Thomas, 44, 108
Bewdley, 29, 69, 98
Beziers, 40
Birmingham, 45, 113, 134, 148, 156, 160, 161, 173, 186, 200–1, 205
Blaenafon, 196
Bloomfield, George, 105–6
Blue Line Cruisers, 135, 137
Boatman's Institute, 149
Bolinder, Erik August, 108
Bollington, 86
Borrow, George, 142
Bowes, Leslie, 206
Boulton & Watt, 58, 69, 93, 104
Bourne, J. C., 56
Bournville, 108, 136, 137, 144
Bonthron, P., 13, 186–7
Bowes Committee, 206
Boyle, Thomas, 143
Bradford, 17
Bradford on Avon, 11–13, 17
Braunston, 85, 129, 130, 134, 135, *133*
Brentford, 108, 147, 214, *147*
Brewood, 84
Bridgewater, Duke of, 32, 37, 40, 41, 42, 43, 45, 54, 67–8, 72, 90, 176, *7, 40*

Bridgnorth, 37
Brindley, Anne, 69
Brindley, James, 7, 42, 43, 44, 46, 47–8, 50, 54, 55, 56, 60, 66–9, 76, 85, 87, 90, 93, 98, 113, 200, 212, 221, *67*
Bristol, 13, 19, 29, 35, 72, 135, 206, 207
British Transport Commission, 163, 205–6
British Transport Docks Board, 217
British Waterways Board, 9, 14, 137, 166, 176, 191, 206, 207, 208, 209, 210, 212, 218, 220, *162, 217*
Brooks, Alan, 173
Brunel, Isambard Kingdom, 12, 72, 77, 120, 156–7, 160
Brunel, Marc, 85
Bunbury, 107
Burns, Robert, 117
Bury, O. R. H., 159
Butterley Ironworks, 70, 77, 105, 189

Cadburys, 126, 136–7, 163, 173, *114*
Caldon Low, 97
Caldwall Lock, *52*
Camden Town, 160
Canals:
  Aberdare, 162
  Aire & Calder, 35, 36, 98, 155, 160, 163, *96, 112, 170, 215*
  Ashby, 163, 201
  Ashton, 98, 163, 197, 209
  Basingstoke, 54, 111, 169, 179, 209, *169, 208*
  Birmingham, 45, 48, 68, 76, 83, 85, 86, 94, 96, 100, 101, 108, 129, 132, 135, 142, 157, 159, 160, 163, 200–1, *78, 95, 138*
  Birmingham & Warwick Junction, 132, 161
  Birmingham & Liverpool Junction, 50, 76, 131
  Bradford, 162
  Brecon & Abergavenny, 84, 86, 87, 90–3, 163, 195, 196, 211, *62, 72, 194*
  Bridgwater & Taunton, 163, *104*
  Bude, 89
  Calder & Hebble Navigation, 66, 201, *111*
  Caldon, 82, 84, 97, 210, 211
  Caledonian, 47, 58, 71, 76, 83, 104, 105, 201, *75, 112*
  Canal du Midi, 40
  Chester, 46, 107, 163
  Chesterfield, 163, 210
  Crinan, 181–2, 201, *202*
  Coventry, 50, 54, 68, 94, 105, 106, *141, 166*

Cromford, 77, 84, 93, 163, *60, 157*
Derby, 70
Droitwich, 68, 162, 211
Dudley, 85, 90, 132
Edinburgh & Glasgow Union, 82, 93
Ellesmere, 42, 47, 57, 70, 71, 75, 94, 98, 131, 179, 189, *76*
Erewash, 70
Exeter, 32, 100, *31*
Forth & Clyde, 66, 68, 94, 97, 99, 117, 125, 162, 180–1, *66, 183*
Foss Dyke, 37, 163
Glamorgan, 84, 114, 162
Glamorganshire, 155
Gloucester & Sharpness, 94–6, 137
Gotha Ship, 77
Grand, 69–70, 160
Grand Contour, 216
Grand Junction see Grand Union
Grand Union, 47, 56, 70, 71, 83, 85, 89, 94, 97, 102, 118, 129, 130, 132, 137, 146, 149, 152, 159, 160, 161, 163, 164, 168, 172, 175, 185, 186, 189, 214, 219, *49, 88, 95, 137, 150, 168, 175, 184, 188*
Grand Western, 162, 163, *59*
Grantham, 162, 163
Gravesend & Rochester, 163
Huddersfield Broad, 163
Huddersfield Narrow, 47, 56, 57, 83, 85, 98, 163, 210, 211, *108, 209*
Kennet & Avon, 11–19, 35, 50, 58, 77, 82, 84, 85, 87, 93–4, 120, 131, 156, 163, 169, 180, 205, 206, *11, 15, 16, 204*
Kennet Navigation, 36, *193*
Lancaster, 53, 54, 59, 77, 82, 83, 93, 163, 178, 180, 201, *181*
Languedoc, 40
Leeds & Liverpool, 46, 47, 57, 77, 80, 82, 83, 84, 86, 87, 94, 96, 101, 120, 131, 159, 160, 163, 171, 178–9, 199, 219, *72, 107, 110, 120, 187*
Lee Navigation, 214, *212*
Leicester & Northampton Union, 59, 161
Liskeard & Looe, 202
Llangollen, 47, 79, 82, 83, 87, 142, 163, *32, 87*
Macclesfield, 83–4, 86, 163, 197, 199, *84*
Manchester, Bolton & Bury, 116, 158–9, 163
Manchester Ship, 40, 53, 58, 78, 82, 98, *58*
Mersey & Irwell, 163, 178
Monmouthshire, 163
Montgomery, 131, 163, 210
Neath, 162
Nottingham, 163
Oxford, 47, 53, 59, 68, 77, 85,

86, 105, 126, 129, 137, 197, 219, *45, 64, 72, 140, 141, 186*
Peak Forest, 77, 82, 83, 85, 89, 93, 98, 129, 163, 196, 197, 209, *197*
Pocklington, 163
Regent's, 108, 130, 131, 132, 149, 160, 161, 182–5, 206, *9, 103, 177*
Rochdale, 7, 47, 50, 70–1, 93, 120, 130, 162, 197, 198, 201–2, 210, *71, 108, 198*
Rolle, 202
Royal Military, 167
St Helens, *see* Sankey
Sankey, 37, 155, 163, *156*
Selby, 68
Sheffield & South Yorkshire Navigation, 121, 213, 216
Shrewsbury, 75, 82, 113, 131, 163
Shropshire Tub Boat, 83, 88–9, 163
Shropshire Union, 50, 55, 56, 83, 84, 86, 87, 94, 107, 113, 131–2, 137, 162, 163, 176, 189, 200, *85, 103, 119*
Somerset Coal, 15, 89, 163
Staffs & Worcester, 35, 47, 48, 55, 68, 69, 80, 83, 84, 90, 98, 107, 129, 135, 199, 206, *52, 111*
Stourbridge, 35, 97, 163, *112*
Stover, 163, 202
Stratford, 79, 82, 90, 93, 94, 163, 186, 189, 205, 207–9, *60*
Swansea, 163
Tavistock, 83, 90, 202
Tennant, 162
Thames & Severn, 85, 90, 162, 210, 222, *90*
Trent & Mersey, 45, 48, 56, 68, 69, 77, 78, 82, 83, 85, 86, 88, 90, 97, 108, 113, 129, 139–40, 163, 179, 197, 198–9, *89, 103, 130, 146, 189*
Tyrone, 88
Union, 162
Ulverston, 163
Warwick & Birmingham, 161, 186
Warwick & Napton, 161, 186
Weaver Navigation, 90, 160, *89*
Wey & Arun, 211
Wilts & Berks, 210
Worcester & Birmingham, 6, 84, 87, 135, 200, 207
Canal Pleasurecraft, 206
Canterbury, 30
Carter, Charlie, *143*
Cartwright, Nell, 142–7
Charlestown, 65
Chester, 35
City Basin, 173
Claydon Yard, 105
Clayton of Oldbury, 126, 132, 135, *133*
Clifton, 67

86, 105, 126, 129, 137, 197,
Clough, Arthur Hugh, 158
Clowes, Josiah, 75
Coalport, 89, *128*
Coalville, 145
Collier, Henry, 158
Collins, Christina, 142
Company of Watermen & Lightermen, 26
Constable, John, 39, *38*
Cornish, Margaret, 171, 173
Cotes, V. Cecil, 185
Courtenay, Hugh, 30
Coventry, 106, 137, 173, 221, *220*
Cromford, 70
Craft of the Inland Waterways, named: Albion, 39, 117, 124, 125, *110;* Alecto, 118; Alexandra, *187;* Amy Howson, 117, 122; Anzac, *66;* Avocet, *119;* Bournville I, *114;* Charlotte Dundas, 117, 180; Colin, 205, *154;* Comrade, 39, 93, 117, 122, 125; Cyclops, 181; Dabchick, *119;* Enid, *118, 137;* Friendship, 116; Gypsy Queen, *183;* Humber Enterprise, *215;* Iris, 205; Jason, 206; Jay, *120;* Little John, *123;* Mabel, *188;* Mendip, 137; President, 116, *91;* Rattler, 118; Shamrock, 116; Travers, 108; Tilbury, 108; Tyseley, 129; VIC 32, 117, 125, *202;* Victory, HMS, 116; Waterwich II, 180, *180;* William, *118, 137*
Croydon, 72
Crosley, William, 84
Cunliffe, Sir Foster, 42

da Vinci, Leonardo, 32
Dalswinton Lake, 117
Danks, Samuel & Co, 135
Darby, Abraham, 37, 84
Darvall, William, 36
Darwin, Charles, 44
Darwin, Dr Erasmus, 44
Davidson, Robert, 163
de Mare, Eric, 8, 219
Defoe, Daniel, 28, 36
de Salis, Henry Rodolph, 23, 101, 132
Devonport, 69
Diesel, Rudolf, 108
Docks and Inland Waterways Executive, 163
Doggett, Thomas, 26
Dowley, 80
Dublin, 69, 70, 169
Dukinfield, 98, 197, *97*

East, Sir Gilbert Augustus Clayton, 22, 23
Eddystone, 65, 69, *65*
Edinburgh, 162
Ellesmere, 47, 71, 94, 131
Ellesmere Port, 98, *76*
Eskdale, 72
Etruria, 44, 45, 69, 97
Evesham, 207

Exeter, 30
Eynsham, 26, *24*
Eyre, Frank, 203

Fairbairn, William, 181
Faversham, 108
Fay, S., 159
Fellows, James, 132
Fellows, Joshua, 132, 135
Fellows, Morton & Clayton, 101, 116, 118, 121, 126, 132–5, 137, 142, 150, 161, 163, *91, 133*
Flatford Mill, *38*
French, Daphne, 171
Fulton, Robert, 88, 89

Garrick, David, 67
Gayford, Eily (Kit), 171
George III, 211
Gilbert, John, 42, 68
Giles, Francis, 179
Gloucester, 29, 136
Goole, 98, 125, 217, *96, 170*
Gould, John, 205, 206, *154, 204*
Gower, Lord, 42, 43
Graham, Thomas, 158
Grahame, Thomas, 181
GUCCC, 119, 126, 129, 171, *100*

Hadfield, Charles, 8, 203–4
Hadley, John, 36
Hambleden Mill, *22*
Hanson, Harry, 140
Harland & Wolfe, 119, 129
Harrison, Norman, 121
Harrow Road Bridge, 183
Hawkesbury Junction, 105, *75, 143*
Hazeldine, William, 189
Head, Sir George, 176–8, 179
Henshall, Hugh, 46–7
Hugh Henshall & Company, 129
Henshall, John, 69
Henry I, 32
Henry VIII, 30
Herbert, A. P., 205
Horseley Ironworks, 85
Houston, William, 179–80
Hore, John, 36
Hull, 36, 217
Humphries, Jean, 141
Hutchings, David, 208
Hutton, W., 45

Imperial Chemical Industries, 126, *124*
Inclined planes: Combe Hay, 89; Foxton, 83, 89, *88;* Hay, 83, 89; Hobbacott Down, 89; Ketley, 88; Marhamchurch, 89
Inland Waterways Association, 170, 203–5, 206, 207, 208, 209, 216
Institution of Civil Engineers, 77
Ipswich, 38
Ironbridge, 37

James, Noel, 148
James, Rene, 148
Jerome K. Jerome, 21, 23
Jessop, Josias, 77
Jessop, William, 7, 47–8, 49, 55,

66, 68, 69–72, 75, 76, 77, 93, 104, 189, *69*
Jinks, Danny, 148
Jones, Frank, 153, *154*

Keadby, 218
King, John, 28
King's Cross Goods Station, *103*

Ladyshore Boatyard, 116–17
Lancashire & Yorkshire Railway Company, 158
Langley Mill, 70
Leamington Spa, 97, 175, 186
Liverpool, 35, 132, 142, 155, 168, 169, 171, 179
Llandogo, 37
Llangollen, 71, 142, 176, 179, 192, 205
Locks: Aldermaston, 211; Banavie, 83; Banbury, *174;* Bank Newton, *187;* Bingley Five Rise, 57, 80–1, 84, *107;* Boulter's, 21, 23, 25, 27, *21;* Bratch, 80, 81, 84, 96, *81;* Bulls, 204; Caen Hill, 58, 84, 87; Caldwall, *52;* Chadbury, 207; Cottistock, *39;* Evesham Town, 208; Fort Augustus, 83; Foxton, 83, 89; Greenberfield, 87, 199; Hatton, 83, 87; Hillmorton, 171–2; Tardebigge, 84, 87; Thurlwood, 88; Tyrley, 87; Watford staircase, 83, *184;* Wigan, 193; Widcombe, *19* London, 32, 35, 37, 71, 83, 129, 132, 134, 156, 161, 168, 173, 182, 186, 206, 216
Longbotham, John, 46, 77, 80

Mance, Brigadier General Sir Osborne, 169–70
Manchester, 40, 41, 47, 78, 129, 132, 134, 155, 177, 196, 198, 201, *198*
Manpower Services Commission, 210
Marsworth, *137*
Mathew, Francis, 32, 35
Menai Strait, 77
Merthyr Tydfil, 155
Mikron Theatre Company, 9, 129, 139
Miller, Archibald, 53
Moritz, Charles P., 139
Morton, Frederick, 132
Morwellham, 83, 90
Museums: Black Country, Dudley, 116, *91;* Boat, Ellesmere, 116; Cotehele Quay Maritime, 116; Dolphin Yard Sailing Barge, Sittingbourne, 116; Ironbridge Gorge, 83; National Waterways, Gloucester Dock, 116; Canal, Nottingham, 116; Waterways, Stoke Bruerne, 117, 216

National Trust, 208
Naviglio Interno, 32
Newcastle on Tyne, 36, 38, 216
New Way Holidays, 206
Nickalls, Joseph, 23

North Ferriby, 28
Norwich & Lowestoft Navigation Company, 163
Nottingham, 59, 132, 161
Nurser's Boatyard, 135

Oldbury, 86, 132
Orwell, George, 178
Otley, 57
Outram, Benjamin, 70, 77, 93
Owen, Jess, 153
Oxford, 25, 26, 35, 47, 149

Paddington, 129, 142, 169, 183
Pagett, Arthur, 37
Painted Boats, 129
Palmer, Graham, 208, 209
Palmer, J. E., 160, 161
Perth, 65
Peterhead, 76
Pickfords, 126, 129–34, 142, 168, 182
Pinkertons, 111
Plas Kynaston Ironworks, 76, 189
Plot, Robert, 24
Plymouth, 65
Pontypool, 195
Portree, 76
Portsmouth, 72
Poynton, 129
Pownall, J. F., 216
Preston Brook, 48, 142, 198
Purcell, Alex, 151

Railways: Cromford & High Peak, 77, 84; Great Central, 159; Great Northern, 159, *103;* Great Western, 11, 14, 16, 131, 132, 156, 163, 183, 186; Lancashire & Yorkshire, 202; Leeds & Selby, 179; Leeds & Thirsk, 57; Liverpool & Manchester, *156;* London & Birmingham, 56, *49;* London Midland & Scotland, 163; London & North Eastern Railway, 163; Middleton Colliery, 155; North Midland, *157;* Southern, 163; Stockton & Darlington, 68, 155; Surrey Iron, 72; Wilts, Somerset & Weymouth, 12
Reading, 36, 206, 207
Redbrook, 37
Rennie, John, 14, 50, 55, 60, 70, 77, 83, 85, 93, 155, *77*
Reynolds, William, 75, 88
Richards, J. M., 8
Ridout, Margaret, *see also* Cornish, 175
Rivers: Ant, 39; Aire & Calder Navigation, 25, 36, 37, 77, 80; Avon, (Bristol), 11–17, 19, 37, 77, 82; Avon, (Warwickshire), 37, 207–8, 209, 210; Avon, (Wiltshire), 27; Blackwater, 39; Bure, 39; Calder, 37, 65; Ceiriog, 71, 189; Cherwell, 35, 47, 86; Churnet, 97; Clyde, 39, 125; Dee, 35, 37, 42, 43, 71, 189; Derwent, 37, 70, 163; Don, 37; Douglas, 37; Exe, 30; Foss Dyke, 32; Frome, 15; Great Ouse, 37; Great Stour, 30; Goyt,

77, 197, *197;* Hull, *127;* Humber, 28, 39, 121, 122–3, 161, 217, *93;* Irwell, 37, 40, 41, 42, 67, 78, 155, 156; Kennet, 28, 36, 37, 211; Lark, 37; Lea, 32; Lune, 82, 93; Medway, 37, 39; Mersey, 37, 39, 40, 43, 48, 123, 155, 160; Mersey & Irwell, 42; Mississippi, 181, 217; Nene, 39, 201, *39, 201;* Ouse (Yorkshire), 37, 98; Ouse (Norfolk), 32; Parret and Tone, 37; Rother, 167; Sankey Brook, 40; Seine, 214; Severn, 6, 28, 29, 35, 37, 43, 69, 72, 78, 84, 89, 122–3, 135, 160, 163, 199, 207, *128;* Shannon, 69; Stour (Suffolk), 37, 39, 47, 69, 98, 187–8; Stour (Worcs), 35, 37; Taff, 155; Tamar, 83, 90, 116; Tay, 65, 76; Tees, 155; Tern, 75, 189; Thames, 21–7, 28, 29, 35, 36, 37, 39, 43, 72, 102, 124, 160, 176, 192, *21, 35;* Tone Navigation, 163; Torridge, 202; Trent, 37, 39, 43, 69, 86, 121, 139, 160, 161, 27, *123;* Tyne, 38, 155; Ure, 163; Usk, 87, 93, 195; Waveney, 32; Weaver, 37, 78, 123, 125, 199, *124;* Welland, 37; Wey, 37; Wye, 37
Robertson, H. R., 153
Rolt, L. T. C., 8, 86, 116, 188, 203, 204, 205, 206, 208
Romney Marsh, 167
Rotherham, 217
Royal Engineers, 169, 207
Royal Society, 60
Runcorn, 43, 48
Rutland, Duke of, 86
Rye, 167

Saltley, 132
Salvation Army, 149
Sampford Peverell, *59*
Sanders, John Owen, 135
Saxon, John, 139
Schofield, Fred, 122
Scott, Sir Peter, 205
Seabrook, 167
Seamen and Boatmens Friend Society, 149
Severn & Canal Carrying Company Limited, The, 126, 135–6, 137, 163, *135*
Shardlow, 69, 98
Sharp, George, 57
Sharpness Docks, 218
Shaw, George Bernard, 169
Shaw, Rev Stebbing, 54, 179
Sheffield, 145
Shipley, 80
Shipton on Cherwell, 197, *72*
Shrewsbury, 37
Simcock, Samuel, 77
Skinner, Joe, 116, 117, 137, 138
Skinner, Rose, 116, 137, 138, *141*
Smeaton, John, 47, 56, 60–6, 68, 69, 70, 82, 99, *65*
Smiles, Samuel, 46, 47, 60, 69
Smith, Emma, 171, 173
Smith, Francis Pettit, 117

Smith, George, 144–5, 148
Smith, Captain R. L. H., 203
Southey, Robert, 58, 105
Southport, 179
Southwark, 37
Sowerby Bridge, 47, 201–2
Statute of Sewers, 30
Stephenson, George, 68, 72, 120, 155, 156, 160
Stevens, Mr Caggy, 108, 150
Stonehenge, 27
Swindon, 210
Symington, William, 117

Tamworth, 135, 173
Taplow Mill, 23
Tate & Lyle, 108
Taylor, John, 25, 90
Telford, Thomas, 42, 47, 50, 56, 58, 60, 70, 71, 72–7, 83, 84, 85, 86, 94, 98, 116, 189, *51*
Tewkesbury, 207, *29*
Thomason, James, 158
Thurston, E. Temple, 186, 188, 196–7, 200
Tintern, 37
Tom Puddings, 98, 124–5, 217, *125*
Tramways: Brecon & Abergavenny, 86; Cromford Wharf, 84; Froghall Basin, 84; Glyn Valley, *87;* Llanfoist, 84; Penydarren, 84; Whaley Bridge, 85
Trevithick, Richard, 105, 155
Trew, John, 32
Tring, 56, 83, 146, *49*
Tunstall, 145
Tunnels: Barnton, *146;* Blisworth, 71, 85, 151, 168, 185, *55;* Bramhope, 57; Brandwood, 90; Braunston, 142; Butterley, 70; Dudley, 85, 90; Gosty, 90; Harecastle, 48, 56, 69, 76–7, 85, 148, 179, 211; Islington, *54;* Netherton, 85; Sapperton, 85, 90, 211, *90;* Standedge, 47, 56, 85, 211; Whitehouses, 189

Victoria, Queen, 149

Walkers of Rickmansworth, 119
Ward, Henry, 148
Ward, Sister Mary, 149, 150
Waterson, Alex, 116–17
Waterways Recovery Group, 208–9, *210*
Watt, James, 56
Wedgwood, Josiah, 43–5, 67, 69, 79–80, 108
Weedon, 168
Weeland, 35, 36
Wet Earth Colliery, 42, 67
Wheeldon, Tim, 15
White, Peter, 9
Williams, Edward Leader, 78
Willow Wren, 126, 137
Woolfitt, Susan, 149, 170, 171–3
Worcester, 29, 30, 136
Wynne, Sir Watkin Williams, 42

Yarranton, Andrew, 35
Yarwoods, 119, 129
Young, Arthur, 29

224